T0349358

CARVER CLARK GAYTON

Odyssey of a Seattle Native Son

Foreword by Brian Carter

Documentary Media, Seattle, WA

ODYSSEY OF A SEATTLE NATIVE SON

by Carver Clark Gayton

First Edition
Printed in South Korea

Documentary Media LLC
books@docbooks.com
www.documentarymedia.com
(206) 935-9292

In collaboration with

HistoryLink
admin@historylink.org

(206) 447-8140

Author: Carver Clark Gayton
Foreword: Brian Carter
Editing and book production: Tori Smith
Book design: Marilyn Esguerra
Editorial Director: Petyr Beck

Available through the University of Washington Press

uwapress.uw.edu

ISBN: 978-1-933245-73-7
Library of Congress Control Number: 2024952076

Photo Credits: All images courtesy the Gayton family archive except where noted.

Carver Gayton *by Quincy Jones*

CONTENTS

FOREWORD

BEFORE MEETING THE MAN, I was privy to the lore of Carver Gayton. University of Washington football star, scion of the illustrious Gayton family, FBI agent, Boeing executive, and anointed community leader. Our paths crossed in the Spring of 2004 as he led the effort to open the Northwest African American Museum (NAAM) at the Colman School in Seattle's historic Black neighborhood, the Central District. Carver swept into NAAM's temporary offices at One Union Square thunderously talking into his always-present earpiece and furiously working a Blackberry. He walked with an energetic bounce that read like brashness and captured my attention because of its sureness. As an unpaid intern from a blue-collar Yakima family, the authority and purpose he exuded were qualities I desperately coveted. After extending a warm welcome, Carver moved on to the meeting in the big office, and I returned to my desk determined to one day make the world see me in the same light.

Under his stalwart leadership our team humbly stood on the shoulders of those who came before, guiding NAAM to its opening in 2008. Carver and I stayed in contact as my career took me to other museums in the region and eventually to my current position as executive director at 4Culture. As a funder, I now support the great number of theaters, community groups, museums, and creative individuals who nurture King County's rich and deep cultural ecosystem. In this work, I am both guided and driven by the inimitable example Carver set during those early years of my career and beyond.

Twenty years of friendship with Carver have shown me how fundamentally I misunderstood the relationship between lore and man. There is not an inevitability to the era-shaping experiences and accomplishments recounted in this autobiography. The poise and conviction I first saw in Carver all those years ago were wages earned for a lifetime in service of elemental values—loyalty, kindness, and duty. I've had the privilege of watching Carver translate these ideals into action; the honor of witnessing the construction of an individual life acutely responsive to the needs of the whole. Carver's story has been a life undoubtedly marked by humanistic missteps and uncertainties, but he has always been profoundly cognizant of the inextricable linkage between what came before, what is, and what will follow. This appreciation of personal context, refracted through decades of leadership roles, honors, and achievements, reveals a consistent theme: a willingness to step forward, to attempt, to dare. Not because he foresaw outcomes he's now lauded for, but because he realized the danger inaction posed for those without the power of his positionality.

The lesson I've learned from Carver is that we must embrace the heavy responsibility bestowed on us all to compose a meaningful chapter in the book of our times. The gift he gave me is the understanding that we can't read it before it's done.

Brian J. Carter
Executive Director, 4Culture

INTRODUCTION

BEFORE I WAS OLD ENOUGH to attend school, my mother read books to the younger siblings of which I was one. The stories included King Arthur adventures, African American Uncle Remus folklore, and traditional children's fairy tales. She also included discussions of Black leaders such as scientist George Washington Carver and Civil Rights leader W.E.B. Du Bois. Invariably, the discussion would go back to the fascinating story of our great-grandfather Lewis Garrard Clarke, my mother's grandfather.

Mom would pull out of her small bookcase an old, dilapidated, plum-red book entitled *The Key to Uncle Tom's Cabin* by Harriet Beecher Stowe, Stowe's followup publication to her earlier *Uncle Tom's Cabin* that commented on slavery in America. Mom would turn to the section describing George Harris, the rebellious quadroon slave and lead character in *Uncle Tom's Cabin*, whom Stowe modeled on the experiences of Lewis Clarke. Mom read from *The Key* as follows:

> With regard to the incidents of George Harris's life, that he may not be supposed a purely exceptional case, we propose to offer some parallel facts from the slaves of our personal acquaintance.
>
> Lewis Clarke is an acquaintance of the writer. Soon after his escape from slavery, he was received into the family of a sister-in-law of the author, and there educated. His conduct during this time was such as to win for him uncommon affection and respect, and the author has frequently heard of him spoken of in the highest terms by all who knew him.
>
> The gentleman in whose family he so long resided, says of him in a recent letter to the writer, "I would trust him, as the saying is, with untold gold."

Lewis Clarke

Lewis G. Clark Boston Mass

Copyright

LEWIS G. CLARK,

THE ORIGINAL GEORGE HARRIS OF UNCLE TOM'S CABIN,

Was born in

MADISON COUNTY, KENTUCKY, MARCH 15, 1815,

On his Grandfather's plantation, on Silver Creek, is brother to J. M. Clark, of Cambridgeport, the Messenger in the U. S. Sub-Treasury.

I do not pretend that my story is at the level of importance as Lewis Clarke's life. However, Lewis's striving over his lifetime to tell the public about his family, the major challenges that led him on his life's pathways, and the intertwining of the vicissitudes of race, are part of my life's journey.

Lewis Clarke had a profound impact on me and later in my life, when I discovered the narrative of his experience of slavery and his escape in *Narrative of the Sufferings of Lewis Clarke During Captivity of More than Twenty-Five Years*, I would dedicate a good part of my life sharing his story, which I present in more detail in Chapter 34 "Honoring My Muse."

In July 2009, I received an email from a man named Greg Wilson who was doing historical research. He attached an article from the *Washington Post* dated May 12, 1890. It was titled "Once a Famous Slave, the Original George Harris of Mrs. Stowe's George Harris is in the City." The extensive article indicated that Clarke had been invited to come from Oberlin, Ohio, where he lived at the time, to speak about his experiences as a slave and his memories of Harriet Beecher Stowe to the congregation at the 19th Street Baptist Church in Washington, DC.

Clarke was quoted as saying that he continued to receive numerous invitations from around the country to speak on such topics despite being *seventy-five years old!* The 1890 article was particularly interesting because it said that Clarke was in the process of "getting out a book on his life" and that he would be going to New York and Philadelphia to work out the details. My own extensive investigations have not revealed to me any published autobiography later in life, but my search continues.

Clarke's intention to write his autobiography inspired me to write my own, with the hope of having better luck ensuring its publication. I do not pretend that my story is at the level of importance as Lewis Clarke's life. However, Lewis's striving over his lifetime to tell the public about his family, the major challenges that led him on his life's pathways, and the intertwining of the vicissitudes of race, are part of my life's journey.

Race is a common theme throughout my own odyssey and an important factor in the evolution of my life and that of my family's. My initial thought was not to emphasize the subject of race in this writing, but I concluded it is unavoidable. Dealing with the issues of race and bloodlines is simply a fact of life for me, and generally for most other Americans of African descent. This issue encompasses the full spectrum of my emotions, from exhilaration and pride to agony and anger. I suspect most Whites would be surprised and confounded by this assessment.

In writing this book, I have reflected on 80-plus years of experiences. Through my unpremeditated odyssey, I have discovered patterns of learning and ways of walking in this world that have been exceptionally valuable to me and hopefully will be valuable to others.

PART I

FAMILY ROOTS

CHAPTER 1

Paternal Family Roots

MY FRATERNAL GRANDFATHER, John Thomas Gayton, referred to by most as J. T. Gayton, was born in Benton, Yazoo County, Mississippi, in 1866 on the Delta of the Mississippi River. He was the son of former slave David Gayton and his wife Betsy. David became a cotton sharecropper after emancipation as did J. T. and his siblings (Debra, Litho, Jefferson, Susan, and Lewis) when they came of age.

For the most part, slaves were not allowed to keep family names from Africa. Often, parents would provide given names to children which were in fact true family names. It is interesting to note that the only sibling of J. T.'s that had a non-European given name was his sister, Litho. We found that "Litho" is a major family name of the Bantu people. The Bantu live on a tributary of the Congo River in the northeast section of what is now the Republic of Congo.

I never could reconcile why he felt such shame toward himself and family members who were subjected, through no fault of their own, to the evil Jim Crow South.

DNA tests of my parents show that our family has bloodlines from that region of West Africa.

J. T.'s mother died when he was nine. Soon after, David married Amanda (Manda) Williams in 1875. According to J. T., he and his brothers and sisters did not get along with Amanda and all left home, one by one, while in their teens. Their stepmother encouraged them to do so.

During this time, J. T. became concerned with the rise of the Ku Klux Klan and the Knights of the White Camellia—race-hate organizations in Yazoo County. Also, J. T.'s stepbrother, Angelo Jennings, disappeared under mysterious circumstances. J. T.'s family assumed that Angelo was a victim of the Klan. These factors, and the family's unpleasant relationship with Amanda, convinced J. T. he had to leave Mississippi. That opportunity came through his relationship with one Dr. Henry Yandell.

Dr. Henry Yandell, a boyhood friend of J. T.'s father, lived in Yazoo City. The doctor was a former officer of the Confederacy. In 1883, Dr. Yandell employed J. T., then age 17, as his coachman, valet, and "collector" (as in: bill collector). Yandell and J. T. moved to Seattle in the Territory of Washington in early 1889, which became a state on November 11, 1889. Yandell later served as the first coroner for King County, Washington.

*J. T. Gayton,
my paternal
grandfather,
circa 1898.*

*Magnolia
Scott Gayton,
my paternal
grandmother,
circa 1898.*

After four months in Seattle, J. T. left employment with Dr. Yandell and began working a variety of jobs. He became a deputy sheriff during Seattle's Great Fire of 1889, a painting contractor, barber, bellboy, and waiter. At that time, Seattle was booming due to all the building construction taking place after the fire. While working in these jobs, he studied bookkeeping at Wilson's Modern Business College. He had no formal education beyond the fourth grade prior to business school.

J. T. was hired as the first Black steward of the exclusive Seattle Rainier Club In 1901, where, he said, members "felt very kindly toward him." He also hired out his services as a caterer for many social functions and dinner parties for prominent families and leading citizens of the city at a time before Seattle's hotels began offering private dining rooms. J. T. was described as an "artist in that sort of work" by *The Seattle Republican* newspaper on March 7, 1902. They added that ". . . he handles more banquets, wedding parties and social gatherings than any other caterer in the city."

In 1904, he accepted an appointment as court messenger and court bailiff for the US District by Judge Cornelius E. Handford, the first US District Court judge after Washington became a state. The position satisfied a long-time interest J. T. had in the law, although he took a cut in salary.

He was appointed by President Franklin Delano Roosevelt as librarian for the US Circuit Court of Appeals in Seattle in 1934. By the time he retired in

1953, he had served under every Federal District Court judge to preside since Washington's admission to statehood.

J. T. married Magnolia Scott in January of 1899. She was born a mulatto in Nashville, Tennessee, on June 15, 1880. Her parents died when she was very young and she was adopted by a White Methodist minister and his wife, The Reverend and Mrs. Scott. They moved to Seattle where Magnolia met J. T. The union produced four children: John Jr., the eldest and my dad; James; Louise; and Leonard.

J. T. was a powerful personality within the family. He set standards for his children by example and laid down absolute rules. A Gayton should not be seen on Jackson Street, regarded as the rough Black neighborhood in Seattle. Also, a Gayton should not accept welfare. Family members were expected to go to church, preferably the more conservative First African Methodist Episcopal Church (FAME), of which he was one of the founders.

When I was a child, J. T. came across to me as austere in his appearance and personality, yet those close to him said he had an engaging sense of humor and was a delightful raconteur. J. T.'s boisterous laugh, often called the "Gayton Laugh" by those outside the family, was inherited by his children.

His wife Magnolia, Maggie to J. T. and Nonnie to the grandchildren, had a personality that was a stark contrast to J. T.'s. She was quiet and very sweet, yet stately. Nonnie had a Mona Lisa smile which reflected that she was comfortable and confident within herself, yet very approachable. She stood at least four inches taller than J. T., but the height difference did not take away anything from J. T.'s very straight posture. In fact, by the way he carried himself he always appeared taller than his actual height. Magnolia had no problem with J. T. being the center of attention. In fact, she reveled in observing his bigger-than-life personality. But she never came across as being subservient.

J. T. was remembered by many as looking more like a judge than the Federal Court judges for whom he worked. In public, he dressed impeccably in bow tie, pince-nez eyeglasses attached to a black silk cord, and dark suits with vests showing his gold watch and chain. I often saw him wearing spats over his always-shined shoes. He walked with a cane as a style statement. The canes matched his suits. In the spring and summer, he wore a yellow rose in his lapel plucked from the family garden.

On weekends his home was filled with visiting neighbors. No invitations were necessary. Those who came by were the "who's who" of the African American community in Seattle. Nonnie would have pots of food simmering in their downstairs kitchen, having been prepared the day before, not knowing who was going to show up, nor the number of people. The bill of fare generally consisted of red beans and rice, ham, collard greens, fried chicken, cornbread, potato salad, lemonade, and peach cobbler with homemade ice cream.

J. T. would greet visitors with a ceramic multi-colored pitcher in the likeness of a bird with a liquor concoction. He'd ask, "Would you like something from the Blue Jay?"

Grandpa Gayton would end such gathering dancing the "cakewalk" or the "quadrille." Both dances were popular at the time. I especially liked the cakewalk which evolved from slavery days. The slaves would mock the ultra-proper masters by leaning back, high stepping, and strutting to music. J. T. would have everyone in stitches laughing at his theatrics. My dad and uncles would oftentimes join him. The quadrille, similar to square dancing, was for couples and much more sedate than the cakewalk.

My mother would get aggravated with Dad when he would come home late afternoon on a Saturday after spending most of the day at Grandpa's and Nonnie's—and after stuffing himself with Nonnie's wonderful southern cooking. Mom's cooking was more influenced by the bland cuisine of Spokane and Vancouver, BC, where her family lived for a while. In other words, Mom's meals could not compete with her mother-in law's. I occasionally felt like a co-conspirator, having been with my father on many of those Saturdays.

J. T. was highly regarded in the Seattle community. In addition to helping found the First African Methodist Episcopal Church (FAME), he played a primary role as chair of its finance committee in saving the institution from declaring bankruptcy in the middle 1930s. He served on the first board of management for the East Madison Branch of the Young Men's Christian Association's (YMCA) formed during the depression years. He was a long-time supporter of the King County Colored Republican Party. The Republican Party was the party of choice for most Black leaders in America from the Reconstruction years after the Civil War until the Second World War.

J. T. and Nonnie instilled a sense of pride for their race and culture within their children. Black peddlers would go door to door in the city's Central District (CD) during the early days, selling their books and pamphlets about African Americans. These publications would always be available in the Gayton home. J. T. and Nonnie would make sure the children read them. Seattle libraries and schools did not have such literature available.

Although J. T. had enormous pride in being "a race man," he did not see himself as a civil rights leader. After all, he worked most of his adult life within the White power structure and knew his limitations as a race activist within that work environment. But he made sure that his integrity as a Black man remained intact. His cordiality was not to be interpreted as being meek.

From the time he arrived in Seattle in 1889 in his Beau Brummell attire, J. T. attempted to separate himself from his roots in the South as a cotton-picking farm boy in coveralls. Clearly, he wanted to be as far away as possible, emotionally and physically, from what he and his family experienced in Yazoo County, Mississippi.

He did not reveal much about his childhood experiences. While he obviously worked in the cotton fields of "Captain Johnson"—the owner of the property where he had lived—he had no particular pride in doing so. He often had derogatory remarks to make about others who did such work. He called both Blacks and Whites he disliked "Negro sharecroppers" or "White sharecroppers."

As a child, I had no idea what a sharecropper was, but I knew it was *bad*, at least in J. T's mind. He reveled in the fact that he knew very little, if anything, about farming, even though his father had made a living as a sharecropper and farmer.

As I grew older and became aware of the meaning of the term, I could not understand why Grandpa was so hateful toward himself and his own relatives. As a man, I could understand why he wanted to have a better life in the north, but I never could reconcile why he felt such shame toward himself and family members who were subjected, through no fault of their own, to the evil Jim Crow South.

My father, John Jacob Gayton, was born December 27, 1899, in a small home near 9th and Madison Streets in Seattle but was raised in a home on 26th and Madison Streets. He was the first child baptized in the First African Methodist Episcopal Church. His godmother was Susie Revels Cayton, daughter of Hiram Revels, the first Black US senator. My father attended Longfellow School and

My father, John Jacob Gayton, and my mother, Virginia Clark Gayton, circa 1960.

Franklin High School. His mother's health was frail and so the family moved to the "countryside" for several years and lived on a five-acre homestead in Hazelwood, a small community across Lake Washington, west of Newcastle. That move took place during Dad's junior year at Franklin and meant he had to take the ferry to Rainier Beach and then the Interurban Rail to Franklin during the school year.

He worked in the summers as a screener in the coal mines of Newcastle and Coal Creek, alternating between walking and horseback riding back and forth from home. He missed military service by a few months because World War I ended just as he was about to be drafted.

My father was blessed with the gift of a wonderful singing voice. Between jobs and family obligations he took singing lessons at the Cornish School on Capitol Hill in Seattle. He even had a manager, Mr. MacGuder, who would set him up with singing engagements around Seattle, mostly at local churches. His primary venue was the First African Methodist Episcopal Church at 14th and Madison.

Dad also served as the president of the FAME choir for over twenty years. He often bragged that the noted Black tenor Roland Hayes heard him sing on a visit to Seattle and urged him to study in England. My father also sang on the radio when it first began broadcasting, accompanied on the piano by his sister Louise.

Around the same time, he was making a name for himself as a singer, and seriously thinking of studying abroad, he met young Virginia Clark. He married her on April 26, 1926. They would raise eight children: Guela, Sylvia, John Cyrus, Gary, Philip, Carver, Leonard, and Elaine.

Over the years my dad would often say he "had no regrets" about his decision to marry Mom and give up a budding singing career. However, the fact that he made that statement so often convinced us kids there was a wee bit of regret over the missed career path.

Dad had a variety of jobs over the years, including dog catcher, deputy sheriff, laborer, caterer with his father, and postal guard for the main post office at 3rd and Union. Oftentimes he worked several jobs simultaneously to support his large family. He was especially proud he never had to go on "the dole" (i.e. welfare) during his lifetime. This was quite an accomplishment considering most of his children were born during the Depression years when the unemployment rate for the general population hovered around 50 percent and virtually *no employment* was available for Blacks.

Despite having the burden of raising such a large family, he took the time to become deeply involved in his community. He was a lifetime member of the First African Methodist Episcopal Church and served on the Steward Board as president of the choir and as a member of the board of trustees. He was a staunch member of the East Madison YMCA where a room was named in his honor. He was a member of the National Association for the Advancement of Colored People (NAACP), The Seattle Urban League, and President of the Chorus, which was sponsored by the Christian Friends for Racial Equality.

CHAPTER 2

My Maternal Side

My maternal great-grandfather,
Lewis Garrard Clarke, circa 1890.

MY GREAT GRANDFATHER, Lewis Garrard Clarke, was an escaped slave and abolitionist leader. His son, Cyrus Clarke, was born in Windsor, Ontario, Canada, in 1863. Cyrus married Guela Johnson in Spokane, Washington, in 1900. Guela went to Nashville, Tennessee, to have my mother delivered because Blacks were not welcomed in the hospitals in Spokane. My mother, Virginia, was born August 26, 1902. Also, in Nashville, her grandmother was able to assist in the delivery. They returned to Spokane when Virginia was two months old.

Lewis Clarke encouraged all of his children to get a good education. This was not available to him as a slave. He had escaped to Canada in 1859, but he grew disappointed with the education his children were offered. This was the main reason he and his family left Canada in 1874 and returned to Oberlin, Ohio, where the schools were integrated and more highly regarded. He made sure that his children were supported financially for their education.

Virginia graduated from Spokane's Lewis and Clark High School in 1919. Her family then moved to Vancouver, British Columbia. That same year she travelled by train to Washington, DC, to attend Howard University, the famous Historically Black College. Her trip was an unforgettable experience. Her father had worked for years as a porter on the Canadian Pacific and Great Northern

My maternal grandfather, Cyrus H. Clark, 1900.

My maternal grandmother, Guela Johnson Clark, 1900.

railroads and was able to contact some of his Black porter and waiter friends about my mother's upcoming trip. They made a point to take special care of the young teenager during the three-thousand-mile sojourn. Over the years, Mother often mentioned that she was treated like a princess by her father's friends during the entire trip and felt like a member of a wonderful extended family.

Virginia attended Howard for three years, staying at the home of her maternal aunt Violetta (Lettitia) Clark Baker, daughter of Lewis Clarke, and her uncle Henry Baker who graciously paid her tuition. From the early 1900s through the 1920s, Violetta and Henry Baker were regarded as among the Black social elite of Washington, DC.

Henry Baker was a distinguished scholar and, in 1875, the second Black to be accepted into the Naval Academy in Annapolis as a cadet mid-shipman. But after two years he dropped out because of the racial mistreatment he encountered. In 1877, he was appointed "copyist" in the United States Patent Office. Henry attended the Ben-Hyde Benton School of Technology in DC from 1877 to 1879. Baker subsequently entered the Law Department of Howard University in 1879, graduating at the head of his class in 1881.

Henry and Violetta married in May 1893 in Lexington, Kentucky, where Violetta's famous father, Lewis Clarke, lived at the time. They lived in Henry's home on 6th Street NW in Washington, DC. They did not have children, which was a primary reason for their interest in having their young niece come to Washington, DC, and live with them while she attended Howard University.

While with the Patent Office, Baker published a manuscript which appeared in *Twentieth Century Negro Literature – Or, A Cyclopedia of Thought on the Vital Topics Relating to the American Negro,* dated 1902. Baker's manuscript, *The Negro as an Inventor,* traced the history of patents by African Americans from the time the United States came into existence. The list of "Colored" inventors within the manuscript was furnished for the Paris Exposition of 1900. For this work and other highly recognized writings for the Patent Office, the *Cyclopedia* declared Baker among ". . . one hundred of the most scholarly and prominent Negroes in America" whose writings are included within the book. Other writers were such notables as Booker T. Washington, George Washington Carver, Mrs. Paul Laurence Dunbar, and Rosetta Douglass Sprague, daughter of Frederic Douglass.

Violetta attended school in Oberlin, Ohio, after her mother Emiline Walker Clarke passed away. Violetta then continued school in Detroit at the home of her aunt, Martha Clarke, widow of her father's brother Cyrus Clarke.

In her late teens, Violetta taught school in Lexington, Kentucky, where her father lived. She excelled as a teacher but, wanting to do more, accepted a position as a clerk in the Department of Civil Service, in Washington, DC. The position was secured through a competitive examination of sixty applicants. Her outstanding achievement was announced in African American newspapers throughout the nation. She held that position until she married Henry Baker.

In 1898, Violetta entered the Sauver Institute of Library Economy at Amherst College in Massachusetts. She was appointed a few years later as a librarian in the US Library of Congress where she worked for more than twenty years. According to Henry, during those years at the Library, Violetta compiled from the records what was considered the most complete index of the literary productions of Black women in this country and around the world. It was her intention to complete and publish the collection. However, she passed away in 1923 before she could finish the project. My efforts to recover the unfinished manuscript have met with negative results. Violetta made groundbreaking accomplishments as a woman and as a Black woman.

My mother started at Howard University in 1920 and focused on math and German courses. She was taught by African American intellectual giants such as philosopher Alaine Locke, "Dean" of the Harlem Renaissance; poet Paul Lawrence Dunbar; historians Charles Wesley and Carter Woodson, founder of Black History

Week. While there, she had the good fortune to work at the Library of Congress as a messenger at the same time as her aunt did. A US senator from Washington, Wesley Jones, recommended her for this appointment.

While at Howard, Virginia became engaged to Lee Terry, a young medical school student. Her engagement and her schooling were cut short when Aunt Violetta became very ill and was unable to continue to send Virginia to school. My mother, obviously heartbroken, left Howard in 1921 to live with her parents in Vancouver, British Columbia.

My mother, Virginia Clark, preparing to enter Howard University in 1920.

The three-thousand-mile distance between the betrothed led to the deterioration of their relationship. Terry and my mother remained lifelong friends even though the engagement ended.

Mom stayed in Vancouver for a couple of years. She had difficulty finding a job and decided to move to Seattle where opportunities were greater. She had a friend in the city, Clara James, who had graduated from the University of British Columbia and was attending the University of Washington School of Pharmacy. Clara convinced Virginia to live with her at the Phillis Wheatley Young Women's Christian Association (YWCA) in Seattle off the corner of 22nd and Madison Street—in the heart of the African American community. The YWCA allowed Black women to rent in this facility, but not in their downtown facility.

Mom found work as a machine operator at a hat manufacturing establishment. She sent some earnings to Vancouver to assist her parents. Her father was ill and had financial difficulties.

It just so happened that my father lived with his parents just blocks away from the YWCA, near 26th and Madison Street, an area where there was a small business center with a variety of shops and stores. The "Y" on Madison was a popular venue for young African Americans for weddings, social events, and community meetings. It stands to reason that they met there, and soon afterwards fell in love and married.

CHAPTER 3

My Early Years

MY FAMILY LIVED in several residences before moving into Madrona, an all-White neighborhood of Seattle, in early 1938. My mother and father had five children at the time, and my mother was pregnant with me. I was born on October 18th. Two more children would be born within the next eight years.

My parents were strong believers in racial integration and equal rights and were members of the National Association for the Advancement of

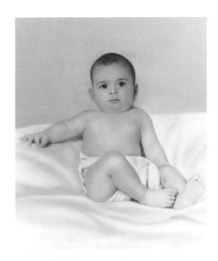

Carver Clark Gayton, 1938.

Colored People (NAACP). So, the move into Madrona was not surprising. They expected some push back from some of the White residents.

Push-back came. Our welcome into our new home was not hospitable. Rocks and bricks were thrown at the house and epithets, including "nigger," were yelled at family members by youths and adults alike. Mom and Dad were willing to endure the hardships because the move brought them into a more upscale neighborhood, and just a block away from the highly regarded Madrona Elementary School.

There was less animosity toward the family as time passed, but the move started a gradual change in the complexion of the neighborhood. Our family precipitated what became known as "block busting." By the late 1960s, that section of Madrona became predominately African American as a result of the "great migration" of Blacks from the South coming into Seattle during World War II, along with Whites moving out of the Central District to the suburbs away from their new Black neighbors.

As the sixth of eight siblings, I tended to have a comfort level of being buried in the middle of the clan. My older brothers and sisters accused me of being spoiled by my mother because I was the only kid who had a four-year span between the next oldest, Phil, and the next youngest, Leonard. Hence, Mother had more free time with me.

I don't deny having been spoiled by Mom. I had a very deep affection for her. One added connection with her was that my middle name "Clark" was her maiden name. I also felt pride in the fact that my father gave me the name "Carver" after the well-known Black scientist, George Washington Carver.

I do not recall any family members calling me Carver very often during my early years. As the story goes, my playmate, a young White girl next door, had difficulty pronouncing "Carver." So, she started calling me "Butch," and it stuck. To this day my oldest friends and family members still call me Butch. My mother never called me Carver; it was always "Butch" or "Mister."

It was not until high school that I adjusted to my given name, which earlier had seemed too formal to me. Appreciation and pride in my name gradually came about after I gained greater knowledge of the scientific contributions George Washington Carver made and how respected he was throughout the world. I grew to have great pride in the distinctiveness of the name, and I am grateful Dad gave me that name.

There were no Blacks living near our home in the Madrona neighborhood during my early years. My parents, very aware of that drawback, made it a point to make sure I had contact with other Black children and our culture through the church. Since my dad did not have a car until I was in my preteens, the family would walk the two-plus miles to First African Methodist Episcopal Church regardless of the weather.

It was difficult for my mother to get the entire brood ready for Sunday School and the morning services. A primary motivation was the ever-present switch from the backyard lilac tree. She did not have to use it often. The mere *threat* of using it was enough of a message. The tree was never able to reach its full height and width over the eighteen years we lived in our Pike Street home because Mom regularly pulled branches off the abused tree for one infraction, or another, committed by the siblings. The boys were the primary perpetrators.

Some of my earliest memories as a child came from attending the church. I was intrigued with FAME. I got to be with other Black kids, many of whom became lifelong friends. The older church members would invariably say when they saw me, "You must be a Gayton! Which one are you?" All of us had features that reflected the blend of both parents. But there were too many of us for them to remember our names!

Some of the more memorable events at church were during the holidays. On Easter and Christmas, I was terrified because the younger kids were expected to recite a memorized "piece" or verse from the Bible—usually one sentence in length—in front of the entire congregation. It always was reassuring to have Mom in the front row to help me when I slipped up on a word or two!

During those early years, the songs performed by the choir and sung by the congregation tended to be traditional hymns and "Negro" spirituals. This was befitting of the more conservative FAME Church, compared to the Baptist churches, for example. I was very proud to see Dad in the choir, particularly when he performed his beautiful tenor solos.

Both Dad and Mom preferred the spirituals and hymns. Neither were enamored with gospel music, which I really enjoyed. They would turn off the radio whenever it was tuned in to a gospel station, considering it not "respectful" and "too common." However, by my teenage years, my parents began to enjoy listening to the great gospel singer Mahalia Jackson, especially when she sang "Take my Hand, Precious Lord" which she performed at Martin Luther King's funeral. They even purchased one of her albums.

The most fun for me at church was on Christmas Eve. Brown bags of nuts, fruit, and candies were passed out by a Black Santa Claus to each of the children, followed by the singing of Christmas carols. The first time I remembered a Black

The Gayton family at the First African Methodist Episcopal Church, circa 1948. J. T. and my father are in the front row with babies in their laps. I am on the far left front, just to the inside of my brother Gary.

Santa handing out the treats, I thought it was peculiar. I assumed everybody knew that the *real* Santa was White. Perturbed, I said to my mother, "That isn't a real Santa!"

Mom hesitated to respond and finally said, "Well, Santa couldn't come. And that's Santa's helper."

Growing up in a predominately White city and being incessantly exposed to White media, I remained suspicious.

The church picnics held at the Woodland Park Zoo grounds or Seward Park were also memorable. The fried chicken, potato salad, and watermelon were great treats. We also had a variety of competitive racing events, and the older kids and young adults played softball. These gatherings were an intermingling of folks, socially and economically. This was not necessarily determined by the Black community, since all Blacks were forced to live within the red-lined Central District confined by discriminatory housing covenants. The unintended positive result was a close-knit, almost classless, African American community.

I recall a wide variety of complexions and features of the congregants as a child compared to church members today. I have no scientific data to support my recollection, but I remember a larger proportion of Black church members in the 1940s and 1950s who, like my mother, were light skinned with Caucasian features and had straight hair, like my mother and my maternal grandmother.

I've noticed in later years at FAME fewer numbers, proportionately, of mixed-blood Blacks in attendance. I assume in current times, with more freedom to move from one section of the Seattle Metropolitan area to another, more White-looking Blacks may be passing for White elsewhere.

Color was not an issue in our family as much as it has been in many other Black families. My dark-complexioned father and White-looking mother never commented on one person's color being better than another. Such discussions would never have been tolerated. Five siblings have lighter complexions like mine and the three others had my dad's skin color.

First African Methodist Episcopal Church gave me a spiritual grounding that has not faded. In addition, the cultural and political aspects of the Church established a comfort zone for me while growing up that contributed to making me proud of who I am as a Black man.

———

Equally important as the church, our family developed several quasi-rituals creating a glue that kept us a close-knit entity. I also enjoyed special one-on-one times with either my mom or dad. These were especially memorable because with our large family my parents could spread their attention only so far over the course of a day.

One family ritual was discussions at dinner time led by Dad followed by after-dinner stories and quizzes with Mother. None of the children could miss 6:00 p.m. dinnertime unless one was sick in bed or in the hospital. The older children were given a bit of leeway but had to inform either parent of a legitimate excuse before the "bewitching hour" of 6:00 p.m.

Dad would sit at the head of the table with a stack of dinner plates in front of him, and he served the helpings of food for each of the eight to ten family members around the table. Conversations would range from politics, race, and church, to gossip in the neighborhood. The only way anyone could get a point across was to talk *loudly*. As a result, the younger ones had a difficult time being

...all Blacks were forced to live within the red-lined Central District confined by discriminatory housing covenants. The unintended positive result was a close-knit, almost classless, African American Community.

---

involved. Consequently, I did a lot of listening. A great deal of laughter was interspersed throughout.

During one meal when I was about four years old, I got frustrated because I could not express myself in a humorous way that would garner everyone's attention and appreciation. I decided to take care of that by yelling out, "Hey, hey Dad—Dad, you're stupid!"

I was waiting for uproarious laughter. Instead, the conversations stopped cold, and all eyes were on me. The silence seemed like an eternity!

Finally, my mother said, "Butch, that was not a nice thing to say about your father. Now say you're sorry."

I said, "I'm sorry, Dad."

My father said, "That's all-right son, but don't say that again."

My brothers and sisters put their hands to their mouths to muffle their snickers. After Dad's admonition, the laughter and conversation picked up again like nothing had happened, but I was devastated and wanted to disappear! My first attempt to become a recognized member of the family clan was a disaster.

Despite the embarrassment of my faux pas, I continued to relish the conversation and laughter at dinnertime. From that time forward, I very seldom thrust myself into these family conversations. I did not become withdrawn, but I had a greater comfort level as an observer, and this is an apt characterization of my personality to this day.

My father was the focal point at dinner with his knowledge of current events, which came primarily from the radio, local newspapers, local and national Black newspapers, and magazines. While most comments from the children seemed directed toward gaining his favor and approval, my lifetime interest and appreciation of political and social issues began at our family dinner table.

————

While my father was the center of attention for the family at dinner time, my mother held court most evenings. She would read fairy tales and nursery rhymes to us when we were very young. As we grew older, she read stories from such books as *King Arthur's Court* and *Treasure Island* as well as humorous selections like those from Joel Chandler Harris' collection of *Uncle Remus* tales. During these evenings, the radio was turned off. We did not have a television in our home until the early 1950s.

The after-dinner gatherings also included my mother giving us quizzes gleaned from the latest monthly issue of *Parent's Magazine,* first published in 1926. The magazine popularized scientific knowledge on child development to help parents rear their children. The quiz questions were grouped according to age ranges. I was the only kid in my age group. Answering the questions was exhilarating and fearful at the same time, because I would be devastated if I was wrong. Nevertheless, I wanted to achieve a high score.

As the evenings evolved, the conversations became less structured and led into discussions of Negro leaders of the past. These included the great poetess Phillis Wheatley who lived during colonial times; the inventor George Washington Carver; educator and writer Booker T. Washington who founded of Tuskegee Institute; architect Benjamin Banneker who had a major role in planning the layout of the nation's capital in Washington, DC; the great abolitionist Frederick Douglass; poet Paul Laurence Dunbar; National Association for the Advancement of Colored People (NAACP) founder W. E. B. Dubois; Black Nationalist Marcus Garvey. This also included patent attorney Henry Baker, chronicler of Negro inventors during the 19th century, who happened to be my mother's uncle.

Many other books in our home were used as references during the evening conversations. Few, if any, of these outstanding contributors to American culture and history were ever discussed in the schools my siblings attended. Of course, Mom often brought up her grandfather Lewis Clarke and read about him from Harriet Beecher Stowe's *The Key to Uncle Tom's Cabin*. I particularly remember her reading:

> *Lewis is a quadroon, a fine-looking man, with European features, hair slightly wavy, and with an intelligent, agreeable expression of countenance.*

> *The reader is now desired to compare the following incidents of the life of George Harris. His mother was a handsome quadroon woman, the daughter of her master, and given by him in marriage to a free White man. A Scotchman, with the express understanding that she and her children were to be free. This engagement, if made sincerely at all, was never complied with. His mother had nine children, and on the death of her husband, came back, with all these children, as slaves in her father's house.*

Mom would emphasize that our great-grandfather, Lewis Clarke was an important figure in American history, and that a well-known author incorporated his life experiences as a slave as part of one of our country's most famous novels.

I thought that was "pretty neat," but nothing more than that. I did not realize at the time that Stowe had quoted huge sections of a book that Clarke had published in 1845 about his experiences as a slave. She included them in *A Key to Uncle Tom's Cabin*. References in *The Key* made mention of a "narrative," but I'm assuming the family thought of that as word-of-mouth stories rather than a published book. It was evident that my mother was unaware of the book also, because it wasn't until decades later that the family found out about Clarke's historic publication through a distant cousin[1].

––––––

I relished mornings when I was alone with my mother and the older children were off to school; I was too young to attend. She would have the radio on, invariably listening to Don McNeill's *Breakfast Club*, a broadcast from Chicago. Part of the program featured a grand band march, usually composed by John Philip Sousa, like *Stars and Stripes Forever*. When the march started Mom would say, "Come on, Butch—let's march!"

We would strut to the beat of the music all over the kitchen. At the end of the music, she would grab me and belt out, "Squeeze me as hard as you can,

Mister!" She would follow with, "You can do better than that!" She made me feel so, so special!

The early morning radio shows we listened to also included the well-known African American singing group, The Golden Gate Quartet, who sang her favorite Negro spirituals and old jubilee-style gospel songs. The Quartet had a nationwide radio show and had the honor of singing at President Roosevelt's inauguration in 1941. I also recall a country and Western station that featured the (White) Sons of the Pioneers.

Music was a fundamental part of our lives as a family. The first twenty years of my life, I never needed an alarm clock. Instead, Dad's beautiful tenor voice would awaken me as he would hit the proper key on the piano and sing the scales—or he launched into spirituals, such as "This Little Light of Mine," "Little David Play on Your Harp," or "Sometimes I feel Like a Motherless Child," among others. Often, my older sister Guela or Sylvia would accompany him on the piano.

What a way to begin the day! I did not fully appreciate how blessed I was being exposed to that kind of magnificence on a daily basis until I left home to marry.

It is still incomprehensible to me how my mother was able to handle all of her household responsibilities during the time most of the children lived at home. She washed clothes in an old wringer washing machine, hanging them to dry on an outside clothesline or in our basement. She cooked meals, cleaned up the house, got us ready for school, and on and on. Although she doled out some chores to the older children, the bulk of the work needed around the house was left up to her.

Nevertheless, she found time to tend to the small "Victory Garden" of vegetables in our back yard, which was promoted by President Roosevelt to enhance our food supplies for the war effort. She was also able to maintain a lattice of sweet-pea flowers, iris, flag crocuses, and many other flowers and plants. To this day, all that I know about flowers I learned from my mother as a child.

The only time I remember my mother crying was when her mother, Guela Johnson Clarke, passed away on March 24, 1947. It seems like she cried for week straight. I was eight years old. When I saw her cry, I began to do the same. Although it did not resonate with me at the time, she was seven months pregnant with my sister Elaine, which probably added to her remorse that her mother would not see her new grandchild.

Mrs. Clarke was my favorite grandparent because I often slept overnight at her apartment near 24th and Madison Streets. At nighttime, she let her gray hair down and I would brush it. It went all the way to her waist. When I got out of line, she would stare at me with her pale blue eyes and shake her finger at me, and I knew she meant business! All in all, she had a caring but strict personality.

Many years after Grandma's death, when Mom was going through some very difficult emotional episodes, she would ask me, "Butch, do you think I will ever be as sweet and loving as Grandma was?"

I said, "Of course, Mom."

Mom could not be a shrinking violet and raise eight children. She had to use a switch more times than I can count. However, in the winter of her years, she was the exact image and demeaner of Grandma. I was so blessed having those two strong and loving women in my life.

PART II

SCHOOL DAYS

Ms. Chamberlin's kindergarten class at Madrona Elementary School in 1942. I am in the middle of the back row.

CHAPTER 4

Madrona Elementary and Meany Junior High Schools

I REMEMBER CLEARLY my first day of entering kindergarten at Madrona Elementary School even though I was only four years old. Our family home was one block away from the school. Mom had my older brother Gary take me to Miss Winifred Chamberlin's classroom. Gary was a fifth grader and becoming a young leader, and brother Phil was a third grader at the time.

Gary held my hand knowing that I had trepidations about leaving my mother's side. He introduced me to Miss Chamberlin who had a sweet and very comforting personality. She knew of the Gayton family through interactions with my mother as well as having my two older brothers in her class. Miss Chamberlin was one of the most caring and sensitive individuals I have ever known. My brothers and I

I did not know what to call it at the time, but I was being "tracked" for my remaining time in the public school system because I was not considered "college material."

---

were the only African Americans attending Madrona during the early 1940s, and the way Miss Chamberlin brought us into that all-White environment set a tone for us to truly enjoy the formal world of learning. From kindergarten through college, I never had a person of color as a teacher or professor.

Miss Chamberlin was a skilled photographer and took many pictures of students through the years. Many of the photos showed students holding her pet guinea pig or rabbit. One of her pictures was a true gem—of brother Phil holding the guinea pig. The picture could have been featured at a photography exhibit. Mom had it framed and displayed it in the family living room.

As a beneficiary of Miss Chamberlin's teaching, plus the value of early childhood education, my year in kindergarten provided me with a foundation and an appreciation of learning. Ms. Chamberlin was the prototype of a caring teacher who dedicated her life to children and the art of teaching. She made learning fun. Miss Chamberlin followed my career Long after my kindergarten year. From time to time, she would call me on the phone to congratulate me on some recognition or activity she'd seen written up in the local newspapers.

My pleasant experience of kindergarten did not transfer to my first grade. My teacher, with her black dresses with high-laced collars and a broach, along with her gray hair tied in a bun, depicted a woman who was austere in personality as well as appearance. Technically she was an excellent teacher, but she attempted to utilize fear as a motivator—an approach that never worked on me as a child nor as an adult. Her grim nature was intimidating to me.

During one class session, she leaned over to me and in a very harsh tone and whispered, "I do not trust you at all."

I did not respond, but her words made me more fearful than ever about her. I had no idea what triggered her remark; I tended to be reserved, and I never acted up in class. I felt bad. I was worried and confused.

When I arrived home, I moped around the house and waited for a quiet moment with my mother. I did not mention the incident, but finally I asked her, "Mom, what does 'not trust' mean?"

She said it meant not being dependable, and not believing a person to be honest.

I replied "Oh." I never told her what had happened. I was embarrassed and ashamed, but I did not know why, or what I had done wrong as a five-year-old. I just knew that a person of authority disliked me. It was especially hurtful not knowing what I had done.

The remaining school year was not a happy one for me. Looking back, I wonder if my being the only child of color in her class set off a deep-seated racist and hateful remark from a woman not accustomed to having Blacks in her classroom. Whatever her reason, the confidence I had in myself in Miss Chamberlin's class receded.

A welcome respite from some of the tensions I was beginning to feel at school came from discovering new friends and having adventures in the neighborhood after school and on the weekends. During excursions to the vacant lot kitty-corner from our house, I could catch and examine lizards and garter snakes. I also picked blossoms from the dogwood trees, the scotch broom, and bluebells for my mother. I made it a fun ritual, especially on May Day, leaving a bouquet of flowers at our front door, ringing the doorbell, then hiding in the back yard and waiting for her to exclaim her surprise and delight.

I started playing with kids my age on the block, like Betty Jane who lived next door and was several years younger than me. She was the one who for some reason named me "Butch," which caught on with family members and long-time friends and has stuck to this day.

Another early friend was Olé. He was one of several Sundberg family brothers who lived a few doors from us. Olé was intellectually challenged. He had the maturity level of a four- or five-year-old, which was my age when we first started playing together. He was much taller than me and probably twelve years my senior. He had a speech impediment and did not attend school. I do not recall other kids making fun of his speech impediment or slow thinking. He was part of the group of kids who lived on the block. He was my partner when we explored the vacant lot or flew our kites together. We had fun playing cops and robbers, and cowboys and Indians.

Around the age of six, I was allowed to go to Madrona Park with Olé or my brothers, usually Phil. The park, four blocks from our house, was a major gathering place especially for the boys in the neighborhood during the 1940s. The Gayton's were still the only Blacks in the area then. On any given day at the park, the ethnic make-up of the kids was comprised of the Gayton's, Scandinavians, and Sephardic and Ashkenazi Jews, some of whom were immigrants from war-torn Europe.

Olé and I expanded our circle of friends to include Jim and Micky Ellis whose dad was in the famous Seabees during the war, and Bill Mickle—all of whom were White.

The only girl in the group was Nancy. She was smart, pretty, and very athletic. She was deaf and mute. We had some difficulty understanding her speech, but it was not an overwhelming issue. When we played basketball, we all wanted to be on her team because she was a good athlete. It is interesting to note that our little group respected the two kids with disabilities. I do not recall any of us making fun of or looking down upon either Olé or Nancy. That mindset must be attributed to the upbringing by our parents.

All of the families within at least a six-block radius of the neighborhood knew of our close-knit little group. We were together for approximately five years. We got together every spare minute over those years. Summers were particularly special. We made many discoveries as we trekked through various vacant lots on the way to Madrona Beach on Lake Washington to go swimming. On the especially warm days, we would stay on the beach all day until we saw the historic steamship *Virginia V* chug past the beach at 5 p.m. That was the signal for us to head back through the woods and hills to our homes. None of us had bikes, at least any that were workable. We walked everywhere.

When we were not at the beach, we would gather in the front yard and play hide-and-seek or mumblety-peg, an outdoor game using pocketknives. Our version of the game was to attempt to stick the knife in the ground by flipping from the nose, the ears, and the shoulders. Whoever stuck the knife in the ground the most won the game.

Toward the end of summer, many of the vacant lots near our homes were filled with wild bushes of ripe blackberries. My mother encouraged us to pick them for making blackberry cobbler, pies, punch, or blackberry jam. We would carry our bowls and small ladders. Sometimes we took the wooden leaves from our dining room tables to mat down the prickly vines so we could reach the sweetest and blackest berries! There were four primary lots that we harvested each year. For the jam, Mom would cook the berries, pour the mixture into Mason jars, and seal each with paraffin wax. The jars would be placed in our cool basement for consumption during the winter. My buddies and I would go through the same process every summer.

Sometimes we would be daring and raid the Rainier and Bing cherry trees in the back yards of homes we had mapped out. Occasionally, we were chased out of the yards, and at times we fell from the branches, squashing the cherries we had stuffed in our pockets, the sugary juice sticking to our pants and legs! The owners of the trees usually knew the culprits and would chase us off in a perfunctory manner as if our mischievousness was an expected ritual. Those were different times indeed! If kids today did the same, they more than likely would be arrested or shot at.

It was not unusual for our little group to take short cuts through the neighbors' yards to reach our destinations. One evening I was with four of the neighbor boys and my younger brother Leonard, who was about six at the time. We were trudging through a yard and as one of the taller guys passed by a window of an apartment house he suddenly blurted out, "Oh my god. Look!"

The rest of us had to get on our tiptoes to see a middle-aged woman undressing. We had never—at least I had never—seen anything like it. It was almost like she was putting on a performance for us. Not more than a couple of minutes had passed when a police car flashing its lights drove up in the driveway!

My friends and I took off running in all directions. I ran up a hill and didn't stop until I was four blocks away from the apartment house, and suddenly realized that *I had left Leonard behind*. The poor little guy was slowly walking toward home. I felt terrible. I put my arm around him and told him not to mention anything to Mom about our episode.

This all happened on a Saturday, which was bath day for the younger siblings. When Leonard and I entered the house that evening, Mom told us to hurry up and get undressed to take our baths. When we were in the tub together, which was a usual practice, she asked where we had been. I told her we were playing at the Saint Teresa playground which was six blocks from where the police confrontation took place. I gave Leonard a hard stare to make sure he was on board with the story line.

My fib worked. I never heard any negative feedback about what happened that evening, but I had many sleepless nights afterwards, especially thinking about the danger my little brother was exposed to.

The lazy summer evenings with my buddies left pleasant recollections. We might meander around the neighborhood watching the sunset, or we'd sit on our family porch gazing at the stars and talking about anything that came into our minds. We had no inhibitions concerning the subject matter, but mostly we bantered about the latest radio show, such as the action hero Captain Midnight, the sci-fi show Dimension X, The Lone Ranger, The Shadow Mysteries, or Sergeant Preston of the Yukon.

As the sun went down, we would look at the stars and try to pick out the Big and Little Dippers and the Milky Way. We would look in amazement at the shooting stars! From time to time, we would sleep together in our "fort" that we built in the vacant lot across the street from our house. Basically, it was a 7-foot-deep by 6-by-6-foot-wide hole in the ground, covered with boards, a rug, and dirt, with a small entrance to crawl in and out. It survived two summers until big Olé jumped on it and the entire top collapsed! Luckily no one was inside.

———

I was clearly aware of my Black heritage and the fact that I was different from my close-knit band of friends culturally, but in no way did I consider myself inferior to them. Their parents did not show any trepidation about me associating with them. I only have one recollection of a racial incident occurring among my friend group. The incident happened when I was about nine years old.

I was moving away from my friendship with Olé as I became more involved in school, and my pool of friends began to broaden to include other White and Jewish kids. I noticed that Olé was befriending a new boy who lived a few blocks from me and also attended Madrona School. One day I saw the new boy, Norton, and Olé together near the school, and Norton was whispering in Olés ear. Then Olé ran up to me and said loudly with his speech impediment, "Bute (Butch), you a niddah (nigger)!" Then he ran back to Norton who laughed. They both walked off giggling as they looked back at me.

I called out, "Olé, you do not know what you are saying. It's not good for you to say that word! Don't say it again."

Regrettably, that was the beginning of the end for my friendship with Olé. I felt bad. The fun years we had together became a memory of the past. Olés innocence regarding racism was over. We both moved into the mainstream and reality of American life.

Olés family moved out of Seattle within a year. Interestingly, the Sundberg family sold their home to a Black family from Arkansas. They became the second Black family to move into our immediate neighborhood. Thus, the beginning of the "second great migration" of Blacks from the South began to manifest in Seattle.

The issue of race became more of a factor in my school life by third grade. One morning I was walking across the Madrona School playground before school and two of my classmates, Neal and Steve, were playing hopscotch. I casually asked if I could join them, and one snidely remarked, "No, go away."

I was mad and sulked. I thought they brushed me off because I was Black. As I walked away, I murmured under my breath, "dirty Jew." To my surprise, Neal heard me. And he said, "I'm going to tell Miss Nadeau"—our classroom teacher.

I have no idea what possessed me to say what I did, or how I knew they were Jewish. Nevertheless, the deed was done.

After roll call, Miss Nadeau asked me to step outside the classroom. I was petrified. I had never been in trouble at school, aside from the mystifying experience with my first-grade teacher two years earlier. Miss Nadeau, a pleasant but no-nonsense middle-aged woman looked me straight in the eyes. She said, "Neal told me what you called him 'a dirty Jew' because he wouldn't let you play with him and Steve."

I said meekly, "Yes, I did."

She continued, "Carver, how would you like him to call you 'a dirty . . .'"

I braced myself, waiting for the horrifying and painful epitaph that my parents did not allow anyone in our household to utter even in jest. "NIGGER" rang through my mind.

But she made a dramatic pause and said "...a dirty Negro?" Which was the acceptable term for Blacks in those days.

I exhaled in relief! I replied, "No, Miss Nadeau, I wouldn't like that."

She took me by the hand and said, "I want you, Neal, and Steve to go outside with waste baskets and pick up the trash on the school grounds until the bell rings. And while you're outside, I want you to apologize to the boys." I followed Miss Nadeau's order, and Steve and Neal accepted my apology. Neal was stern with the admonition that I never say that again. The whole drama left me with mixed feelings of remorse, but I gained enlightenment and appreciation of the sensitivities of others.

Looking back, I consider the way that Miss Nadeau handled the situation as masterful. She understood the cultural and racial sensitivities of each of us. If she had handled the situation differently, it could have blown up to be a school and community crisis. Her commonsense instincts represent a model for us all when we face similar circumstances.[2]

Throughout grade school, I did not feel academically challenged and, as a result, did not receive very high grades. Nevertheless, for the most part, I enjoyed my teachers and the relationships I had with the other students. I was a popular student and was bestowed the highest accolade a boy could receive in elementary school during the 1940s in Seattle: captain of the School Boy Patrol for my sixth and last grade at Madrona. I liked being liked! My brother Gary received the same recognition five years earlier.

During the '40s there was a nationwide paper shortage. My school began an annual paper drive to encourage recycling. As captain of Patrol, one responsibility I had was to check in the stacks of papers to be recycled. I was approached by a few of my friends, asking me to set aside some popular comic books during the paper drive. I knew it was wrong to give the comics to my friends—I never kept any for myself—but it curried their favor, which bonded my relationship with them. Nevertheless, I felt some guilt.

I was beginning to wean away from my relationship with my old "crew" of Jim and Micky Ellis, Olé, and Bill Mickle. I started to develop new relationships with boys who lived farther away from the family home. Dick was one of my news friends. He was taller and heavier than most boys his age, including me. Some considered him somewhat of a bully, probably because of his size. However, he never bullied me. We often played softball and touch football together at Madrona Park and generally got along fine.

One summer afternoon, my next older brother Phil, looking flustered, rushed up to me as I was sitting on our porch. He blurted out, "Butch, I need a favor from you." I thought this was serious because, as the younger brother, I was usually asking favors and questions of him.

As a flattered eleven-year-old, I said, "Sure what's up?"

He said, "Dick and I were at the park a few minutes ago and he called me a 'nigger'!" I thought to myself, *Shit. This is serious.*

Phil went on to say, "Since you two are the same age, you have to fight him for me."

I said, "But he didn't call me the name."

Phil responded, "Since I'm four years older than him, I can't fight him— because it wouldn't be fair."

Phil never explained what led to the name calling. The clear implication was that if I did not fight Dick, I would have some repercussions from Phil. I was between a rock and a hard place. I reluctantly agreed to fight Dick.

Phil said he would set up the fight later that afternoon on a side lawn of Madrona Park, next to the street. I was pleased that Phil wanted me to help him out of a jam, but I had no desire whatsoever to fight Dick who was built like a man.

Phil worked out the arrangements and the three of us met at the park. Dick and I said "Hi" with both of us being non-plussed by the whole situation. Phil explained the rules. Since Dick was bigger than me, he would lie on his back on the ground and I would be on top of him, and Phil would say "Go," and the fight would begin.

As soon as Phil said "Go," Dick flipped me over and was on top of me with his knees imbedded between the bone and muscle of each of my upper arms. I cried out, "What do I do now? I can't move!"

Looking perplexed, Phil said, "OK, Ok, Ok. Let's do this again. Dick, you let Butch up, and Butch you get back on top of Dick."

We went through the same ritual three more times with the same results. Finally, a flustered Phil said, "This isn't going anywhere. Let's stop."

I was so grateful. As Dick and I said goodbye, Phil shook his finger at Dick and said, unconvincingly, "Let that be a lesson to you, Dick!" Phil and I walked home together in silence, while I rubbed my sore arms.

My social transition of unconsciously weaning myself away from my group of White friends in the Madrona neighborhood and becoming more involved with Black kids was enlightening as well as adventurous. I was feeling my way through these new relationships and finding a level of comfort as I transitioned to Meany Junior High in the fall of 1950.

I became a bit distraught when I learned I was assigned to a woodshop vocational class when most of my sixth-grade friends were assigned Spanish or French language courses. I did not know what to call it at the time, but I was being "tracked" for my remaining time in the public school system because I was not considered "college material." Looking around, I did not recognize any of the other students in my woodshop class. Most were poor Whites or Blacks. I became confused, surly, and argumentative. The grades in my classes were above average, but certainly not exceptional. I was assigned second semester to a metal shop class along with my core courses, and I became more disgruntled.

One day I got into an argument with a mean-spirited boy named Bill. He seemed to aggravate everyone in the class. I have no recollection of what the argument was about, but I remember that at the conclusion of it, Bill challenged me. He said, "I'll meet you in the boys' bathroom immediately after school to settle this!" I responded emphatically with a gruff, "No problem! I'll be there!" I realized that his challenge could potentially lead to a fight, which I did not relish at all. However, my pride would not allow me to back down.

We met in the bathroom. Nobody else was there. We stood face to face, yammering threats. I thought I could talk my way out and hoped Bill would back down. Suddenly, out of nowhere, he swiftly hit me in the mouth with his fist. I knew immediately that he had something else in his hand because the blow felt like an electric shock. I stepped back feeling pieces of my front teeth in my mouth. I reached up to my face, felt moisture, and then looked at my hand filled with blood. As Bill rushed out the door, I saw a huge brass ring on his finger similar to what many boys were creating in the metal shop.

I stood there for a minute or so, stunned, with my bloodied hand over my mouth. Then I ran out of the school and continued running from 22nd Avenue and Denny Street all the way to where I lived on 31st Avenue and Pike Street. I didn't stop running until I entered the house. I didn't cry, but feared what my mother would say when she saw my face.

I have no recollection of what she said that evening. But I do recall the shock on her face! My front two teeth were broken in half, and my lips had deep gashes that later left lifetime scars. I also have no memory of what my father said. I had never been in a fight with any of the kids in school or the neighborhood before. What I had etched in my mind was that my face was disfigured for life and that I had to retaliate.

I telephoned Willie Stovall, a tough Black kid who lived in Madison Valley, whom I recently befriended at Meany. I told him to get me a big brass ring and to let Bill know that we would meet after school the next day at the outdoor basketball court to continue the fight. Word got around school the following day about the plan. I floated through the classes in a haze, anticipating the fight. I had no fear whatsoever. I only had revenge on my mind. Bill was White and about the same size as me.

After the bell for school dismissal rang, Willie met me in the boys' bathroom and gave me his brass ring. It was a bit too big for me, but I was not concerned. I took off my regular shoes and put on the tennis shoes I brought with me to school. I was prepared for battle.

Willie and I walked out of the restroom side by side to the outdoor basketball court, which was filled with what appeared to be half of the enrollment of Meany! Bill was already there. Willie asked if Bill and I were ready and we simultaneously and loudly said, "Yeah!" Willie said, "Let's get it on!"

The punches flew. I did not feel any of his blows. I was attempting to hit his front teeth. A couple of times Bill said, "Are we done?" and I said "Yes." And as he began to walk away, I hit him from behind each time. I got the best of him as the fight moved outside the court onto the side entrance of the school. The fight ended when Willie knelt behind Bill and I pushed him over Willie's back. Bill struggled to get back up, but it was apparent that Bill had had enough.

Prior to the fight, I was fundamentally considered a non-entity. After the fight, they saw me as a "tough guy" with the result of me having more Black friends.

At that point, the school's music teacher ran out. She rushed over to Bill and wrapped her arms around him. Looking sideways toward me, she screamed, "What have you done to him, Carver?"

I had a hard time figuring out her reaction since my face looked like a truck had rolled over it from Bill's sucker punch the day before! Immediately, Miss Peterson, the tall Swedish assistant principal, came toward us and told me and Bill to follow her to the office so she could find out what led to the fight. I was oblivious to her scolding, but neither of us were suspended from school.

The next day, Bill came to school with a broken arm in a plaster-of-Paris cast. I kept looking to see if any of his front teeth were broken. I subsequently learned that I had chipped a couple of his back teeth. When I confronted Bill, he was as ornery as ever and spit out, "Gayton, I'll shove this cast down your throat!" I laughed and walked away, feeling somewhat satisfied that Bill had paid the price for what he had done to me.

However, I had years of flashbacks of that fight with Bill. These memories always reignited the hatred I had toward him. I was also disturbed by how enraged I became during the fight. I was prepared to do everything possible to maim him, with no consideration of fair play. I rationalized my actions by saying to myself that fairness was not a consideration for him when he sucker-punched me with his ring. I am grateful that I have not felt such rage since that horrific afternoon.

One interesting outcome of the fight was how I was looked upon with greater esteem by the Black boys in the school. Prior to the fight, I was fundamentally considered a non-entity. After the fight, they saw me as a "tough guy" with the result of me having more Black friends.

Miss Peterson decided to make me one of her personal projects. She evidently felt I was on the verge of becoming a juvenile delinquent or a dropout because of the fight. She gave me some responsibilities to help me to stay on the right track and out of trouble. She asked me to be a courier for the school's lunchroom receipts. I took these to the Administrative Service Office of the Seattle Public Schools approximately three miles away two to three times a week. I was given a satchel of money and bus tokens for the round trip. Also, she asked me to work with Mr. Lee, the highly regarded gym teacher, to raise and take down the Stars and Stripes several days a week. I did this with another good friend from the neighborhood, Gordon Golliette, who happened to be White.

Miss Peterson really knew how to read me. Those two projects certainly boosted my self-esteem. I was so proud to tell Mom and Dad about my important assignments. I never was fully sure if Miss Peterson's actions were initiated exclusively by her or whether she worked in concert with my parents to come up with the plan. The peculiar thing about this whole drama is that I have no recollection of my parents admonishing or consoling me about the fight. What I did know, without my parents having to tell me, was that what I had done was out of character for how a "Gayton Boy" should comport himself. Their silence was deafening.

The damage to my teeth was more extensive than initially diagnosed. The blow to one tooth drove the root into my jaw creating an infection. I was sent to Dr. Groves, the family dentist, the only Black dentist in Seattle at the time. Dr. Groves was not trained as a dental surgeon, but he conducted the surgery as best he could. He had to cut off the root of the tooth as well as a portion of my jaw to eliminate the infection. I had to make at least three visits, and all were especially painful. The Novocain injections were ineffective. My screams led him to slap me several times. I never told my parents. It was clear that the cost for the dental work must have been exorbitant, and my parents did not have dental insurance. The dental bills, along with the financial burden of raising eight children, must have been overwhelming for my father.

As a result of the fight, I became more withdrawn. My swagger declined. The jagged and discolored teeth made me embarrassed to smile. I was reluctant to approach girls because of my appearance. I asked my mother several times if there was any way to get the teeth fixed, and she would say, "Butch, there is no need to have it done until you finish football," which I started playing during my freshman year at Garfield High School. After a while I quit asking her, realizing that such a procedure would be a prohibitive expense.

Around the time of the incident, I began having a vision or dream that recurred for many years. In the dream, I am sitting across from my father at our kitchen table, and we are alone in the room. My father looks at me disdainfully and says in a near whisper, "I do not like you." I do not react with fear, but I am confused, not really knowing if I actually see him and hear what he is saying. To this day, I am at a loss as to whether that scene was a nightmare or reality. I've been telling myself for over 70 years that the whole scene was a figment of my imagination because what I thought he said was completely out of character for him. Growing up, he did not show great affection, but he was *always* kind to me. I never felt neglected, and as I grew older, he seemed genuinely proud of me.

———

My remaining year at Meany continued to be less than uplifting. My academic performance became mediocre, and I was feeling uncomfortable and distant around other students at the school. I would occasionally attend school-sponsored "sock hops" on Friday evenings, and I learned how to do the popular dance among the White kids called the "Avalon." I reluctantly would ask no more than two of the White girls to dance and was turned down fifty percent of the time. Only two or three Black kids would show up because the records played were usually Top 40 tunes without Black performers.

During a break at one of the Spring hops, I walked outside to get a breath of fresh air. It was early evening and nearly dark. As I turned a corner of the school building, I was jumped by four "greasers"—White guys from the school with leather jackets and chains, their hair greased back to form "duck tails." My arms were held back by one of the bigger toughs in the group, and he yelled, "This nigger was following a White girl. Let's take care of him."

I said, "What are you talking about?" I had no idea any girl was outside. I recognized one of the guys who I considered a casual friend. His name was Jack Chamberlin, and he occasionally helped me with my paper route. I had not realized Jack was hanging out with such a band of losers.

Jack told the big guy who was still holding my arms, "This is Butch. I know him. He's ok. Let him go."

I was not particularly afraid, probably because I just considered them "wanna-be-gangsters," but that was the last sock hop I attended.

Branching out to new friends, I was invited, quite often, to the home of Jimmy Hatfield, a sixth-grade classmate. He lived one block away from Madrona Park. Jimmy's home also became quite popular with other boys in our class because Jimmy's parents owned one of the first television sets in the neighborhood. Additionally, his father was an executive with KIRO radio and had dozens of our favorite radio programs on shellac discs. I enjoyed visiting Jimmy's home. I felt welcomed by him as well as his parents.

One day toward the end of the school year, our sixth-grade classroom was abuzz about an impending party that was to take place at Jimmy's home. I was surprised that I was practically the only kid in the class who didn't know about it, especially since it was to be held at the home of one of my best friends. I was confused and hurt.

I confronted him, and he was upfront about me not being invited. He did not have an explanation. I was devastated and became indignant. I told him, "You are one of my best friends. You obviously made a mistake. I will be there!" I was surprised by my own arrogance. Jimmy did not object. I thought, *what could I have done to Jimmy to be so betrayed?*

Preparing for the party, I dressed in my best church attire: slacks, sport coat, my best shoes, etc. When I arrived at his home, I was greeted pleasantly by his mother who didn't seem surprised to see me. I arrived a bit later than the others and noticed that I was one of the last guests. Looking around the living room I immediately realized I had made a mistake. Of the three Black kids in our class, I was the only one in the room. But even worse, all of the kids were *paired off* by boy and girl! I was the odd boy out. No girl for me.

As the evening wore on and several games took place, I felt even more uncomfortable when "spin-the-bottle" began. The idea of the game was that when the bottle stopped spinning, whichever couple the top of the bottle pointed at would give each other a kiss.

With the assistance of Jimmy's mother, and by unanimous acclaim, I was appointed the permanent bottle spinner. I was the only one of the kids who was

Jimmy's party, whether I consciously thought of it or not, marked the beginning of a social separation between me and my White friends when the opposite sex came into the picture.

---

not paired off. Also, being the official "bottle spinner," I was not allowed to kiss any of the girls.

I felt more humiliated than angry. I was the first to leave the party. But I gave Jimmy the benefit of the doubt. Up to that point in our lives, Jimmy and I had had a colorblind relationship. In my mind, the racist sex configuration of the party was too sophisticated for eleven-year-old Jimmy. Obviously, Jimmy's parents planned the pairing of the White kids.

Jimmy's party, whether I consciously thought of it or not, marked the beginning of a social separation between me and my White friends when the opposite sex came into the picture. I gravitated toward social activities that included girls and boys at the predominately Black Eastside YWCA and the YMCA. I also joined the Youth Choir and Youth Usher Board at my family church, the First African Methodist Episcopal Church.

My close friends became almost exclusively Black. John Bass started attending First African Methodist Episcopal Church (FAME) with me regularly. We joined the Youth Choir and the Youth Usher Board. Although we were God-fearing young men, God knew that a primary interest for joining the groups was to meet the girls who were also members. Invariably, after the weekend practices for the choir and the usher board, we would go to the home of someone in the group to listen and dance to the latest rhythm and blues hits.

My first bit of intimacy with a girl happened outside the home of one of these gatherings. I was attracted to a pretty girl my age named Bonnie. As we were talking, she suggested that we kiss. I began shaking in anticipation and I started kissing with my lips closed, as I had seen actors in the movies. I thought to myself, *this isn't working right*, because she kept trying to stick her tongue through my closed lips. She stopped and said, "Haven't you ever French kissed?"

I said, "What's that?"

She replied, "Now relax and open your mouth and let me show you."

I was a happy thirteen-year-old, and I've been relaxing ever since.

———

One Sunday afternoon service at FAME, the Youth Usher Board was on duty and my friend John and I were the ushers for one side of the congregation hall. A young preacher and his choir from Tacoma were the program guests. FAME in those days was regarded as the more sedate and conservative of the African American churches. The FAME choirs tended to sing more hymns and spirituals rather than gospel music, and the sermons were more cerebral than emotional.

But this young preacher and his choir were not at all products of the FAME conservative tradition. John and I liked the up-tempo, soulful music of the visiting choir, like the rhythm and blues tunes being played at the parties we attended.

The electrifying gospel songs set the stage for the preacher. His message soared! After fifteen minutes or so, he began chanting while a call and response cadence took place between him and the swinging organist. The emotion within the congregation was rising. He chanted in rhythm: "The devil is among us, uh . . . he is everywhere, uh . . . we must be strong, uh . . . here he comes, uh . . ."

The choir members stood up, raised their arms, and started shouting "Preach! Preach! Yes, Lord! Thank you! Thank you!" Suddenly the preacher ran from the podium, jumped off the stage and began running up and down the aisles while the organist went off on his own furious, syncopated tangent. As the preacher ran, he kept looking back with a fearful expression while swatting his hand toward the rear, shouting "Get back! Get back! Get back! Get back, Devil!" His robe was flowing as all the eyes of the congregation were fixed on him. John and I were mesmerized.

A large lady in the choir loft worked herself into a trance and fell on the brass bar of the loft. Four male members of the choir tried to lift her up delicately and tastefully as possible, to no avail. Finally, each of the men took one of her limbs and carried her through the church spread eagle. All of this was happening while the preacher continued to run up and down the aisles, swatting the imaginary devil.

John and I looked at each other and broke into uncontrollable laughter! I was on my knees, laughing. One of the adult deacons walked over and admonished us for our "shameful behavior." He also informed us that our services were no longer needed. John and I continued laughing as we exited the church.

———

Changes in the racial makeup of the neighborhood made building more relationships with Black friends feel natural and unforced. The home of Olé Sundberg was now occupied by John Bass, who was my age, Mr. and Mrs. Williams, and their four sons. John, bright, athletic, and gregarious, became one of my new best friends and remained so through high school.

Around the same time, another Black family, originally from Texas, moved in three blocks from my home. Within the family was a son, Royal (Roy) Dotson, who was also my age. Roy was a natural athlete who excelled in both football and baseball during our high school years. He had a great sense of humor and a commanding personality. What probably attracted me most to him was his street smarts. He was mature beyond his years. When he was twelve, Roy went to Alaska with his father as a laborer on a construction project. The fact that he was allowed to do that with his dad gives one the sense of how precocious he was physically and mentally. Roy and I remained good friends until the day he died at the age of sixty-two. I am also the godfather of his first child, Rochelle.

The Bakers were another Black family who moved in six houses south of John Bass's home. King Baker was also the same age as Roy, John, and me. We became the new "crew" in the area, but we maintained a fringe relationship with the initial group of my White friends.

King Baker tended to be more of a loner than my other Black friends. Much of that was because John, Roy, and I were more involved in sports than King. However, he was the one who admonished me one day by saying, "Butch, you have to become more 'hip'." He continued, "If you want to know what's happening, you have to show up at the 'free for all' house parties that go on in the CD (Central District) on the weekends."

King was describing the Central District as mostly the area a few blocks from us in the Madison Valley area, between Cherry Street and Madison Street, where most of the Black families lived. King also influenced my dress style by wearing pegged pants with thin suede belts and suede shoes. I was intrigued, to say the least.

I began attending the house parties he related to me, and they were eye openers! The parties were all Black affairs. As a twelve-year-old new to the scene, I was clearly one of the wallflowers. But I learned how to do the "slow drag" and "off time" swing dance at the small private house parties given by the mother of another new Black friend, Wesley Graves. The get-togethers at Wesley's home were arranged between his mother and several other mothers, such as mine, who had known each other for many years. In other words, they were from older Seattle families. As a result, the kids invited were me, Carrolle Fair, Pat Winston, Carolyn Purnell, and Bobby Johnson. We were considered kids from "nice" families, or longtime Black families, in the eyes of our parents. For example, Carrolle Fair's great-grandfather, William Grose, was one of the first Black residents in Seattle, having arrived in the city in 1860, ultimately becoming one of Seattle's wealthiest residents. These private, pre-teen, and early teen affairs were chaperoned primarily by Mrs. Graves, but the other mothers were encouraged to assist her.

Although the parties always had the excellent cooking of Mrs. Graves and were pleasant, I looked forward to the more adventurous free-for-all parties introduced to me by King Baker where parents were nowhere to be seen. They were usually held in the basements of homes and were crowded. No invitations were sent out. Kids found out about them by word-of-mouth. The records played were the latest rhythm and blues of the day purchased from the Black-owned Little Record Mart on the corner of 22nd and Madison. Such records were the precursors of rock and roll tunes that took off in popularity during the mid-nineteen fifties.[3]

———

Around this time, I wanted to be more socially independent, and not depend exclusively on the small "allowance" I would get periodically from Mom for chores I did around the house and yard. I worked mostly during the summer as a paper boy delivering *The Shopping News*, *The Seattle Times*, and the *Seattle Post-Intelligencer*. I also worked a variety of jobs including selling milk bottles for five cents each, washing dishes at Mrs. Steiner's Bohemian Bakery on 34th Avenue in Madrona, and cleaning homes for wealthy families who lived near the Tennis Club in Madison Park. Most of the jobs were hand-me-downs from my brothers, Gary and Phil. Often, I would work with each brother separately to learn the ropes, then they would pass the jobs on to me.

One of the more challenging jobs I had was taking over Phil's morning *P.I.* paper route the summer of 1950. The route was between Union and Madison Streets covering parts of 23rd, 24th, and 25th. The area I covered was comprised almost exclusively of Blacks, who happened to be poor and/or lower middle class. Through June, July, and August I *lost* money, because about a third of the residents could not or would not pay for the delivery of the paper. It was not untypical when a man answered the doorbell, for him to say, "Boy, I didn't order the God-damned newspaper. Don't you come back here again!" And then slam the door. Invariably, I would owe money out of my pocket each month to the *P.I.*

Once, Phil asked me to come with him to collect for *The Seattle Times*. His paper route hit the homes on 30th Avenue off Pike Street, an area of mostly lower- or middle-income Whites. At one home, a young White man answered the doorbell, looked us up and down and yelled to his wife, "Honey, there are two snow bunnies here collecting for the *Times*! What should I tell them?" Phil and I looked at each other and shook our heads. We did not show anger because we needed the money and got it. Despite the indignity, we had to laugh about the fact that White racists had as many derogatory names for us as we had for them—but "snow bunnies" was a new one.

For the most part, having a paper route was a positive experience. For example, I recovered a young pigeon on a house porch with a broken wing. I took the bird home, put a splint on the wing, built a small coop, and nourished it with bird seed until it was strong enough to fly. The bird kept coming back for food for the next *five years*. I was very proud of myself, especially since few in the family expected the bird to survive.

The morning paper routes on the Seattle ritzy "Gold Coast" on Lake Washington, near the Seattle Tennis Club, were obviously enjoyable—and quite a contrast to the homes less than a mile away in the predominately Black neighborhood. I actually *earned* money during the summers because the White wealthy customers paid their monthly bills for the newspaper subscriptions, and more often than not gave tips. Occasionally, a butler would come to the door with rolls of dimes or quarters on silver trays to pay when I rang the bell. The homes were luxurious, and during the summer months their backyard patios would often have tables of fruits and candies left over night. I would occasionally indulge myself with a banana, assuming such goodies were left on purpose for the paperboy.

Another fond experience of my morning paper route was walking along the corner of 23rd and Madison Street around four o'clock in the morning when I'd hear the blues and jazz bands and singers still performing at the Washington Social Club! A few of the tunes I heard included classics like The Clover's "One Mint Julip," James Moody's "Moody's Mood for Love," and the risqué "Hey Mrs. Jones," by Jimmy Forrest. Quincy Jones reminisces about his collaboration with Ray Charles during the late '40s and early '50s. He says the Washington Social club was one of the venues where they played.

In the early dawn with my paper bag over my shoulders, I was in heaven listening to those sounds! I yearned for the day when I would be old enough to go into that club and witness such gifted musicians! After hearing such soulful music, I had no problem at all finishing my route.

CHAPTER 5

Garfield High School and Football

I ENTERED MY FRESHMAN year at Garfield High School in 1952. John Bass was still an eighth grader at Meany. We maintained contact, though not as frequently as before. At Garfield, I reconnected with my friend Royal (Roy) Dotson, also a freshman. Roy had a dark complexion and was fairly tall and very muscular. I gravitated toward him because he was street wise, had a great sense of humor, and was very comfortable around girls. He smoked unfiltered Lucky Strike cigarettes from the time he was twelve and would continue to do so until his untimely death at age 62.

Roy and I walked to Garfield and back nearly every day, a total of four miles, until we graduated. We talked about everything. It was a great way for me to start the day. We did not have a great deal in common regarding our family backgrounds, but we had mutual respect and appreciation for what we each represented. Not only did I admire his rapport with girls, but he was relaxed around kids as well as adults. He had a ribald sense of humor that kept me in stitches.

I was fascinated by his large extended family with Texan roots. His mother's southern cooking opened a new world of cuisine that contrasted with my mother's blander cooking. I witnessed in awe the weekend-long parties at Roy's house with plenty of drinking and soul food as well as his uncle playing Texas blues on the guitar. His stepdad and his friends worked hard as construction laborers all week and couldn't wait until Friday. They stayed true to the old blues lyric: "The eagle (depicted on coins of the era) flies on Friday, and Saturday we go out to play."

In those days, Friday was payday for laborers across the country, and the beginning of night parties which often lasted through Sunday night. Such partying gave rise to blues songs like "Call it Stormy Monday," made famous in 1947 by blues-great T-Bone Walker.

I observed that Roy connected with me because of my stable family situation and the fact that schoolwork came relatively easily to me, though I was not an exceptional student. Decades later at Roy's funeral, I was surprised to find out from his widow that he regarded me as a "chick magnet" and liked to hang out with me because of that. In no way did I see myself in that light. In fact, I took mental notes of how *he* related to girls.

Hanging out with Roy also gave me "legitimacy" among the "Black brothers," particularly those who lived on the other side of town, south of Jackson Street. Roy's family had lived in that section of the city before they'd moved into the Madrona district. Because of Roy's build, fearless appearance, and swagger, no one from the Jackson Street area would ever challenge him. Roy was not a bully, but he could easily have been one. He was a boy-man who looked older than his age when he was a young man, but then looked younger when he was middle-aged. His appearance did not change much over the years. Given my light complexion and non-generic Black features, hanging around Roy with his classic Black features may have further "legitimatized" my "Blackness." I certainly did not think along those lines as we grew up together.

I remember walking home after school with Roy one day and relaying that almost every day after freshman football practice, Speedy Bryant, from the south side, was trying to egg me on into wrestling with him. It was playful at first, but it was clear he wanted to rachet it up. Speedy was much bigger than me, but I held my own. When I gave him a few crunching tackles during football practice, he decided to back off. He didn't like getting hit. As I told this to Roy, he said something that described his outlook on life: "Butch, my dad always told me, 'Step on. Or *be* stepped on. Do not let anyone take advantage of you.'"

The way he spit out his statement was chilling. I never witnessed Roy fighting anyone. But the way he carried himself, along with his muscular physique, said it all: "Don't mess with Roy!" I was going to stay close to Roy Dotson.

My interest in football started in the late '40s, and especially in the early '50s, when football-greats running-back Hugh McElhenny and quarterback Don Heinrich were playing for the Washington Huskies. Each became college All-Americans and National Football League standouts, with McElhenny ultimately being inducted into the NFL Hall of Fame. I never played organized football until my freshman year at Garfield. During middle school, I'd played sandlot ball at Madrona playfield. At that time, I felt I had to hit guys harder than others because I was small for my age and had to prove myself.

As a teenager, I would walk from the Madrona neighborhood to the U of W stadium to watch the Huskies practice. I was in awe of the ambience of the beautiful U of W campus and the majestic stadium. An added thrill was when I walked through the dark tunnel between the football locker room and onto the sunlit playing field. I'd imagine the stadium full of sixty thousand fans, cheering the football players as they ran out of the tunnel onto the field before each game. What a rush that had to be for the players! Never in my wildest dreams, in 1950, did I see myself ever playing football for the University of Washington—or for any other university. Such a thought was simply unimaginable.

My negative experiences at Meany Junior High School had left me somewhat rudderless with no real sense of direction. As a result of the fight, I considered my face deformed, and no girls were interested in me. With the exception of John Bass and Roy Dotson, I didn't have close friends. School classes were non-eventful for me, and I was not significantly challenged by my teachers because they didn't have great expectations of me. I received C grades for the most part, with an occasional B.

I was extremely happy that I made the freshman football team at Garfield.[4]

Toward the end of my first year at Garfield, something piqued my interest in the trophy cases in the halls of Garfield: the name "Homer Harris" was etched on various trophies. They included recognitions covering record-breaking achievements in football, baseball, and track. He was All-City in *all* of the sports he participated in—and was named as captain or inspirational winner in those sports as well! Certificates related to his academic achievements were also displayed in the cases.

I had vague recollections over the years of my parents talking about him, mentioning that he attended Garfield in the mid-1930s and was a good friend of a few of my uncles. Mom and Dad would point out that he was an outstanding athlete at Garfield and attended the University of Iowa where he also excelled in football. After graduating, he had completed his Medical Degree at the acclaimed African American Meharry Medical School. From there he'd gone on to Chicago where he was a practicing dermatologist.

Needless to say, I was impressed by the stories I'd heard about Doctor Harris, but I became an even greater admirer after seeing his trophies and certificates at Garfield. I thought Dr. Harris had done it all. He obviously was the highest achieving student athlete to ever graduate from Garfield. I did not consciously tell myself that I wanted to emulate Homer, but I was certainly fortunate to be aware of his achievements. There's no question that he remained on my mind from that time forward.

My interest in football grew through my sophomore year. I believed I had the tools to become a member of the varsity squad despite my 145 pounds and five-feet-eight inches. As my sophomore year was coming to an end, I decided to watch the University of Washington's 1954 Spring, inter-squad game. As the game progressed, I noticed Garfield's head football coach, "Swede" Lindquist, standing on the side-lines. He was tall, gray-haired, heavy set, and a bit gruff. His demeanor, physique, and old school style of coaching intimidated many of the players at Garfield. I had not talked with him very often during my first two years there. Nevertheless, I hesitantly walked up to him and said, "Hi, Coach. How are you? I'm really looking forward to the turn out for the varsity in the Fall."

He began laughing and said, "Gayton, you're too small. You should stick with track like your brothers. The Gaytons are meant to be track men."

I replied, "Coach, I like track. But I'm still turning out for football."

Swede guffawed and said, "OK Gayton, I'll see you in the Fall," as he continued to laugh." He obviously got a kick out of my chutzpah. I surprised myself by challenging him. In hindsight, I do not know if he was testing my commitment. His remarks didn't give me much assurance about making the squad.

Fall of 1954 was the start of my junior year at Garfield. I was provided with my football gear for the turn out of the varsity squad. I started out on third string and as always, I put out a great deal of effort in the basic drills of blocking, tackling, and the sprints toward the end of practice. I alternated on the third string as a fullback. Swede utilized the old-style, straight "T" formation. The role of the fullback in the formation was primarily as a blocker and punter on offense, and as a linebacker on defense. It was not considered a flashy position, but I enjoyed the role even though I was only 145 lbs. For such formations, the fullback was usually the heaviest in the backfield.

John Boitano, the relatively new assistant coach and legendary three-sport star athlete from Ballard High School, brought a contrasting approach of coaching to Lindquist's. John was much younger than Swede. He had an outgoing personality and would joke with the players, but on the field, he had high expectations. He laced his machine-gun patter with more expletives than Swede but intertwined them with jokes. John called me aside from tackling drills one afternoon and said:

Butch, (Coach Boitano always called me by my nick name. Swede, on the other hand, would yell out "Gayton") we just found out that Charlie Jordan [the starting fullback on the Varsity squad] broke his leg in practice yesterday. And I told Swede that you should replace him on the starting unit. You've been doing a good job during the drills, and I think you can do the job. Don't disappoint me. I'm going out on a limb for you.

I was dumbstruck! I could not believe what he was saying. Coach Boitano recommended me rather than three other guys ahead of me! I would be one of only three juniors as a starter. During that one practice, I went from third-string Junior Varsity to first-team Varsity. I felt badly for Charlies Jordon. He was an excellent athlete and was destined for recognition on a team that would make history by the end of the season.

I got the impression from Swede that he and Boitano had been talking to each other about me for some time, but there was no question that Boitano's recommendation was the clincher. Swede liked my grit but initially had some trepidation about my small size, especially as a fullback who would need to block for the team's star player Tommy Huelett, a superb quarterback.

Swede watched me in some initial drills and seemed pleased but pulled me out of the drill to talk about improving my blocking technique. He said I should use my forearm for blocks from time to time to keep attackers away from the quarterback. He formed his arms in a horizontal winged position with his fists touching and approached me. Then he swung his right forearm into my solar plexus! I was surprised by the blow and did not have my stomach muscles flexed. The resulting pain was excruciating. I began to feel dizzy.

He said, "That's the way you should do it! How do you feel?"

I gasped and barely whispered, "I feel fine," and trotted back to the huddle. I looked back and Swede was smiling. He obviously got a kick out of my toughness. I wasn't going to give him the satisfaction of knowing I was in pain. I can imagine the number of players he applied that punch to as a test of their grit. Never again while I played ball at Garfield did Swede ever question my courage and toughness.

The first game of the season against Cleveland High School. I was knocked out cold by a defender who attempted to jump over me to get to Tommy Huelett. I stopped the defensive end, but on his way up he kicked me in the helmet, and I immediately fell face down. The team managers said I was knocked out for around five minutes! They added that, in my delirium, I was cussing out the coach. I had no recollection of that episode. Later that evening, our family physician, Dr. William Lacy, came by our house to check out my concussion. He gave me the go-ahead to play in the game the following week. As far as I know, that was the only concussion I had during my high school and college years playing football.

I was knocked unconscious in the first Garfield Varsity football game against Cleveland. What a way to start off my football career 1954!

That 1954 season, Garfield went on to win the city championship and tie Kent-Meridian High in the annual Thanksgiving Day Championship Game at Seattle's Memorial Stadium. It was the first football championship for Garfield in seventeen years, since before World War II! Deservedly, the injured Charlie Jordan was named the Inspirational Award winner for the team that season. Record breaking quarterback, Tommy Hulett, was named to the All-City team along with other Garfield players center Lenny Peterson, and end John Newcomb. During that season my primary responsibility was to block for Tommy and to sniff out runners as a linebacker on defense. I loved it!

All-City, and mythical State Champs, celebrating in 1955. I am in the middle, and am the team captain.

The marching group for the BonTemps, an all-Black social club affiliated with Neighborhood House, often performed in Seafair events during the middle and late 1950s. I am third from the left and was president of the group.

Garfield was back on top as a football powerhouse within Washington state! This contributed to students seeing me as a football "star" during my junior year; hence, I became more popular. Girls, both Black and White, began calling me on the telephone. It was hard to believe that just a year earlier I regularly prayed, "Please make it possible, God, for me to have a girlfriend."

The attention made me feel better about myself, and I began to concentrate more on my studies, which resulted in my being placed—for the first time—on the academic honor roll. Although I generally enjoyed school over the years, and had a particular affinity for social studies, I never developed a passion for any subject until the second semester of my junior year.

Mrs. Marian Eskenazi, a recent English Literature graduate of the University of Washington, taught Language Arts. I was enrolled in her class and was initially turned off because her course of study emphasized the plays of William Shakespeare. Within a couple of weeks, Mrs. Eskenazi pulled me aside and read me the riot act. She told me my schoolwork was not up to her standards and that I needed to improve. She went on to say that I was a bright boy and, academically, I was not meeting my potential. She expected more from me and said, in essence, that she'd stay on my back until I started to improve!

I was shocked by her frankness. Up to that point, no teacher had ever said that I had more academic potential than I demonstrated. But I responded to her challenge and surprised myself by how well I did in her class. I gained a true appreciation of the works of Shakespeare. As my term project, I even memorized and presented an extensive soliloquy to the students and received an "A" grade for her class.

Marian Eskenazi was the most inspiring teacher I had while attending Garfield High School. I kept in contact with her through her later years.

Because of that class, years later while on a business trip for The Boeing Company in 1993, I made a point to visit Kronborg Castle in Denmark, the setting for Elsinore Castle in Shakespeare's *Hamlet*. Mrs. Eskenazi and I kept in contact until she passed a few years back and whenever I have the appropriate opportunity, I mention her as a primary influence on my life and career. She taught at Garfield for only that *one* academic year. Serendipity? By the end of my junior year, I was feeling fortunate about how life was treating me. Academically, I was doing better than ever. I was regarded as an above-average athlete on the football and track teams. Several friends, Black and White, convinced me to run for senior class president. Surprisingly, I eked out a win against Herb Schoenfeld. Girls were noticing me. My prayers were being answered.

———

While I attended Garfield, my grandparents Nonnie and J. T. were both bedridden. Evenings, my dad would drop me off at their place. I'd stay nights and care for them. In the morning, Dad would take me to school. Other siblings were not involved in this, only me. Having that responsibility bonded me more with my dad. He trusted me!

During that same period, Dad would take me with him to get the family Christmas tree each year, usually on Christmas Eve. Unfortunately, all the trees we saw looked like Charlie Brown's scraggly tree! But once we put everything on it, it was beautiful! That was my favorite time of the year to be with Dad.

The summer of 1955, before my senior year, was especially memorable. My family moved a few miles south of the Madrona neighborhood to the Mount Baker district. After spending my entire life in one home and enjoying it, I was peeved by the decision. Not only was I taken out of my comfort zone, but I had the fear I might have to attend Franklin High School, Garfield's biggest academic and athletic rival! I was relieved to find out that our new house was on the border of the two districts, and I was allowed to remain a Garfield Bulldog.

One June afternoon, my mother got off the phone after an animated conversation. She called out, "Butch, I need to talk with you."

I sat down with her in the dining room, and she said, "I just talked with Homer Harris's wife, Dorothy. You know of Homer. He's the outstanding student athlete from Garfield who is now a physician. He, his wife, and two daughters are now living in Seattle. Mrs. Harris wants you to come over to their home and meet Homer's stepdaughter who's your age. Her name is Hope, and she will be staying here just for the summer."

I could have been knocked over with a feather. I'd been hearing about Homer Harris my whole life. His incomparable athletic and academic achievements at Garfield were legendary. His name on various plaques and trophies made my eyes glaze over. It never entered my mind that this living legend would ever come back to Seattle, much less did I dream that I would be invited to his home to meet his stepdaughter. Frankly, meeting his stepdaughter did not resonate with me as much as having the opportunity to meet Dr. Harris. (I had to stop referring to him as Homer.)

When I went to his home and Hope answered the door, I temporarily forgot about Homer because Hope was a girl to behold! She was extremely pretty. Being a bit nervous, I commenced with non-sequitur small talk until I was introduced to Homer and his stately wife, Dorothy.

By that point I couldn't talk at all. I was dumb struck by all that he represented. He reminded me, in appearance, of my brother Phil with his reddish-brown smooth complexion and wavy brown hair, along with his sharp features. I thought there could never be a better representative for the dermatology profession.

———

I became a senior in 1955, the same year that fourteen-year-old Emmitt Till was lynched in Mississippi for whistling at a White girl at a grocery store. Interracial after-school social interaction between Black and White boys and girls was frowned upon by the parents of both races. Among Blacks, Black guys dating White girls was considered outright dangerous. This was not an isolated state of mind in much of White America. It was an extreme example of what, today, we tend to call "White privilege" and more pervasive "White superiority" in Mississippi.

To my parents' chagrin, one spring evening two attractive White girls I knew from school came to my house, and I invited them in. I was as surprised as my parents. Mom and Dad got up from their chairs in the front room. They started marching slowly up the stairway to their bedrooms, looking back over their shoulders with unsmiling faces toward me and the girls, without saying a word. I had no doubt about how they felt.

I talked with the girls for a few minutes, and they gave me a small box of chocolates and then they left in their car. Neither parent talked about the visit, but a statement by my dad a few days later let me know where he was coming from.

"I can't understand these young colored boys going out with White girls when they can have their choice of colored girls in any shade of complexion, type of hair, and facial features they desire."

This was a not-too-subtle reference to my mother, who did not have what would be generally regarded as a Black feature on her entire body. However, she could proudly trace her Black blood lines back to the times of slavery. She felt the same way as my father. There was no question of the preferred direction they had concerning my taste in girls. Remembering that scene, I can't help but chuckle. I do not believe my parents fundamentally changed their perspective on the mixing of races. Although there is no doubt that they became more tolerant over time.

I added a job during the spring of my senior year. I worked weekends at Dick's Drive-In taking orders and preparing hamburgers and milkshakes. Following graduation, I was able to work five days a week. Since the drive-in was kitty corner from Garfield and in the Central Area a wide variety of customers would come by—including Blacks, Whites, Asians, wealthy, poor, small-time hoodlums, pimps, prostitutes, et al. I enjoyed the banter and the intended—and unintended—humor. The weekends were especially fun and interesting. The experience at Dick's exposed me to the wide variety of people and personalities of the area. I almost felt guilty receiving my monthly checks from the owners for those wonderful months I worked at Dick's.

Senior year was a whirlwind of fun, excitement, and achievement. Our football team went undefeated within the city. That accomplishment was topped off with a victory over Kirkland's Lake Washington High School at the annual Turkey Day Championship game held at Seattle's Memorial Field. Our team, arguably considered the best football team in the history of the school, was ranked by a few polls as the number one high school football team in the state.

Garfield had seven players selected to the All-City first team including two African Americans (John Bass and me), a Nisei (Billy Ishida), and a Jewish Holocaust survivor (Alex Chevalier). What a statement regarding the positives of cultural diversity! Billy, an outstanding running back, and I were selected as All-State players. Billy was named as the team's most inspirational player, and I was selected as team captain.

Aside from my honors as an All-City and All-State fullback, I was especially pleased that my coach, Swede Lindquist, was quoted in a November 1956 issue of

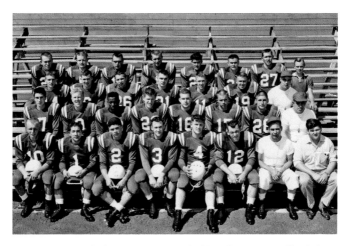

Me, #2, sitting in the front row next to my buddy and teammate, Billy Ishida, #1. We were selected to play for the All-State Star West team.

the *Seattle Post-Intelligencer*: "...naming his top players after twenty-seven years in the game, Coach Lindquist picks Bob Wooten and Dale Holmes of Marysville; Lee Stout, Dave Brougham and Bill Ristine of Broadway; and Carver Gayton of Garfield." His recognition of me was humbling considering the outstanding football players he coached at Garfield for twelve years.

I was floating on air from all the personal recognition I received that season. I enjoyed the game along with the camaraderie of my teammates. I was certainly cognizant of the fact that we had an outstanding team and deserved the awards, but I had no expectation that I would be singled out for receiving any personal awards.

Topping off our historical season, Darrell Royal, then the head football coach at the University of Washington, came to Garfield's recognition ceremony along with two of his assistants to congratulate the team for its accomplishments. A U of W head coach had never recognized a Garfield team in such a manner!

The series of recognitions emboldened me to think seriously about the possibility of playing football for the University of Washington Huskies. I started badgering Coach Lindquist to put in a good word for me with Darrell Royal to give me a full ride (full tuition and a stipend for books and living expenses) to play football at the U of W. Initially, Swede waved me off by saying I was too small. I was beginning to soften him up at the start of the spring track season my last semester of high school.

He backed off a bit by saying, "Gayton, if you add ten pounds to your 160 pounds, then I'll approach Coach Royal about recruiting you."

I started gaining weight and even increased my speed as a 440-yard dash runner and a sprinter—placing third in the All-City 440 and anchoring Garfield's 880-yard All-City relay, leading the team to second place. I was the second fastest runner on Garfield's track team and was selected by my teammates as "...their Greatest Inspiration During the Season." At the end of the season, I told Swede that I had gained ten pounds and was ready to talk with Coach Royal. Swede said he would get back to me. A couple of weeks later I cornered him again. He sighed, shook his head slowly, and said "Ok! Ok! Gayton. I give up. I'll call Coach Royal and set up an appointment with him."

I was recruited by Coach Darrell Royal to play for the U of W on full scholarship. I had no interest in playing football with any other university.

The meeting with Royal was short and to the point. He had a congenial smile and said in his slow Oklahoma drawl, "Carver, Coach Lindquist has told me about your work ethic, desire, and determination. I've decided to give you the scholarship. And I guarantee you that I will continue

I graduated from Garfield in 1956.

that support each year if you maintain that attitude. Congratulations!"

He did not mention my athleticism, which was fine. He admired my work ethic and positive attitude. That perspective of me encapsulated the core "attributes" that I would strive toward my entire adult life.

The Squad in Later Years

HERBIE SCHOENFELD CONTINUES to be a great friend. Herb is a scion of the pioneer Schoenfeld family, which made a fortune in the furniture business. Herb was the Yell King at Garfield our senior year—as well as in our senior year at the University of Washington when we won the 1960 Rose Bowl, in which I played. Herb has been involved in a variety of very successful businesses ventures over the years. I am proud of the fact that we have continued to remain in touch to this day.

In later years, Tommy Hulett became internationally renowned as the rock concert promoter and founder of Concerts West. His company promoted the concerts of Jimi Hendrix, Elvis Presley, Elton John, and Eric Clapton among many other stars.

The squad of twenty-two also included: Martin Selig, a hard-nosed linebacker who ultimately became the commercial building developer whose business transformed the skyline of Seattle; and outstanding linebacker Alex Shevalier [Sytman] who delivered my son, Carver Clark Gayton, Jr., eight years later and went on to become a nationally recognized cardiologist.

I thanked Swede profusely for lining me up with Coach Royal. The year before, the thought of becoming a Husky was a vague far-fetched dream that I considered unattainable.

I did not think of the historical implications of coach Royal's decision at the time. I became one of no more than five Blacks on the entire Husky football team to receive a full ride. I was also the only player on our illustrious Garfield team to get a four-year ride to what we now call a "Division I" football program. I was a wide-eyed, seventeen-year-old who had an insatiable desire to become a Husky football player, and I became one. Racial and/or social implications never entered my mind. It was all about a dream coming true.

I was pleased I remained on the honor roll as my senior year drew to a close. My accumulative grade point average was over 3.0 for my last two years but I certainly was not enough of an academic star to be a member of Garfield's Gold Seal Honor Society. Nevertheless, I was selected to be the class commencement speaker! I was extremely proud that the Commencement Committee, comprised

I was a graduate of Garfield High School's Class of 1956. I was senior class president and selected to be the commencement speaker.

of students as well as teachers, wanted me to be the representative for the class. The speech I delivered emphasized how sincerely grateful I was to have had the opportunity to attend Garfield.

Up until graduation day, life seemed to move too slowly for me. But from that point forward the years seemed to have flown by.

My high school football experience was topped off by playing fullback in the East-West All-State game in Spokane in August of 1956. Despite spending a week in a Spokane hospital with heat stroke from our squad's practice sessions, I surprised everyone by punting a football sixty-five yards in the air! I'd never kicked a football that far before or since. Coach Royal was in the stands, and I suspect that he thought he had a diamond in the rough by providing me with a scholarship. I never kicked in another game.

✥

CHAPTER 6

College at the University of Washington

I BEGAN WORKING at the University of Washington Athletic Department in the summer of 1956 as part of my "grant-in-aid" football scholarship. Several incoming freshmen football players were part of our work contingent tasked with sweeping out the Hec Edmondson basketball pavilion. As the start of classes drew near, our work crew was approached by the Assistant Athletic Director Jim Wiley. He said that several incoming freshman football players on the Washington State University campus had given their commitment to play for the U of W instead but had, reportedly, changed their minds.

Mr. Wiley said he had information indicating that the athletes had been pressured by WSU officials to change their minds. He asked three of us if we would join a group of upper classmen to talk with those athletes. He hoped we could talk them into leaving the WSU campus before classes began—to come to the University of Washington.

I regarded the proposition as far-fetched and dangerous. But I volunteered to go with the car caravan because Wiley had proposed it and because I wanted to prove I was a committed Husky. Two other freshmen bought into the scheme. Wiley emphasized that we could not talk to anyone about our plans.

The three cars left late one weeknight evening in the last week of August. Our intention was to reach the WSU campus before sunrise the next day. We knew that the three ball players we wanted to bring to Seattle were staying in one of the campus dormitories. The plan was for three of our group to surreptitiously go to the target dorm at dawn, bring the players out, meet at noon with the rest of our group on a designated street, get picked up, and drive back to Seattle with the athletes. It seemed like a workable, cut-and-dried plan.

At noon, I was waiting on campus with two of our guys at the agreed upon spot on a small hill. The other contingent, I found out later, was having trouble locating one of the athletes in the dormitory. I was getting nervous, because by 12:20 p.m. the other members of our group had not arrived.

At about that same time that the car arrived—*without* the players we expected to come to Seattle—I heard a rumble. I looked over the hill and saw about 40 football players, and what appeared to be two coaches leading them, coming toward us. We were surrounded by the football players before three of us could take off in the car. Three massive linemen applied full nelson grips from behind to our necks and arms while the whole group was yelling and screaming at us with all sorts of expletives.

One of the two coaches yelled, "Let's shave their heads and paint them orange—and drop them off in Colfax!"

I found out later that Colfax is where the county jail is located. Luckily, the head football coach, Jim Sutherland, belatedly arrived and told his players to let us go. He told us to "Get the hell out of here and don't come back—or we *will* follow up on the Colfax suggestion!"

We jumped into the car and drove off, not knowing what happened to our "co-conspirators" or the players we attempted to "rescue."

Sixty miles outside of Pullman, we heard news reports on several radio stations about our aborted "kidnapping." Insult was added to injury when reporters indicated that University of Washington officials had no knowledge of the prank and insinuated that it resulted from over-zealous students, with no authorization whatsoever from the University.

The next day there was a bright red front page headline in *The Seattle Times:* "Cougar Coach Accuses U of W Students of Player Raid." One of the U of W players had his engagement by his WSU co-ed fiancé broken because of his actions. None of the players that our group sought out decided to attend the University of Washington, nor did they remain on the WSU football squad beyond their freshman year.

That was my introduction to the University of Washington campus. While a lot of folks had a great laugh over the episode, it certainly was not a very auspicious beginning.

The beginning of my frosh football season started with a taped interview I had with a Pacific Coast Conference official about payments I may have received above and beyond what was stipulated in my grant-in-aid agreement. This process resulted from what had been called a "slush fund" organized by downtown Seattle business boosters to sweeten the pot for "exceptional" blue-chip football and basketball players enrolled in the University. The fund was obviously in violation of National Collegiate Athletic Association (NCAA) rules. Exposure of the operation in 1954 ended the coaching career of Head Football Coach John Cherberg and dashed the rumored political aspirations of the well-known and respected businessman Torchy Torrance. Football great Hugh McElhenny, a recipient of the fund, was not exaggerating when he was purported as saying that he took a cut in pay when he left the University to play professional football.

Frankly, I felt somewhat special being interviewed, because I did not consider myself an "exceptional" recruit worthy of any treatment above and beyond the rules. The University of Washington was the only college I wanted to attend, and did not expect nor was offered, funds beyond my grant.

Fall quarter, with classes and frosh football commitments, was a challenge for me. The reading and composition expectations of the English and social science courses were a rude awakening. However, the courses provided a solid academic foundation for my undergraduate experience. I continue to utilize the English literature texts and novels in the course syllabus as insights for my life to this day.

I was initially intimidated by many of my frosh football teammates because of their size and recognition as stars from their respective high schools. To my surprise, I emerged as the starting halfback and leading ground gainer for the team by the end of the season. I began to realize that I could compete at the top levels of intercollegiate football.

At the end of the season, Head Coach Royal accepted an offer to become the head coach at the University of Texas. His five-win and five-loss season

Surprisingly, the 1960 Rose Bowl marked an historic year of Black participation in the Rose Bowl. Ray Jackson, George Fleming, Joe Jones, and I represented the largest number ever of frontline Blacks to ever play in game.

record was quite a success after the NCAA imposed sanctions against the slush fund program. Additionally, Royal did an excellent job recruiting a number of exceptional athletes to play the following fall. He was ultimately inducted into the National Collegiate Athletic Association (NCAA) Hall of Fame for his college coaching record.

Soon after Royal's departure, Athletic Director, George Briggs, announced that 29-year-old Jim Owens was going to replace Royal. Owens was an exceptional, young coach with a bright future. He had the backing of football luminaries such as Coach Bud Wilkinson of Oklahoma, and Coach Bear Bryant of Texas, where Owens was his assistant coach. In the early and mid-1950s, the best college football in the nation was being played in the Southwest, i.e., Texas and Oklahoma.

U of W 1960 Rose Bowl winners (Carver, second row, fourth from the right).

Owens, like Royal before him, was willing to test the waters in the North where programs had not been exposed to coaching *racially integrated* teams. I was curious about how Coach would treat the Black players. It's important to note that there were no more than five Black players on the team at the time. The result of Royal and Owens coming to Washington transformed, for the better, Pacific Coast Conference/Pac 12 college football over the next thirty years.

During my years playing under Coach Owens, from 1957 through the 1960 Rose Bowl, I was pleased that I was an occasional starter and ultimately earned varsity letters each of those years. I was plagued with a variety of injuries, starting with a torn rotator cuff in my left shoulder during my sophomore year. My junior year, I played the entire season with it torn. Chains and leather straps held my arm in the shoulder socket during practices and games. In my senior year, just minutes into our second game of the season with the University of Idaho, I tore ligaments, tendons, and cartilage in my left knee and was considered out for the season. I reinjured the knee at least four more times over the ensuing two and a half months trying to get back into the line-up. However, I never was able to recover more than twenty percent of the original strength of my leg.

This basically ended my football career.

Nevertheless, I was pleased to have played in the 1960 Rose Bowl game against Wisconsin, which we won by the score of 44 to 8. My leg was taped from my groin all the way down to my toes. I had no high expectations for my performance. My main concerns were not to fumble the football the couple of times I took a handoff, and not to drop the punt I caught toward the end of the game in front of the one-hundred thousand fans in the stadium and the millions of folks watching on television!

The abrupt end of my football playing days was emotionally devastating. I could endure the physical pain, but not being able to fulfill the high expectations I had for myself, my teammates, and sports writers haunted me for several years—even though four years before I had been completely satisfied just being on the team.

For a hometown kid who did not expect to ever play a football game in Husky Stadium, I was pleased with what I contributed to Husky football, despite not being able to reach my full potential. I have great pride being a member of a legendary team of 48 players, the first Husky Football team ever inducted into the Husky Hall of Fame.

I was not academically engaged during my undergraduate years—not as engaged as I should have been. Much of that had to do with the injuries I sustained. However, I enjoyed the history and English literature courses I took. U of W History Professor Thomas Pressly also made a big impression on me. He was able to bring history to life through his lectures and utilizing primary sources of memoirs and journals as assigned reading. Rather than emphasizing just facts and data. Professor Pressly's approach emphasized the experiences and feelings of real people.

The professor who challenged me the most philosophically and psychologically was Professor Sophus Winther who taught American Literature. During my sophomore year class with him, Winther would occasionally express his dislike of big-time athletic programs at universities and the high salaries of head football coaches. I was taking his course at the same time Jim Owens had just been hired as head coach and was making more money than the President of the University! Dr. Winther's continuous rants on the subject led me to forego wearing my letterman's sweaters to his classes. Dr. Winther could not understand how he, who had been internationally recognized for his writing and research, would make *less than half* of what Owens earned.

Sports Editor Georg Meyers and Press Book Commentary on Gayton

In a *Times* article by Sports Editor Georg Meyers in April 1958, Meyers wrote:

Carver Gayton, halfback, the most improved player on the team at the end of the 1957 season... in early [spring] workouts is dodging tacklers (or knocking them down) as though the five months since the end of the 1957 season were a weekend.

In an October 21, 1959, article in *The Seattle Times* after my injury in the Idaho game, Meyers pointed out:

A shoulder injury kept Gayton out of scrimmage last spring. Despite the handicap of lost time, he was in the starting line-up of the Huskies opening game at Colorado and was the day's outstanding runner.

In the Rose Bowl Official Program, January 1, 1960, referencing the Huskies 1959 season, Meyers wrote:

Disgruntled fans who had cussed the Huskies split-T plunge and punt offense abruptly were delighted if not dazzled by a "swing T" attack with flankers, wingbacks, unbalanced lines and the forward pass as a tool of deception rather than desperation. .. Still, after 23 years of not going to the Rose Bowl, indoctrinated skeptics said the Huskies had: "No Speed." They were nearly right. Carver Gayton the fleetest Husky, scampered at will in Washington's opening victory, 21-12 over Colorado, then was injured. Lacking a break-away runner, the Huskies had to be satisfied with touchdown runs of 25 yards by George Fleming against Idaho (23-0) 30 by Ray Jackson yards against Utah (51-6) and 30 yards by Don Mcketa, for the loan goal crossing against Stanford (10-0)

In the *Press Book: 46th Rose Bowl: Wisconsin Badgers vs Washington Huskies* my profile is described as follows:

#23 Carver Gayton (160, 5'10" Senior). Lettered as a sophomore and junior and was headed for a great season this year until injured in a game against Idaho. Was considered lost for the campaign, but through sheer determination kept working out and finally rejoined the squad for the California game and saw a few minutes of action against the Bears. Small and elusive, he has fine speed and breakaway ability and is hard to bring down. He was an 'All-Stater' in high school. Majors in history and plans to teach.

The press book also reflects that I remained at the top of the Husky running backs regarding yards per carry, which averaged 5.0 yards for my three varsity years.

Nevertheless, his discussions and assigned readings by Joseph Conrad, Ernest Hemmingway, D. H. Lawrence, William Faulkner, and Henry James, among others, led me to be more introspective and self-analytical and my writing more precise and thoughtful. I only received a "C" grade from Professor Winther, but the grade was irrelevant. It was my most valuable course in terms of learning more about human nature and the complexities of life.

I never had any further contact with Professor Winther after taking his class. Professor Pressly, on the other hand, was very friendly and the ultimate Southern gentleman. He volunteered to write a letter of recommendation for me in 1961 when I was under consideration for hire as one of the few Black social studies teachers on the secondary level within the Seattle School system. There is no question that his letter helped me to be hired by Garfield. Professor Pressly and I maintained contact over the years, and I was indeed honored when he was in the audience at Kane Hall on the U of W campus in the spring of 1997 when I received the University of Washington Alumni Association's Distinguished Service Award from President Richard McCormick.

Looking back at my formal educational experiences, I would have appreciated class discussions and perspectives of African American literature in the curriculum. This never happened. Alas, that was another place and time in American history and race relations. All through my school years—from grade school through graduate school—I never had a person of color as a teacher or professor, nor were other Black students *in any of my classes* throughout my college years! I had to depend upon having access to books and publications about the Black perspective from what my parents had at our home library or what I sought out on my own.

Despite my enlightening academic experiences at the University, my emphasis on football—and its abrupt end with my knee injury—made me suddenly realize that I had no sense of a pathway forward in my life. Although I would graduate with a Bachelor of Arts degree in History and a minor in English, I chose teaching as the most likely a job I would eventually seek out because I couldn't think of anything else of interest that related to my course work.

One uplifting thing occurred in my senior year at U of W: I had my teeth taken care of after football season. I paid for the operation with funds I had saved from college jobs. The dentist did an excellent job. I could smile for photographs again!

PART III

INTO THE UNKNOWN

CHAPTER 7

Marriage and Teaching at Garfield High

I HAD STARTED DATING Mona Marie Lombard beginning my junior year at the University of Washington. I had known her since high school. She was two years younger than me and attended Holy Names Academy, an all-girls' Catholic school. She was crowned Queen of her senior prom and had asked me to escort her. From that point forward we dated regularly.

Mona was a striking Creole beauty, whose family came to Bremerton from New Orleans in the 1940s and from there eventually moved to Seattle. The Lombards were a traditional and devoted Catholic family. Their social life was focused around a small close-knit Creole Catholic community. I began taking Catholic confirmation classes at the end of my junior year at the U with the intention of ultimately marrying Mona. Because of Catholic guidelines in those days, a Catholic could not marry a non-Catholic.

Having been born and raised within The First African Methodist Episcopal Church, I was not overly excited about joining her church. But I loved her and intended to marry her. While my parents never voiced any concerns, I am sure they were a bit disappointed that I moved away from the family church.

After my career-ending knee injury in the September 26th game against Idaho Coach Owens hired me as a graduate assistant coach. The job provided a small salary and covered tuition costs for graduate courses that would lead to a teaching credential.

I was still living at home at the time and my mother said I would have to start paying rent—even though I had no job, and my football stipend was miniscule. I felt a bit hurt, but she was justified in asking since I would be turning 21 that October.

Mona and I were engaged by the end of the fall of 1959. I had no job offers or plans for my life. Marrying Mona seemed to be the logical thing to do. I shake my head remembering those days. We were married in August of 1960.

––––––––

My first encounter with blatant institutional racism as an adult took place while I was searching for an apartment for Mona and myself. I looked in the newspaper for rental ads in areas near the university. I would call on the phone and arrange to look at the apartment, but when I arrived at the residence, the proprietor's response would be that the apartment had just been leased. Occasionally, they would be up front and say, "We do not rent to coloreds"— blatant, up-front racism. It woke me up to the real world my family and I would have to deal with for the rest of our lives. After many attempts, I was able to lease a one-room apartment with a Murphy bed in the U District.

The stress of going to school, student teaching, and coaching wore down my system and I contracted mononucleosis toward the end of the football season. I was too sick to accompany the team to Pasadena to prepare for our second straight Rose Bowl, this time against the University of Minnesota. It was scheduled for January 1st. My role as a graduate assistant coach ended.

By Christmastime, I was bedridden with strep throat and the mumps. I literally was on my back in bed from December through February. Mona was working part time as a nurse's aide. She became pregnant and ultimately had to quit because she had "morning sickness" all day, every day, until she delivered our daughter! No money was coming into the household.

By March, my health was beginning to improve, and we celebrated when two of the jobs I applied for came through.

I started working as a substitute teacher for the Seattle Public School System during the day and as a maintenance electrician at The Boeing Company for the 5 p.m. to midnight swing shift at night. Having these dual roles was very tiring mentally and physically, and certainly didn't help the home situation, but I had no other choice. I had a family to support.

One day the Seattle Public Schools[5] sent me to Mercer Junior High School to teach an 8th grade social studies class. As I was leaving at the end of the school day, a tall, gray-haired woman rushed toward me calling, "Carver, Carver!"

Not clearly knowing who she was, I said, "Hi! How are you?"

She replied, "I'm Miss Peterson, the principal here at Mercer and I was vice principal at Meany Junior High when you were there as a student."

I was astonished. I said, "My gosh, Ms. Peterson. I had no idea you were here at Mercer. What a great surprise!"

We started talking and she mentioned the boy with whom I fought back in 1951. She asked if I remembered him. I said, "Of course, how could I forget!" I had had years of nightmares about that encounter, and I dreaded them.

Miss Peterson told me that he had been involved in a series of crimes over the years and eventually convicted of being a habitual criminal. He'd been sentenced to the Walla Walla State Penitentiary for the rest of his life. She said she thought that I might want to know that.

I thought to myself that I was fortunate having only two teeth chipped by this boy. I thanked her for telling me and expressed how much I appreciated all she'd done to get me on the right track regarding school—and ultimately, my life.

I never saw Miss Peterson again. But the flashbacks of the fight and my hatred toward Bill Buckmire stopped on that day. If I had not seen Miss Peterson, the negative energy expended over that incident could have continued for many more years. God, thankfully, works in mysterious ways.

I held that horrendous two-job schedule from March of 1961 until September of that year. I had to support my wife and new daughter, Cynthia Marie, who had been born in June.

I was hired the next fall as an English and social studies teacher as well as assistant football coach at Garfield High school, my alma mater. It was definitely unusual for a new, 21-year-old college graduate to be teaching at a high school in Seattle. Most new teachers my age had to start at the elementary or middle school level. Garfield's English and social studies departments had exceptional teachers, most of whom had been on the staff when I attended Garfield as a student.

One of the fondest memories of my life took place in early September when Martin Luther King, Jr. was invited to speak at Garfield by Frank Hanawalt, the relatively new principal. This opportunity took place after most representatives of government and the major church entities of the city refused to let Dr. King address gatherings at their venues. The Reverend Samuel McKinney, pastor of Seattle's Mount Zion Baptist Church and former classmate of Dr. King's at Atlanta's Morehouse College, brokered the arrangement for Garfield. In 1961, the Civil Rights movement was in full swing and King was considered by most of White America as a flaming, out-of-control radical. The White power structure in Seattle did not welcome Hanawalt's brave decision.

On the morning of the speech, Reverend McKinney contacted me and asked if I wanted to meet Dr. King after his two planned speeches. I was blown away by the invitation. Because the Garfield student body was large, King had to speak twice to accommodate the audiences in the school's small auditorium. Each extemporaneous speech had as its theme the civil rights movement, yet each was different. The speeches were oratorical gems!

I rushed backstage after the last assembly and was introduced to the great man by Reverend McKinney. I remember King as being much shorter than I had envisioned. His countenance was serious, yet he reflected contentment and confidence. His handshake was not firm, and I felt the perspiration on his hand that belied his composed face.

Reflecting on that moment years later, I thought of the concern, and even fear, he must have felt from the continual threats of violence and death that he received. Yet he persevered for the cause. That was the only visit King made to Seattle. I was indeed fortunate to meet him.

––––––

My two-and-a-half years at Garfield were much more enjoyable than I had anticipated. The student body was comprised of approximately 50 percent

"Miss Hart, you should keep an eye on Mr. Gayton. He's teaching our class a bunch of fantasies about the achievements of Negroes in science, literature, inventions, and so on. I just thought you should know."

African Americans, 40 percent White, and the remaining being of Asian descent. There was energy on the campus that was enhanced, in my mind, by the feeling of hope and prosperity initiated by the oratory of President John Kennedy: "Ask not what your country can do for you, but what you can do for your country."

I never felt more positive about the importance of public service and the possibilities of Blacks and Whites coming together for the mutual benefit of the nation. The Central District community around Garfield was still intact. Poverty and the influx of drugs had not yet permeated the neighborhood, and the African American middle class, for the most part, remained in the area. However, Garfield was by no means a Nirvana. The harsh remnants of institutionalized racism within the school and the system itself became clearer to me one day at the end of one of my US history classes.

I had a telephone call from Louella Hart, the social studies department chair, and daughter of Lewis F. Hart, former Governor of Washington. Miss Hart indicated she wanted to see me but gave no mention of why. I went to her room expecting the worst because of the ominous tone in her voice on the phone.

Miss Hart was a large, dignified woman with White hair and a stern, no-nonsense demeanor. When I entered her room, she said, "A student from your class came to me yesterday and said, 'Miss Hart, you should keep an eye on Mr. Gayton. He's teaching our class a bunch of fantasies about the achievements of Negroes in science, literature, inventions, and so on. I just thought you should know'."

I began to sweat, waiting for an admonition from Miss Hart for me to cease incorporating Black history into my course of study. Surprisingly, Miss Hart said,

"I want you to continue to teach just as you are doing. I thought it was important for you to know about what this young man said. I am proud of your teaching."

I gave a sigh of relief and started edging toward the door.

As I was halfway out, she mentioned the boy's name. He was Black and I considered him a model student. I was not angry, but I was deeply saddened! I wondered how many other young Black students in the class and beyond school felt that same way. How did they feel about the complete lack of representation of Black accomplishments throughout United States history? Here's the true sadness: this young man could not visualize himself nor people who looked like him accomplishing the kinds of things I was describing in class.

This episode made me grieve for the hundreds and thousands of young Blacks who limit themselves to thinking that they cannot achieve and be successful in areas of life other than the performing arts and athletics. The lack of self-confidence is ingrained in many kids.

Although that incident took place nearly 60 years ago, I do not see strong indicators that the perspective of that young boy has changed much in the hearts of many, especially in urban, public school districts. This is shameful!

As far as I knew in 1961, I was the only teacher in the school incorporating the Black perspective into the social studies curriculum. Ralph Hayes, the only other Black teacher within the school's Social Studies Department, was highly respected among students and teachers alike. But I was unaware how he was incorporating the Black experience into his course of studies. I was looking forward to working with him, but before the end of my first year at Garfield, Ralph transferred to Franklin.

I was fortunate that my parents' library gave me the opportunity to provide my students with a broader and more honest view of our country's history than most students were exposed to in Seattle Public Schools. Crucial negative factors were not only the narrow historical exposure of his White teachers, but the paucity of Black historical facts and data within the required textbooks. In the minds of Black and White students, whatever was in those textbooks defined "legitimacy." Sadly, not enough parents of Black students were as fortunate as I was to have a mother and father who truly lived and breathed the importance of Black history.

CHAPTER 8

Joining the FBI

My brother Gary and myself in 1963.

I HAD BEEN TEACHING at Garfield High for almost two years when in the early summer of 1963, when I had a discussion with my older brother Gary during a family picnic at Seattle's Seward Park. He had recently been hired as the first African American Assistant US Attorney in the State of Washington. He asked if I was interested in becoming an FBI special agent. I thought he was joking and started to laugh uncontrollably. I said that had never, ever entered my mind.

Surprisingly, he elaborated on his idea. He worked with agents on a daily basis and was impressed with them. He said that US Attorney General Robert Kennedy was on a campaign to increase the numbers of "Negroes" in the Bureau. Gary added that I should consider joining because I'd never lived outside of Seattle and the experience would give me the opportunity to see other parts of the country. I pointed out that I was not an attorney or an accountant, which I understood were minimum requirements for applying. Gary said new guidelines were expanding to include the category of administrative experience and my teaching background could be applicable.

The over-arching hurdle for me was the question of race. I never heard of a Black FBI agent. The chances of me becoming one of the first in the nation were, in my mind, slim to none! I talked with my wife, and we agreed that my acceptance into the Bureau was not likely, but it would be fun to test the waters and apply. I considered Gary's suggestion as a dare, with nothing really to lose because I enjoyed teaching the energetic, inquisitive kids at Garfield and working with the school's excellent staff. I was not looking for any excuse to leave teaching.

I applied to the Bureau in June of 1963. I had almost forgotten about the application until November 14, 1963, when surprisingly, I was asked to come to the Seattle office of the Bureau for an interview and a physical examination. My background investigation had taken nearly six months.

I weighed in at 165 lbs. and was designated a medium-frame build. Under Bureau guidelines, an agent with a medium frame and my height could only weigh a maximum of 161 pounds. I was advised to get down to that weight within the following four days and weigh in again. I was peeved and suspected the demand was some sort of psychological test. But I welcomed the challenge, and for the next three days during my waking hours, I wore a sweat outfit, ate next to nothing, drank no liquids, and jumped rope continuously. I went back to the Bureau office.

When I arrived, the agent processing me said, "Carver, by the way, we determined you actually have a large frame, and you didn't have to lose any weight." I thought, *What is this all about?* I asked to be weighed anyway, and the scale indicated that I had lost five pounds and would have met the medium range standard. I concluded that the agents wanted to know if I was totally committed to becoming a special agent. They were baiting me.

I received a letter dated December 9, 1963, from the United States Department of Justice, Federal Bureau of Investigation, asking me to report on January 27, 1964. It was signed by John Edgar Hoover. It stated:

Dear Mr. Gayton: You are offered a probationary appointment in the Federal Bureau of Investigation, United States Department of Justice, as Special Agent GS 10, $7690 per annum..." The letter concluded, "...should you accept [the appointment] you are directed to report for oath of office and assignment to Room 5231, Department of Justice Building, 9th Street and Pennsylvania Avenue, Northwest, Washinton, DC at 9 A. M. on January 27, 1964.

Sincerely yours, (signed) J. E. Hoover, John Edgar Hoover, Director.

1964 FBI class (Carver, middle row, second from left).

I received Mr. Hoover's appointment letter two weeks and three days after the assassination of President John F. Kennedy.

In the early morning of January 26, 1964, I bade my young family farewell and boarded a 707 Jetliner to Washington, DC. I would not see them again until the middle of the following May. My arrival at the Washington, DC, airport was an eye opener. Coming from Seattle, I had never seen such a large concentration of Black people in my life. Before that time, the largest metropolitan areas I visited were Los Angeles and San Francisco during the years I was playing football for the Washington Huskies. Neither city appeared to have as many Blacks as DC.

As suggested by the Bureau, I registered at the historic Harrington Hotel on Pennsylvania Avenue, a short walking distance from the US Department of Justice. I appreciated the historical significance of the hotel, i.e., "George Washington slept here," but my first impression was that the moniker gave the owners a rationalization not to modernize or to make basic repairs within the building.

The class of 25 new agents were sworn in at the Justice Department in the early morning by Mark Felt, the Bureau's assistant director in charge of the Training Division. This is the same Mark Felt who revealed in May of 2005 that he was the "Deep Throat" informant journalists Bob Woodward and Carl Bernstein utilized for their articles about the Watergate scandal in the *Washington Post* in the early 1970s.

Felt was handsome, had prematurely grey hair, and was immaculately attired. To me, Felt represented the prototypical FBI special agent. He was intelligent, personable, yet serious. I could understand how he rose to become one of the top officials within the FBI hierarchy.[6]

After two days of briefing at the Department of Justice, our class departed Washington, DC, in a bus and we were on our way to Quantico, Virginia, the location of the iconic FBI Training Academy. Our stay of three weeks was steeped in classes of constitutional law, criminal procedures, illegal search and seizures, firearms training, and defensive tactics.

Gabrielle Kirk

During my residence in Washington, I also enjoyed visiting my niece by marriage, Gabrielle Kirk. Gabrielle was a first-year law school student at Howard University. She was fascinated with my stories about the FBI and was amazed with the depth of my knowledge of Constitutional Law and Criminal Procedure Law that I was exposed to through my FBI classes.

Gabrielle graduated first in her class at Howard Law School and later became notable as Gabrielle Kirk McDonald, a Federal District Court Judge in Houston, Texas. In the 1990s, Gabrielle became a judge at the World Court in the Hague, Netherlands. She also served on the International Criminal Tribunal for the former Yugoslavia. She was regarded by many as "The most powerful African American Woman in the World" while serving as President of the Tribunal. She has received honorary doctorates from Amherst, Notre Dame, Howard, and Georgetown Universities. I still remember her as a young girl visiting Seattle in the mid-1950s. It has been mindboggling to see her evolution on the world stage.

The most interesting session we had was a presentation by two FBI firearms experts about the rifle used by Lee Harvey Oswald to assassinate President Kennedy. The experts were on the firing range for at least a week testing the rifle before they spoke to the class. The experts made the following primary observations: 1) Oswald, in their opinion, was the lone shooter; 2) Oswald had to be an expert shot to fire off three bolt-action rounds within the presumed time frame, though it was not an impossible task; and 3) the assumptions that more shots had been fired based on the number of holes in the President's suit were likely incorrect and that the extra holes were because of *folds* in the President's suit. The experts did not lead the class into believing there were more shooters than Oswald. It was sobering and eerie being a few feet away, and seeing the actual rifle used to murder the President of the United States.

The training was certainly beyond my expectations. One of our classmates, Robert Dwyer, an ex-marine captain, noted that the training he experienced at Quantico from the FBI firearms experts was more intense and stringent than any of the training he experienced while he served in the Marine Corps. Before my stint at Quantico, I hadn't fired any gun beyond my Red Rider BB gun when I was a kid. By the end of my training, I and my fellow agents were firearm experts, particularly regarding the use of our Smith & Wesson, six-chamber 38-caliber service revolvers. We were also adept with the shot gun, Thompson submachine gun, the 45-caliber handgun, and the rifle.[7]

After the training, our class came back to Washington, DC, and remained there for a month conducting field work until graduation. In DC, I shared an apartment with three other classmates at 14th and Massachusetts Street across from Dupont Circle, one block away from the Russian Embassy.

During our free time, I had opportunities to experience things I'd never imagined possible, including a meeting I had with Ed Guthman, a Pulitzer Prize-winning former reporter for *The Seattle Times*. He was the communications director for Attorney General Robert Kennedy. Being from Seattle, I contacted Mr. Guthman's office to say hello. I soon received a phone call from him. He told me and the two other new Black agents in the class, Ed Scott and William Lucas, that the Attorney General wanted to meet us.

We briefly met Mr. Kennedy late one morning as he was leaving his office for an emergency meeting. Mr. Guthman invited us into Mr. Kennedy's office where we talked for almost an hour. He showed us a variety of historical items. One was a US Marshall's helmet dented by rioters in 1962 when Robert Kennedy ordered the University of Mississippi to enroll James Meredith as the first African American to attend the University. Another was the first Kennedy half dollar minted by the US Treasury. We also saw the coconut shell Lieutenant John Kennedy wrote on that led rescuers to Kennedy and his crew after his PT Boat 109 was torpedoed by the Japanese during World War II. There were all sorts of colorful drawings by his children pinned on the walls of the office as well. History came to life for me that morning.

Robert F. Kennedy welcomed me with an autographed picture after my FBI training.

Soon afterwards I received a photograph of Mr. Kennedy. "For Carver Gayton. With Appreciation and best Wishes, Robert Kennedy." was penned in his hand.

Guthman subsequently became the managing editor of the *Los Angeles Times* as well as the *Philadelphia Inquirer*. As a result of his work with Robert Kennedy, he was listed as number three on President Nixon's "Enemy List" for many years.[8]

My appetite for jazz music was whetted in DC. I was able to visit some of the city's legendary night clubs, such as The Caverns and Blues Alley, where I appreciated firsthand the artistry of the likes of trumpeter Dizzy Gillespie, pianist Thelonious Monk, drummer "Philly" Joe Jones, and an "unknown" big city blues singer at the time, Lou Rawls. The city offered me a true buffet of some of the best music in the world. I couldn't get my fill.

As the April 1964 graduation ceremony drew near, we were told explicitly by Fred Fehl, our class counselor, that we had to wear dark blue suits and White shirts for the occasion. One brave class member raised his hand and told Agent Fehl that he did not have a dark blue suit. Without missing a beat, Fehl repeated, "All new agents are to wear dark blue suits and White shirts." He went on to say, Mr. Hoover—as in J. Edgar—would be at the ceremony, and that no words were to be exchanged with him when we shook hands other than

"Thank you" when he congratulated each of us. The ceremony was the only time I met the Director.

A day after the ceremony I received notice of my first office assignment: Kansas City, Missouri. The Kansas City Field Office (KCMO) covered western Missouri and all of Kansas state. I had no impression one way or another about Kansas City. Discussions with a few of my classmates indicated that Kansas City was unofficially regarded as a "disciplinary office" for second office agents. Since Kansas City was to be my first office, I wondered if that had any negative implications. Other rumored disciplinary offices included the remote offices of Anchorage, Alaska, and Butte, Montana.

I immediately telephoned Mona and told her to start preparing for the move to Kansas City. Our second child, Carver Clark Jr., was one year old, and Cynthia was nearly three. I had mixed feelings of trepidation, excitement, and curiosity about the new venture. My view of humankind and the world would never be the same after my fourteen months in Kansas City.

CHAPTER 9

KCMO and the KKK

MY FIRST WEEK IN KANSAS CITY would literally start with a bang. The field office was abuzz about a pending trial of a wealthy electrical contractor who had ties with the local La Casa Nostra mob. He was ready to testify as a government witness against the mob and was justifiably fearful that his life was in danger.

His large estate had an electrically wired fence surrounding its acreage and was protected by four Dobermann Pinschers. But before the trial, all the dogs had their throats slashed.

For added protection, the witness outfitted his car in a way so he could start the motor by remote control from twenty yards away—in case someone planted the car with a bomb.

He made the mistake of routinely going to a bowling alley with his wife the same day and time, once a week. After coming out of the bowling alley one evening, he started his car with the remote control. It did not explode, so he and his wife walked toward the car. A car with two men in ski masks sped toward the witness and his wife. One of the masked men got out of the car, pushed the wife aside, shot the witness twice with a shot gun, and then the killers roared off. The car and the gun were found later, but there was no evidence revealed that could trace the killers.

I subsequently found out that there were literally dozens of unsolved "contract" killings ordered by someone other than the actual perpetrator that had taken place in Kansas City dating back to prohibition days. The murder at the bowling alley was no exception.

A day or so after the murder, I was talking with a Black detective from the Kansas City police department and he nonchalantly told me that he had a full description of me, along with details about my background, weeks before I had arrived. He would not reveal his source. That revelation pretty much cancelled out my intention of fading into the woodwork in Kansas City. I was the first and only Black agent to serve in the Kansas City Field Office. Additionally, there were no other Black agents serving in any of the southern field offices in 1964. I was the first Black agent to serve in a former slave-state, and one of no more than ten Black agents serving in the entire nation. Reflecting on my assignment there, I was clearly a test case for how a Black would fare in that environment.

The race baiting started early on with one of the agents. One day he said he wanted to talk with me. He started off by pointing out that it was not part of the culture within the office for any "second office" (veteran agent) to talk with a "new" agent. But he would make an exception and talk with me, implying that I should feel lucky he was doing so. He obviously was trying to feel me out. The conversation was vague, and I have no recollection of talking with him again.

I was assigned to cover a lead on a case with an agent from Virginia. As we drove together, he baited me with questions like: "Why are so many Negroes fat?" "Why do they eat so much greasy food?" "What is it about Negroes that makes them inclined to be gay?" I knew what he was doing. He was attempting to embarrass me and push me to lose my composure. I responded to his questions as if they were intelligent inquiries. I did not become rattled, because if I had, it would be difficult to replace me with another African American if, and when, I was reassigned.

However, I did mention this experience to an agent I had befriended on my squad, Tom Trettis. Tom was a graduate of the University of Pennsylvania Law School. He was a very bright guy with a great sense of humor and one of the best agents in the KCMO office. Tom became incensed by what I told him. He was aware of that agent's racist tendencies. I am not aware of what Tom did after our conversation, but soon the Virginian was reassigned as a "Resident Agent" (RA) in the one-agent small town of Salina, Kansas, in the middle of the wheat fields.

As a disciplinary office, the Kansas City Field Office had a significant number of second-office agents who were there for disciplinary reasons. As far as I could tell, many of those agents had "embarrassed" the Bureau in some way, but their infractions were not so egregious to justify dismissal from service. Rather than have an agent as the focal point of controversy, it was typical to transfer the agent to "disciplinary offices" like Kansas City, Missouri; Anchorage, Alaska; or Butte, Montana.

One example was an agent on the Fugitive/Interstate Transportation of stolen Motor Vehicle (ISTMV) squad with me. He happened to be a scion of the Paul and Joseph Galvin family that founded the Motorola Corporation. He was a very hard-working, excellent agent. He joined the FBI for love of country, and because he admired and respected the agency, not for the salary. He was transferred to Kansas City from the Chicago Field Office because of a run-in with a Chicago cop. The agent had received a hot lead that a UFAP (Unlawful Flight to Avoid Prosecution) fugitive was on his way to O'Hare Airport to board a flight out of Chicago. The agent headed for the airport in his Bureau car and was stopped by one of Chicago's finest for speeding on the freeway. The agent showed his credentials and explained he was in a hurry to apprehend a fugitive. The cop said he didn't care about the fugitive and that he was going to write him up for speeding. The agent shoved the officer away from his car and sped off, preferring to take his chances of not being in good graces with the Chicago police—rather than being written up by Mr. Hoover for allowing a fugitive to escape. The cop reported the incident to his superiors who registered a complaint with Special Agent in-Charge (SAC) of the Chicago Field Office.

The "arrests of most-wanted Federal fugitives" and "dollar value of the recovered stolen property" were priority data elements Mr. Hoover boasted about when he went before Congress to increase, or at least maintain, the Bureau's budget. Therefore, positive working relationships between the FBI and local police departments were imperative, especially for the Bureau. Arrests of fugitives and recovery of stolen property had interstate implications and required Bureau agents to work closely with police offices on a daily basis. When the speeding incident story got back to Washinton, DC, and to Mr. Hoover, the Agent was transferred to Kansas City.

One famous disciplinary transfer in the history of the FBI was that of James Hosty. Hosty and I served on the same squad in the Kansas City Office for about one month. Before he was transferred to KCMO in late 1964, he served in the Dallas, Texas, Field Office when President John Kennedy was assassinated. Hosty, a relatively new agent then, was handling security cases in Dallas. He had the misfortune of having a file open on Lee Harvey Oswald as a "Potential Security Informant" (PSI) which merely suggests that Hosty had an interest in possibly turning him into a Security Informant (SI) because of his Marxist connections.

Contrary to wild allegations of conspiracy theorists, Hosty never had direct contact with Oswald, although Hosty made several attempts to reach him. Apparently, the mere fact that there was this distant connection between Hosty and Oswald when President Kennedy was killed, was seen as possibly embarrassing to Mr. Hoover and resulted in Hosty being transferred to Kansas City.

My conversations with Hosty in the spring of 1965 came to the attention of the United States Senate Committee on Intelligence Activities years later. The Committee was conducting investigations on the assassinations of President Kennedy, Malcom X, and Martin Luther King. My sworn affidavit to the Committee quoted me as follows:

> Hosty stated to me and other members of the squad [Kansas City FBI Field Office Criminal Squad] that Oswald had been a PSI (Potential Security Informant) for an older agent who retired from the Dallas FBI Field Office. He [this older agent] had a PSI file on Oswald, and one of the last acts the agent did before he retired was to deactivate the Oswald file as a PSI because he could never contact him. According to Hosty, when he came into his new job in Dallas, he decided to reopen the Oswald file as a PSI. Hosty commented that as part of his effort to make Oswald a PSI, he left notes at Oswald's apartment, urging him to get in contact with him. Hosty said Oswald did not respond to his notes.

Although it was clear from my affidavit that Hosty had no direct contact with Oswald other than the notes Hosty left at his home, conspiracy theorists— most notably the film director Oliver Stone—attempted to construe my affidavit to support the assumption that Hosty had direct communication with Oswald. This flagrant disregard of the facts in reference to me is reflected in Stone's publication *JFK*, a book utilized as the basis for his film of the same title.

Here's the irony of the James Hosty faux pas. Hosty was attempting to fulfill the guidelines of J. Edgar Hoover by maintaining a case pool of at least two to four informants by opening the closed file on Oswald. Hosty thought Oswald could possibly become a full-fledged Security Informant after reading about Oswald's background in the file. That could not happen without at least some intercommunication. According to Hosty, intercommunication did not take place. The previous agent had closed the Oswald file for that same reason. Had the case remained closed, Hosty would not have been subjected to the embarrassment of having an open file on an assassin of the President of the United States. My impression of Hosty was that he was a hardworking, dedicated agent who got wrapped up in circumstances outside of his control.

––––––––

In early 1964, Martin Luther King was becoming extremely concerned about the rise of violence in the south against Blacks: the assassination of Medgar Evers, Field Secretary of the NAACP of Mississippi; the bombing of the 18th Street Baptist Church in Birmingham, Alabama, killing four young girls; and scores of other similar atrocities. In reaction to this upswing of violence, King confronted officials of President Lynden B. Johnson's (LBJ) administration. As Arthur Schlesinger framed King's argument: "Federal law enforcement agencies . . . were long accustomed to 'working within secret groups and obtaining effective results'" in reducing violence; however little if anything had been done to what was going on within "conspiratorial racist circles. Many of the shocking bombings might have been avoided if such knowledge had been available." [9]

It was clear that the Bureau had not engaged in any effective infiltration of violent racist organizations in the South and the Ku Klux Klan (KKK). However, the FBI had effectively infiltrated the Communist Party of the United States of America (CPUSA) and Mafia.

I had the opportunity to see the effectiveness of the tactics the Bureau utilized to decimate the Communist Party while I was assigned to the Philadelphia office in 1966. I was invited by one of the three espionage agents to witness an overview of logs taken by paid security informants of their account of a Communist cell meeting held in Philadelphia a day or so earlier. The cell was comprised of five members. Three of the members were on the FBI payroll as informants. Each believed they were the only informant in the cell. The logs made continuous reference to how each were true believers of the Communist cause.

During our gathering, the espionage agents handling the informants were laughing uproariously while reading from the written logs about how each PI was pointing a finger at another PI about his danger to the nation. Assuming that this scenario was taking place in CPUSA cells throughout the nation, one could conclude that at best, our government had firm control of the party, and at worst, a case could be made that it was overkill and a waste of taxpayers' money.

Why couldn't the same be done with the Ku Klux Klan? Finally, in June of 1964, Attorney General Kennedy formally recommended to President Johnson that the FBI should use similar techniques against White supremacy groups.[10]

J. Edgar Hoover was known for his racist attitudes. This was not unusual for many Whites of his generation who headed Federal agencies during his tenure as FBI Director. He talked openly about his prejudices against the civil rights movement and Blacks, like Martin Luther King, and against homosexuals and communists. When Robert Kennedy became Attorney General, he found Hoover "rather frightening"—a dangerous man who ran "a very dangerous organization."[11]

However, Kennedy believed he could impose his authority over J. Edgar Hoover. For the first time in his career, Hoover had to take orders from the Attorney General of the United States. As the civil rights movement became a major political factor, Hoover was badgered by Kennedy to hire Black agents. As a result, Hoover hired a handful in the summer of 1963. As you know, I was one of the new FBI special agent applicants being considered that summer.

Every day, it seemed as though a fresh series of racist murders and bombings were taking place in the south. On February 27, 1964, after a race-related bombing of the Florida East Coast Railroad in St. Augustine, Florida, President Johnson ordered Hoover to get on the railroad case. Johnson exclaimed, "I'm not going to tolerate blowing up of people with bombs."[12]

LBJ relied on Hoover to a great extent in national security and praised him often. At a May 8, 1964, Whitehouse gathering celebrating Hoover's 40th year in power and his impending 70th birthday, Johnson announced that he was waiving the mandatory retirement under federal law and promised that Hoover would be director of the FBI until the day he died. Johnson went on to say, "[Hoover] is a hero to millions of decent citizens and an anathema to evil . . . that would subvert our way of life and men who would harm and destroy our persons."[13] Author Tim Weiner points out that, "Lyndon Johnson concentrated information and power in the Oval Office better than any president since Franklin Roosevelt. He admired the way Hoover used secret intelligence. He used the FBI as a political weapon in ways no president ever had done." Weiner continues:

LBJ never used power more effectively than when he ordered Hoover to destroy the Ku Klux Klan in Mississippi, a red-white-and-blue war against the Klan's church-burning terrorists.

Burke Marshall, the chief of the civil rights division at the Justice Department, remembered LBJ saying that "three sovereignties" were involved in the battle: "There's the United States and there's the State of Mississippi and there's J. Edgar Hoover." To handle all three required a combination of brute force and great finesse. LBJ made it work.

On Sunday, June 21, 1964, three civil rights workers disappeared after fleeing a jailhouse in Philadelphia, Mississippi, in their station wagon, with Klansmen hot on their trail. Once they went missing, they were presumed dead. Mississippi saw, on average, twenty-five civil-rights-connected shootings, beatings, bombings, and arsons every month during 1964. But a triple murder— and one that involved two white men from the North—was out of the ordinary.[14]

The burning remains of their car had been found near Philadelphia, and there appeared to be little possibility that the three men were still alive. Hoover told LBJ on a phone call; "We're going to have more cases like this down south, . . . What's going to complicate matters is the agitators of the Negro movement."[15]

Another problem was that many in the local and state law enforcement entities were members of the Klan. The bureau had few FBI agents working in Mississippi. Many long-time agents had close relationships with local law enforcement and were not motivated to investigate out-of-state civil rights workers.

It took a lot of pressure from LBJ, but Hoover eventually got the president's message and opened a full-time office in Jackson, Mississippi, with a Special Agent in Charge (SAC) and a full-time staff, though Hoover remained skeptical. LBJ pressed Hoover on a July 2 phone call:

"See how many people you can bring in there," said the president. "You oughta put fifty, a hundred people, after this Klan, and studyin' this from one county to another. I think their very presence may save us a division of soldiers . . . I think you oughta have the best intelligence system, better than you got on the communists. I read a dozen of your reports last night here 'til one o'clock on the communists. And they can't open their mouth without your knowin' what they're sayin'."[16]

Johnson insisted that Hoover use the same tactics and energy he used against communists, and ultimately, Hoover obeyed. Despite the fact that he saw the civil rights activists as lawbreakers, he moved against the Klan in Mississippi.

On August 4th, 1964, Deke DeLoach, top aide to Hoover, called the President to inform him that the bodies of civil rights workers Chaney, Schwerner, and Goodman had been discovered and their killers arrested. Nevertheless, it took many years for all of them to be convicted for their crimes."[17]

The deep penetration of the KKK in Mississippi led Hoover to authorize a full-blown counterintelligence program against the Klan. COINTELPRO—WHITE HATE was inaugurated on September 2, 1964, two months after the president had told Hoover to pursue the Klan just as he had chased the Communists. WHITE HATE went on for seven years, inflicting serious and lasting damage on the Klan.[18]

Two hundred FBI agents were sent to investigate the case. Every one of them was White. The racial climate in Mississippi was considered too volatile for African American agents to conduct investigations on any aspect of the case within the state. Accordingly, I was not sent to Mississippi.

These agents, many of whom were former Marine combat veterans, worked on the Mississippi killings which led to almost 500 Klansmen being interrogated. The plan was set up as "internal security" cases rather than criminal investigations. As such, they depended on infiltration, surveillance, and sabotage of the members of the Klan.[19]

No one outside the Bureau knew that its Intelligence Division had institutionalized a project called the Counterintelligence Program (COINTELPRO). COINTELPRO had been started against the Communist Party in 1956 with a mission to penetrate organizations not to merely find out what they were doing, but to disrupt and destroy them. Its weapons were rumor, forgery, denunciation, provocation, i.e. "No holds barred."

. . . COINTELPRO demonstrated "the astonishing degree of independence the FBI had gained in the domestic security area. The Bureau was able to initiate an extensive, risky, and highly questionable operation without consulting the attorney general. The COINTELPRO project required only the recommendation of the assistant director in charge of Intelligence Division and the approval of the FBI director.[20]

In 1964, William Sullivan, the assistant director in charge of the Intelligence Division, persuaded Hoover to transfer the Klan matter out of the General Investigative Division and into COINTELPRO.

> The General Investigative Division . . . had Klan informants. Gary Thomas Rowe Jr., for example, had been recruited in 1959. But, after the Klan COINTELPRO began in September 1964, Rowe's FBI case officers told him, "The bureau is declaring war on the Klan. You can do anything you want to get your information." . . . As for strong-arm activities, "Well, you'll have to do what you have to do. No holds barred."

> . . . "We have penetrated the Klan very effectively," Hoover declared publicly in December 1964, ". . . particularly in the States of Alabama, Georgia and Mississippi." Nine months later he reported to the Attorney General that, of the Klan's fourteen state organizations, "we have penetrated every one of them through informants and currently are operating informants in top-level positions of leadership in seven of them." In one state, the top Klansman was an FBI operative. "As a result, we have been successful to date in holding Klan violence in the entire state to an absolute minimum." . . . In the first year of the Klan COINTELPRO, informers accounted for 70 percent of the new membership and, at the end of the year, for about one sixth of the total—2,000 out of 12,000–13,000."[21]

When the COINTELPRO effort was initiated in 1964, there were 14,000 Klan members; by 1971 it had fallen to 4,300 "completely disorganized and impotent individuals."[22]

My pride in the Bureau was at its highest level as a result of the investigation by special agents into the disappearance of civil rights workers James Chaney, Michael Schwerner, and Andrew Goodman beginning in June of 1964. Schwerner and Goodman were White. James Chaney, the only local resident, lived in the nearby, mostly Black town of Meridian, Mississippi. All were in their early twenties and were in the area on behalf of the Congress on Racial Equality (CORE) to assist Blacks to register to vote. The fact that two of the three were White certainly gave more urgency to solve their disappearance.

Scores of agents from throughout the nation were thrust into the investigation, six of whom were from the Kansas City Field Office. One included my best friend in Kansas City, Tom Trettis—a former Marine officer and University of Pennsylvania Law School graduate.

The Bureau involvement led to the discovery of the bodies of the young men in Chaney's car, which was found at the bottom of a pond in Philadelphia, Mississippi. All three had been beaten, shot at least once while in their seats, and the car was set afire before being sent to the bottom of the pond. Of the victims, Chaney, the Black, was tortured the worst before he died. Both of his arms had been broken as well as his jaw, and he was shot three times. The Whites were shot once.

Seven of the perpetrators were convicted for violating the US Enforcement Act of 1870 and 1871, the criminal codes which protected African Americans' right to vote, to hold office, to serve on juries, and to receive equal protection of the laws. Three received sentences from seven to ten years in prison. The ringleader and Ku Klux Klan organizer, Edgar Killen, was not initially convicted of three counts of manslaughter as the result of a hung jury. However, he was found guilty in state court of the three counts on June 21, 2005, and sentenced to 60 years in prison where he died on January 11, 2018.

Several books and movies were produced or published regarding the murders, with the film *Mississippi Burning* loosely based on the incident being the most popular.

The six agents from the Kansas City office sent to investigate the murders were rightfully proud of their accomplishments. The negative view many in the nation had regarding the commitment of the Bureau to conduct a thorough investigation of the murders was substantially allayed. The perpetrators were successfully identified and ultimately convicted. That was a shining moment in the history of the Bureau concerning civil rights matters.

CHAPTER 10

KCMO and My Work

DURING MY YEAR ASSIGNMENT in the Kansas City field Office, I was the only African American special agent operating in the states of Missouri and Kansas. My case load primarily included Interstate Violation of Stolen Motor Vehicles cases, Selective Service cases where individuals failed to register for the draft, and Unlawful Flight to Avoid Prosecution crimes such as murder, rape, burglary, etc., where the perpetrators cross state lines to avoid prosecution.

I usually followed up on leads by myself unless there was the definite possibility of making an arrest. In those cases, I would ask at least one of my squad members to assist me. Whenever my leads made it necessary to go into primarily Black neighborhoods, I felt more comfortable *not* asking other agents to go with me because they were White. Being required to wear a dark suit, White shirt, and a snap brim hat made me stand out anyway in the Black communities. Having a White partner in such circumstances would eliminate any effort of trying to be subtle.

Soon after I arrived in Kansas City, the case of a Black Criminal Informant (C.I.) was made available to me after the previous agent assigned to him was transferred. The informant's file indicated that "Cal" was very productive and reliable. After reading the file, I felt that Cal, being an older, long-term resident of the Black inner city of Kansas City, could at least give me a good feel for the city as well as possibly be, my eyes and ears regarding criminal activities in Kansas City, Missouri.

After my first two meetings with Cal, I felt my presumptions of him were on target. Cal was originally from Detroit, Michigan, and had spent a short period of time in the Los Angeles area before coming to Kansas City.

He related to me an intriguing story of the days he lived in Los Angeles. There he drove trucks carrying illegal drugs between Los Angeles and Mexico for the notorious mobster, Bugsy Siegel. Cal said that Siegel had given him the turquoise and gold ring he'd shown me on his pinky finger. Cal also claimed that he was the first person to find the mobster after he was gunned down in the Beverly Hills home of his girlfriend, Virginia Hill, on June 20, 1947.

Cal came to Kansas City soon after Siegel's murder, which has never been solved. Cal owned a small construction company in Kansas City and dabbled in petty crimes on the side—as he had in the previous cities where he lived. This helped him maintain credibility with the local criminal element.

Cal was about 56 and I was 24. Being much older than me, he made it a point to tell me a great deal about the city's Black community, but more directly about the Black criminal element in the broader Kansas City metropolitan area.

One afternoon Cal and I met outside a tavern in Kansas City, Missouri's (KCMO) central area. He said he wanted to take me inside the tavern to meet a few of the local mobsters.

He said "Now Carver, let me do all the talking, you just have to observe. I will introduce you as my friend from Los Angeles. This will be a good experience for you." We went inside and several surly looking Black guys were standing near the entrance. Cal was next to one and said to him, "I want you to meet Rocky Rogers."

I immediately stuck out my hand to the fellow next to Cal and said, "Glad to meet you, Rocky." The guy shook my hand, looked at me quizzically and grunted an unintelligible response.

Cal continued small talk with the three men. I ordered a glass of coke on the rocks with as gruff and tough tone I could muster. (One of the Bureau's rules for special agents was not to drink alcohol while on duty). We lingered in the uneasy atmosphere a few minutes longer and finally Cal said to me, "Let's go!"

As we went out the door, Cal grabbed me by the elbow and escorted me down the street at a fast pace. He whispered in a low and precise tone, "Carver, *you* were supposed to be Rocky Rogers! I think we blew that one." He hurried me into his car and sped off.

Cal continued on with the understatement, "We need to hold off going into that place for a while."

I weakly responded, "Cal, please give me a clue regarding my alias the next time." That was my introduction to the underworld of Kansas City. I've laughed over the years about that story, but there was no way I could have stayed alive in that town if I repeatedly made that kind of blunder!

Soon after that episode I came close to making another faux pas. Cal had mentioned that one of the more popular jazz clubs in KCMO utilized its basement quarters to hold stolen goods that had crossed state lines. Such activities violated Title 18 of the US Code and thus came under the jurisdiction of the Bureau. To get a feel for the layout of the club, I went inside one evening and sat at the bar and ordered a drink. While at the bar I saw in the mirror in front of me that the proprietor, whom I had met before, was looking at me with a knowing smile.

Within a few minutes a scantily dressed woman wearing a fluffy ostrich feather boa sat next to me and said in a sultry voice, "Today is my birthday." From the mirror I could tell that the club owner was still looking at me. I knew I was being set up. I began to light my long, thin Clint Eastwood type cigar and responded, attempting to be suave, "That's wonderful. How often do you celebrate?" Before she replied, as I was striking the match, the entire matchbook burst into flames! Within a split second I imagined the boa catching on fire and headlines in the *Kansas City Star* newspaper: "Local FBI Special Agent Ignites the Dress of a Woman at a Local Jazz Club."

What actually happened? I immediately clasped my hands over the flaming matchbook. The flames stopped, and I began to sweat profusely. I acted as if I did that sort of thing on a regular basis. I didn't wait to hear the woman's response and casually excused myself, with me not being able to close my hands. With obvious difficulty, I drove home and treated my second-degree burns. It was clear the club owner, knowing I was a special agent, was attempting to put me in a compromising situation with the woman. The experience reminds me of the inept Inspector Jacques Clouseau portrayed by Peter Sellers in the *Pink Panther* movie series.

The information about the suspected stolen property in the basement of the jazz club was passed on to the agent in our office who handled such matters.

It continued to be an ongoing investigation during my required year-long assignment in Kansas City.

One afternoon Cal invited me to his home to meet a friend. The man was the first Black sales representative for a major beer company. His territory was the predominately Black central district of KCMO. I found out from our conversation that we had mutual acquaintances in Seattle. I had no problem telling him I was a special agent. That revelation, along with him becoming a bit tipsy from his drinking, brought out the "macho" in him. Out of the blue, he boasted that he had mob connections in Kansas City, and if he was so inclined, he could have me "wacked" (murdered). I knew he was drunk and laughed it off. But Cal took offense and cussed him out for disrespecting me in his home, demanding that he apologize. He did, and I let the matter go. I never saw the sales rep again.

Cal continued to supply information to me about criminal activity in the area. He wanted to do everything he could to make my introductory year in the Bureau successful. He had never met a Black agent before, and he was proud of our relationship. To his detriment, the word got out among his underworld enemies about his association with me. From time to time the wires in his car were cut, as well as his tires. He also was framed for committing a burglary by a KCMO police informant and put in jail. However, the evidence did not support the accusation, and he was released.

During my time in KCMO, Cal never wavered in his support for me, despite putting his life in danger by doing so. I respected Cal as a human being, but at the same time, as an officer of the law, I had to be on guard knowing that most of his adult life he had been entrenched within a world of crime. I learned a great deal about the mean streets from him, as well as the significance of loyalty and respect. Cal was one of the brightest men I have ever met in terms of his understanding of human nature and his ability to read people. All of that was innate and what he learned in the streets. Cal was a survivor and fundamentally a good man. In my naïve and tender years, he opened my eyes to the fact in life that there are blurred lines between good and evil, between right and wrong. I evolved as a man knowing Cal.

———

My other informant in Kansas City was Charlotte. She was a mixed-race 25-year-old prostitute, who looked more White than Black, and appeared to be twice her age. I met her when following up on a lead for an escaped fugitive. Charlotte was approximately six feet tall and very full figured. She'd tuck her 6-inch barreled revolver inside her bra and no one would notice it. Her language was gruff and foul, used primarily for protection and intimidation. Although she looked Caucasian, her language and demeanor left no doubt that she was African American.

When we first met, she was loud and scary and came across as a bit mentally off-center. The fact that she would often be popping "goof balls" (barbiturates) with one hand and drinking vodka out of a bottle with the other probably contributed to my initial assessment of her mental state. Nevertheless, she gave me good information concerning the fugitive I was tracking down, which resulted in him being captured.

I decided to set up a file on Charlotte as a Potential Criminal Informant (PCI). As such, I was required to touch base with her at least twice a month to keep the file active. Over the next few months, I began to move away from the one-dimensional, horrific impression I initially had of her. I found out that she was from a broken home and went into prostitution as a twelve-year-old while living in Fort Scott, Kansas. As she grew older, she protected herself with a hard, out-of-control persona. When she moved away from that façade, she came across as an innately bright woman who had unbelievable survival skills for living within such a degrading and violent world.

Charlotte talked to me about a variety of subjects. Frequently, she related the difficulties she had with her pimp. As an example, she went into detail one day about him having a relationship with another young woman, and that she was tired of being disrespected by him. She planned on teaching him a lesson. She said that early one morning while lying in bed, she talked sweetly to him. She asked if he wanted her to make him some pancakes, and he replied, "That would be wonderful, honey."

She mixed the pancake batter and then began to heat up maple syrup in a saucepan on the small stove. She then poured lye in the syrup and yelled at him, "I'm going to teach your broke ass to fuck around with another bitch!" She picked up the hot pan of syrup and lye and began to chase him! He leaped out of the bed and ran naked toward the door. As he opened it, she threw the mixture across his back. She didn't say what happened to him, but she didn't care and would work the streets by herself. She was not through with him, however. She contacted his new girl, played up to her, and after a day or so, took her to bed. Charlotte mumbled to me, "No nigger will disrespect me like that man did to me."

Charlotte continued to provide information to me, most of which related to local crimes that I passed on to the KCMO Police Department, and I never found out how the cases panned out. One case that made Charlotte especially fearful related to a Black male friend who was found shot behind his ear on a dark side street near Kansas City's Central High School. She knew it was a drug-related hit, but she did not provide me with further details. The implication was that she was close enough to the victim to fear for her life. In those days the Bureau did not investigate drug related crimes.[23]

To the consternation of my wife, Charlotte would call my house at times during all hours of the night to tell me of her woes or to get me to help her get out of jail. She was convinced that many of her arrests by the KCMO Police Department were basically harassment, because—like with Cal—the word got out about her connection with me. She hated the local cops and would go into her crazy act when they rousted her. She also said they were peeved because she would not be a "stool pigeon" (informer) for them.

During an unguarded moment, I asked her how she avoided having children over the years. She replied, "Carver, I may be an evil, hard-assed, scum of the earth. But I would never be able to live with myself by bringing a child into my God-forsaken world! That would be my worst sin. I am not that evil." That statement blew me away.[24]

———

My successes with Cal and Charlotte led to my being selected to attend the prestigious Informants School at Quantico, Virginia, at the end of my year in Kansas City. In later days, I came across some forgotten notes that I had taken during one of the sessions. The notes were from a presentation by none other than Mark Felt, who would become noted years later as "Deep Throat" during the Watergate investigation. Felt, at the time, had just been promoted to Chief of the Inspection Division of the Bureau. He did not provide substantive information about developing informants. His primary role was welcoming the class as a representative of the top executive echelon of the Bureau.

The class helped me solidify my approach to developing informants. It was about building personal rapport by demonstrating that you *respect* them as human beings. Although I grew up in Seattle's Central District and had met—at least to my mind—a wide variety of folks from different races and socio-economic backgrounds, I was not prepared to meet the likes of Cal and Charlotte, nor the people with whom they associated. I believe the thing they liked about me was that I was fascinated by their lifestyles. I listened intently to what they had to say. I really did not have first-hand experience of knowing that people lived the way they did day after day within a criminal environment.

I do not believe I lost my sense of morality, but I certainly changed the way I viewed people. For example, I admired the raw honesty of Charlotte and the fact that Cal did all that he could for me to respect him as a man. Each could keep me in stitches with their humorous stories and experiences. They helped me to view most people in general as multi-dimensional in terms of their character and mores, rather than as merely *good* or *bad*. Respect is the key. This does not mean agreeing to or trusting all that they say, but rather, respecting them as individuals and being open to listening to new and different perspectives.

I met another middle-aged Black man in Kansas City who was also a product of the streets, but he utilized his mathematical mind to become one of the most powerful underworld figures in the city. His name was Harry. Another agent in the office was a specialist in wiretapping telephone conversations of La Cosa Nostra, i.e., Mafia family members. The agent was Sicilian and spoke the language impeccably and fluently. The conversations the agent tapped were of mobsters talking in Sicilian, the language of the authentic "made men" in the Mafia. He also maintained a log of the conversations. The agent developed Harry as a Criminal Informant (CI) and met with him every couple of months. I got involved because of the importance of the cases this agent investigated; he needed another agent to come as a witness when talking with Harry. Harry was the "kingpin" of the floating crap games in Kansas City.[25]

No one could be as successful as Harry running an illegal gambling operation in Kansas City and not be connected to the mob. I had no doubt that because I was Black, the Sicilian agent felt that Harry, who was also Black, would be more open to discussing his connection with the mob. The agent explained that the conversation with Harry would be pro forma and basically a ritual because there was no way the gambler would tell him about paying off the syndicate in order to operate his crap games. Nevertheless, the agent said this would be an interesting experience for me.

We went to the Criminal Informant's home and the subsequent conversation was fascinating. Harry was a very distinguished looking Black man with a light brown complexion. He spoke in an erudite manner. He asked us to sit down and offered us a soft drink. My immediate thought was, *How could this impressive gentleman be an underground 'kingpin' with Mafia connections?*

The agent started off by saying, "Harry, you know why we are here. Let's get the question out of the way and then we can just talk. Are you paying off the La Cosa Nostra in order to operate your floating crap games in Kansas City?"

Harry did not show any fear or surprise from the question and responded in a bored and matter of fact manner, "I have no idea what La Casa Nostra is, and with that being the case, I could not be 'paying off', as you say, any such organization. I am an independent entrepreneur and report to no one but myself."

The agent said, "Harry, we've gone through this song and dance routine many times before, so your response was expected. Tell me...how are your games coming along?"

He replied, "As a matter of fact, the games are doing quite well."

I was surprised by his response, but the agent told me after the meeting that Harry had no problem talking to us about his gambling since Harry knew that we as Federal authorities had no real interest in the crap games per se. Such crimes were local matters. Our primary interest was Harry's knowledge of the local and national inner workings of the La Casa Nostra.

Once the formalities were out of the way, I asked Harry a series of questions about his gambling business. I was enthralled for the next hour and a half. Harry indicated that his involvement as the organizer of floating crap games, i.e., dice games in Kansas City, began in the 1930s. The only times he personally participated in a game, he said, was after he had watched the players and mentally calculated the statistical probabilities of him being able to win. He obviously was a gifted mathematical genius. Also, he would only allow his dice in the games with his serial numbers to make sure loaded dice were not used. His reputation was such that other gamblers did not question the integrity of the games. Harry was especially proud of his daughter and son who were college educated. His son was a graduate of the Massachusetts Institute of Technology with a PhD in mathematics.

Harry voiced no regrets about his vocation. I've often thought of folks I met during my stint with the Bureau—and what they could have done in the "legitimate" world in the public and private sectors, if not because of the color of their skin. They invariably had the analytical and interpersonal skills to survive and excel within the intricate and dangerous underworld in which they functioned.

Harry made mention of literally dozens of "spot" or "contract" murders by the mob in the Kansas City area from the 1930s through 1964, none of which had ever been solved. His inference was that he was shrewd enough to survive it all.

As our meeting wound down, I understood why my partner agent went through the charade of talking with Harry, knowing full well he would not reveal his connection with the La Costa Nostra. Harry had fascinating stories, and there was mutual respect between him and the agent who, I'm sure, looked forward to talking with him whenever necessary.

———

Toward the end of 1964, about six months after being assigned to the Kansas City Field Office, I was following up on a lead regarding a fugitive who was believed to be residing in Kansas City, Kansas—across the Missouri River from Kansas City, Missouri. After interviewing an acquaintance of the subject, I noticed a storefront campaign headquarters for a person named George Haley who was running for state senator. As I walked by the headquarters, a congenial looking African American man was standing outside. He introduced himself as George Haley. He asked if he could talk with me about his campaign for senator. I agreed, and he talked about his background and why he was running for office.

I was especially impressed that he was the first Black to graduate from the University of Arkansas School of Law. I listened politely, and after a while I explained I could not vote for him because I was a resident of Kansas City, *Missouri*. But I assured him that he impressed me, and I wished him well in his effort to win a seat in the Kansas State Senate. As we continued talking, he asked about my profession. Somewhat reluctantly, I told him I was a special agent of the FBI. He was very impressed and indicated that I was the first Black agent he had ever met. After further conversation, he invited me and my wife to his home for dinner and I agreed. He had a Black friend visiting in town and wanted him to meet me.

Our families met for dinner, and George introduced me to his brother Alex Haley who was a freelance writer for several publications, including *Reader's Digest*, *Playboy*, and *Show Business Illustrated* among others. Alex said he was only planning on staying in Kansas City for a week or so. The primary reason he was in town was to interview an aunt who had in-depth information about the Haley family and their historical roots which could be traced to west Africa. He said he was working on a book about civil rights activist, Malcolm X.

I was fascinated with Alex's ventures as a writer. However, I had no hint at all that what he related to me would lead to the writing of two worldwide bestselling books: *The Autobiography of Malcolm X*, published in 1965, and *Roots: The Saga of an American Family*, published in 1976, which was the basis for the iconic television series, *Roots: The Next Generation*, introduced in 1979.

I maintained a friendship with Alex Haley over the years. When they met, Haley thought my young son, Chandler, was the next Kunta Kinte, a reference to author's Roots saga.

I maintained contact with George Haley over the years. He served in many high-profile positions within the administrations of Presidents Nixon, Ford, Carter, both Bushes, and Clinton. Some of the positions he held included Chief Counsel of the Federal Transit Administration, Chairman of the US Postal Rate Commission, and US Ambassador to Gambia. I reconnected with Alex when he moved to Seattle in 1990, where he died in 1992.

My year-long assignment in Kansas City was coming to an end and I was asked by the Bureau to list three offices of preference in priority order. I listed San Francisco as number one, Seattle as two, and Los Angeles as three. So naturally I was assigned to the Philadelphia, Pennsylvania, Field office! Typical bureaucratic reasoning. My wife, Mona, took the assignment in stride, but she had hoped to live close to her sister's family in the Bay area of San Francisco.

I had thirty days of vacation time before I needed to arrive at the Philadelphia office. I purchased a 1965 Chevrolet Nova in KCMO, and Mona and I set out to Seattle with our children, Cynthia and Carver Junior, to visit our relatives before the long trip to Philly. Mona was expecting our third child, Craig, in March. The trip was a bit uncomfortable for her, but it was a fun experience with sightseeing, warm summer weather, and the fact that we were not rushed for time.

CHAPTER 11

Into the Jungle

A MONTH LATER, the family settled into an apartment in Barrington, New Jersey, a suburb of Philadelphia. On April 1, 1965, I started my new assignment in the Bureau offices across from Penn Square in the center of the city. I was assigned to the Bank Robbery and Fugitive Squad under an excellent boss, Dick Rogge, who in later years became Special Agent in Charge of the Los Angeles Field Office. Most of the squad was composed of ex-jocks a foot taller and bigger than me. I was the only one on the squad who did not carry the macho .44 magnum revolver that agents purchased on their own dime. I stuck with the government-issue .38-caliber Smith & Wesson sidearm.

On my first day in the office, one of the agents handed me a packet of eight to ten photographs of known La Casa Nostra members of the Angelo Bruno Family of Philadelphia and told me to memorize their faces. The agent said there was rumored to be an open contract out on any agent, and that I should be careful about investigating leads in South Philadelphia, the section of the city where most of the Italian community resided. To this day I have no idea of the details behind that warning. Nevertheless, the warning certainly got my attention as to what I could expect in the "City of Brotherly Love."

The Bureau was attempting to build up its image in Philadelphia, particularly within the Black community. As part of that effort, I was asked by the special agent from Mississippi, in charge of community relations within the office, to visit the all-Black Booker T. Washington High School and talk with a group of their Black male students. They were extremely enthusiastic about meeting a Black FBI agent! They were unaware that the Bureau had Black special agents. The meeting was informal, as I talked mostly about my background. The students were exceptionally respectful and very interested in what I was saying. Toward the end, one of the boys asked how I became interested in becoming an agent. I told the story about my brother being an Assistant US Attorney in Seattle, and that Robert Kennedy, the US Attorney General whom J. Edgar Hoover reported to, initiated an effort to recruit Black agents into the Bureau. That's what led me to apply. The meeting ended on a high note with the young men standing and clapping for me. It was a proud moment.

As I was leaving with the community relations agent, he pulled me by my elbow and admonished me by saying that it was J. *Edgar Hoover* that initiated the effort to hire more Black special agents, not Robert Kennedy. I did not agree with him, knowing that in fact that was not the case. I was not asked to accompany him on any further public relations during my remaining three years in Philadelphia.

One of the first leads I investigated was in the Black ghetto of North Philadelphia, better known as the "Jungle." I was in disbelief of what I saw. As far as the eye could see were dilapidated row houses with garbage, walls of graffiti, and abandoned cars. The area was inhabited by extremely poor minorities, most of whom were Blacks and Puerto Ricans. I had never seen such an expanse of poverty before.

Much of what I saw were remnants from the infamous race riots in the "Jungle" during August of 1964, precipitated by allegations of police brutality against Blacks in North Philadelphia. At the time of the riots, Blacks were 18 percent of Philadelphia's population and 40 percent of the inmates in the city's jails and prisons. Hundreds were arrested, and property damage would be $23 million in today's dollars. Tension continued in the "Jungle" throughout the nearly three years I was assigned to the Philadelphia field Office.

In the late Summer of 1965, I followed up on a lead to interview the daughter of a "subject." The temperature was in the 80s with a humidity level of 80 percent. The water hydrants on the garbage-filled blocks were going full blast. A putrid smell of rotting food filled the air. The young girl who answered at the one-room row house apartment was no more than fifteen years old. Her infant baby was lying on an overstuffed chair sucking on a baby bottle of curdled milk. The unkempt, pretty, brown-skinned girl looked helpless and bewildered.

She related to me that she had no idea where the fugitive was living and that she had not seen him in over a year. She came across as credible, and I couldn't help but ask how she got into these dire circumstances. She said that she was sent to Philadelphia by her mother in New York City to live with an aunt because her single mother couldn't afford to support her. Her strict aunt tried to keep a leash on her. However, the girl became pregnant, and the aunt told her to leave.

She did not smile once during our conversation. In fact, she showed no emotion other than bewilderment. Looking out her window, she casually pointed out the local pimp, an attractive woman in her twenties dressed in men's clothes. The girl said the pimp was on good terms with her girls because she treated them with more respect than most male pimps. She showed me a local drug dealer, not far away from the pimp.

The girl didn't indicate she was selling her body or taking drugs. As I left the apartment, I wished her well. As I stood on the top of her stairwell and looked around, I thought that the girl, if not already doing so, would soon be prostituting herself or taking drugs—most likely both—to survive in her environment. Few other options were apparent to me. I couldn't imagine anyone, much less that young girl, overcoming such circumstances. I surmised that the only individuals making a decent living in her neighborhood might be the pimp and the drug dealer. Hopelessness pervaded that block and every other block within a two-mile radius of the young girl's home.

A few months later I covered another lead with a young black woman around the age of twenty who was considerably more mature and worldly than the teenager I'd met earlier. She lived in a one-bedroom apartment with three small children and was on welfare. The fugitive I was investigating lived in the neighborhood, but the woman was not sure of his exact residence. I asked if I could touch base with her from time to time to help apprehend him, and she agreed. I considered developing her as an informant because she seemed to have a good network of what was going on in the high crime area where she lived.

However, a couple of incidents delayed that possibility. After a few months of periodic contact with the woman, I received a call from someone who identified herself as a welfare case worker for the State of Pennsylvania. She wanted to know who I was because she was considering cutting off welfare payments to the woman I was contacting. I asked, "What does that have to do with me and my effort to arrest a fugitive through my contacts with the woman?" She said she did not believe the woman was talking with an FBI agent, and that she'd never heard of a Black being an agent, much less, one being in Philadelphia. (The welfare worker was Black.) She pointed out that if a man was in her life, it was more than likely that he was giving her money. And if that were the case, the Welfare Department would have to cut off payments to her. I assured her who I was and that it would not be necessary to cut off her stipends.

I was not aware of how the welfare system operated during the 1960s, but that one incident—assuming it was typical of how it functioned—contributed to the disintegration of family structure for many poor Blacks in America. In my mind, there was no positive incentive for poor Black males who worked in low-paying jobs (or no jobs at all) to stay with their families. In many cases, welfare policies in states like Pennsylvania led unwed mothers to keep men away from their households and to not marry in order to receive more money from the government.

Although the welfare worker was diligent, or more than likely curious, about the young unwed mother's relationship with a Black FBI agent, she was less focused on girl's lover. He was a married father of six children who maintained a relationship with the woman.

After a month when I had no communication with her, she phoned me to say she had just been released from the hospital. Her lover became enraged one evening, which happened often, and he took a heavy iron lamp and hit her on the head. With blood gushing from her wound, she crawled from her apartment screaming. A woman next door called the police and an ambulance. She was rushed to a nearby hospital and immediately went into surgery. Her life was saved. But the doctor told her that if the wound to her skull was a fraction of an inch deeper, she would have died. There was no indication from the young woman that her attacker was ever incarcerated. I presumed, sadly, that she and the man continued their dysfunctional relationship.

I learned from reports that at the height of the earlier riots, some residents in the Jungle burned down *their own* residences. That was something I couldn't fathom. I had an interview with a woman concerning a fugitive whose apartment was in the area where some of the home burnings took place. She was about thirty years old, holding a baby. Three other infants were in the room. A lady who appeared to be the woman's mother sat on a couch. No man was in the room. This was a typical scenario of homes I saw in North Philly.

I asked her, "Why did so many Blacks in your neighborhood burn down their own homes during the riots?"

She shrugged and said with disgust, "Look around this apartment. It's like most in this area. What do you see that's worth saving? We're sick and tired of not being able to find jobs and not being able to support ourselves like human beings. This place—which we don't own—is not fit for pigs!"

I could not argue with her. The apartment looked like a garbage dump. Exactly like scores of others I'd seen while investigating cases in North Philadelphia. Each time I entered a home, I attempted to not look uneasy or chagrined by the surroundings. I did not want to appear disrespectful or haughty by the families I was visiting.

Each night, as I went home from Philadelphia across the Ben Franklin Bridge to my upper middle-class townhouse in southern New Jersey, I tried to push to the back of my mind what I saw and experienced in those homes and neighborhoods in the Jungle. I never talked with my wife about how my day went. She never would have believed me! I needed a few hours' respite anyway, in order for me to meet the challenges of the next day. But strangely, I never regretted having to start all over again the next day.

After a year in Philadelphia, I decided to attend night school at Temple University to work on a master's degree in education administration, with a focus on kindergarten through twelve programs. The more I witnessed in the poor Black sections of Philadelphia and the negative impact of it on the lives of young Black children, the more convinced I became that my professional focus should be in the field of education.

My Bureau experience was an educational experience in and of itself. It was hard for me to conceive how young Blacks in particular could overcome what they were exposed to every day of their lives: the poverty, dysfunctional families, crime, drugs, health issues, etc. At the same time, I was amazed to witness the *fortitude* of those who were able to overcome such dire circumstances and live fruitful lives. I looked back on the lives of my grandparents and great-grandparents who as slaves, and then victims of Jim Crow laws, endured even

The more I witnessed in the poor Black sections of Philadelphia and the negative impact of it on the lives of young Black children, the more convinced I became that my professional focus should be in the field of education.

worse circumstances. They survived with the help of others. I need to be one of those "others."

I had no timeline for leaving the Bureau. I decided to finish my master's degree yet be open to other possibilities careerwise beyond the Bureau. The Bureau was my non-academic "PhD in *Life*."

———

FBI agents received general training within the first year and a half of employment to enable them to investigate a wide variety of cases. It was not until they were assigned to offices in large metropolitan areas that they focused on narrow fields, such as bank robberies, stolen motor vehicles, "top hoodlum" matters, or espionage, etc. A smaller number were assigned as Resident Agents (RA's) in rural towns and covered all criminal and security matters under Bureau jurisdiction. Occasionally, I was assigned cases outside of the bank robbery/fugitive squad. Some included espionage or top-hoodlum matters. Some concerned background investigations for presidential appointments. For such appointments, scores of agents were assigned to investigate leads regarding the prospective appointees.

The most interesting background investigation related to the possible appointment of Reverend Leon Sullivan as US Secretary of Housing and Urban Development.[26] Although Harvard PhD, Robert Weaver was ultimately appointed to the position, my interviews concerning Rev. Sullivan were very positive and enlightening.

I interviewed Pennsylvania Superior Court Judge Theodore O. Spalding, and he introduced me to many professional Blacks who were his lifelong friends and acquaintances from Philadelphia and South New Jersey.

I enjoyed interviewing Black people whom I had regarded as heroes from the time I was a teenager. They were the crème de la crème of Black Philadelphia.

Among the interesting people I met socially or as an FBI agent were Cecil Moore, Esq., the fiery and admired President of the Philadelphia Chapter of the National Association for the Advancement of Colored People (NAACP); Federal District Court Judge A. Leon Higginbottom, a national leader recognized for initiating affirmative action programs for African Americans; Sadie Tanner Mossell Alexander, Esq., the first woman to receive a law degree from the University of Pennsylvania Law School, the first national President of the Delta Sigma Theta Sorority, and the first African American woman to receive a PhD in economics in the United States; and William Henry Hastie, the United States Circuit Judge of the US Court of Appeals for the Third Circuit.

The most entertaining and energizing interview I had was with Cecil Moore. Moore was considered one of the new breeds of young Turks within the NAACP, who wanted the NAACP to be more militant concerning the rights of Blacks. His sense of commitment to the rights of the poor and Blacks was reflected in these words:

> *I was determined when I got back from World War II that what rights I didn't have, I was going to take, using every weapon in the arsenal of democracy. After nine years in the Marine Corps, I don't intend to take another order from any son-of-a-bitch that walks.*

The most riveting interviewee was William Henry Hastie. At the time of the interview in 1965, Judge Hastie held the highest judicial position attained by an African American. In 1946, he was appointed by President Harry Truman as the first African American Governor of the Virgin Islands, a position he held until 1949. Judge Hastie was a graduate of Amherst College as well as the Harvard University School of Law. While Dean of Howard University's School of Law, one of his students was Thurgood Marshall, who in later years was appointed by President Johnson as a US Supreme Court Justice.

During the interview, Judge Hastie was so precise in the delivery of his words. All of what he said could have been typed verbatim without any grammatical corrections. His straightforward delivery went on for 45 minutes! There was no clearing of his throat, nor any hesitation. Never in my life have I met anyone with such extemporaneous command of the English language! I was in awe partly because I had been hearing and reading about him my whole life. However, even if I had never known about him before the interview, I believe I would have been mesmerized.

Judge Hastie's interview was the last. On my way back to the office in Penn Square, I was pinching myself regarding what I had experienced the past few weeks. Each of my interviewees had legal degrees, most of which were from Ivy League schools prior to the 1940's. They received the degrees during a time when most Blacks were being rejected by predominately White institutions. Not only were their credentials superlative, but they had the intangible leadership and interpersonal skills to be giants in their respective vocations. I was invigorated by the experience of those three weeks! I became pumped up about myself and my career possibilities and being an African American. Also, I became more committed than ever to complete an advanced degree, quite possibly a doctorate in education or the social sciences.

CHAPTER 12

In Danger

Another venture outside of the primary areas of my assigned squad concerned a woman I contacted on a lead for one of my fugitive cases. Her information turned out to be non-productive. However, she mentioned she would like to contact me periodically when she had information that could be of interest to the Bureau. The timing of her offer was fortuitous as I needed to increase my informant case load. I accepted. Her offer was a pleasant surprise since few possible informants came forward with information without a long period of cultivation.

Several months later she called and said she moved from North Philly to one of the Black sections of South Philadelphia, composed mostly of Italians. She had some information that may be of interest and would like to meet.

I went to her new apartment where she had been watching—from her living room window—some interesting activity between the known numbers racket gambling kingpin of the Black neighborhood and "some guys" in a long, black, four-door late-model Cadillac. There were exchanges of packages or papers between the racketeer and the driver of the Cadillac. She said the car stood out because very seldom did such expensive cars drive through that part of town. She gave me the license number of the car and I left.

I suspected a La Casa Nostra connection because, as was the case in Kansas City with the floating crap games, no such operation could exist and thrive in that part of town without the approval and payoffs to the mob. I went to my office and traced the license plate number to a rental agency in South Jersey outside of Camden. I went to the Top Hood Squad (Organized Crime) and provided the assistant supervisor with the license plate information and all that had transpired. He said he would handle the matter from there and would contact the Philadelphia Police Department's "elite" Intelligence unit.

Around three o'clock in the morning, I got a call from the woman who had given me the information. She was screaming uncontrollably, saying she just arrived home after an evening of "night clubbing," and her entire apartment was trashed! She feared for her life and was going back to North Philly to live with friends.

The trashing was undeniably a message to my informant. I was livid about what could have happened to her. I went to the agent in the "Top Hood" squad and told him what had transpired. I asked "What the hell" did he do with the information I gave him. He told me he passed it on to the Intelligence Unit of the Philadelphia Police Department and told them to handle it. It was obvious to me that the Unit was in cahoots with the gangsters in the Cadillac. I was also peeved at the agent for not being more discreet with the information I gave him. Moreover, he came across as being unconcerned by the whole episode, especially the threat to my informant.

I made a point of not telling him the address my informant moved to. I didn't discuss the matter with any other agent because, quite frankly, I became suspicious of both the Bureau and the Philadelphia Police Department in terms of their true relationship with the Philadelphia mob.

I knew I had to tread lightly regarding any follow-up inquiries I made. I was moving into a dangerous area about which I was not being fully informed, especially by my fellow agent in the Top Hood Squad. Nevertheless, I was very interested in talking with the numbers kingpin that my informant identified.

Before my informant's apartment was trashed, I attempted to contact him at his upper middle-class home in the Main Line in Northwest Philadelphia. He was not home, and I left a note under his door with my name and Phone number. In those days agents did not have business cards. He contacted me about a week later, and I asked him to come to my office to talk.

Entering the office, the well-dressed, slim African American was fidgety, his eyes darting from side to side. I invited him into an interview room. He asked what I wanted to talk about, and I advised him of his Miranda rights under the law: "You have the right to remain silent, and anything you do say could be used against you in a court of Law. You have the right to an attorney. If you cannot afford an attorney, one will be provided for you." I said I had reason to believe he was involved in organized crime in South Philadelphia, and that he was doing so to maintain his numbers business in the area. He then blurted out that he had contacted his attorney and advised him to file charges against the Bureau for harassment if the interview was more than an hour long. I said fine.

The man was in his late thirties, very bright, and well spoken. He certainly did not come across as an individual operating on the wrong side of the law. As he began sweating above his upper lip he explained, "I'm a legitimate businessman. My father ran the enterprise before me as did his father. I am sure you and I have a lot in common." He said he graduated from a reputable Historically Black College and joined a well-known African American fraternity. He also spoke proudly of one of the well-known social groups that his wife was a member of and surmised that my wife probably was a member of the same organization.

He was basically pleading for me to understand that the two of us had the same values and interests, and that as a "brother" I should stop "harassing" him. In fact, he suggested that our families should get together socially and quit going through "the cat and mouse games" of false accusations against him. I pointed out that such a scenario was not likely.

Finally, he stood up and reminded me of his earlier warning concerning his lawyer. He remained very nervous and agitated. As he left, he said, "I really hope we can meet again under different circumstances." I was impressed with his intelligence and the fact that his family was able to sustain his "business" over so many generations. I remained fascinated with his unwavering view that he was an "entrepreneur" providing a service for the Black families in that section of the city and had no compunctions about its illegality. It's important to note that the Bureau had no jurisdiction over his numbers activities. Our primary interest was his connection with the mob and the interstate racket implications.

One late afternoon in the Philadelphia office, an agent who handled Away Without Leave (AWOL) i.e. deserters from the armed services cases, asked me to help him pick up a master sergeant with the Marines who'd deserted. Such cases were building up as a result of the unpopular Vietnam War. The agent said he had good information as to the subject's whereabouts and that "the apprehension shouldn't take long."

I agreed to assist him and felt that the arrest would help build "statistics" that agents always sought to bolster their performance evaluations. The arrest of the muscular 5'10," 250-pound African American master sergeant, as predicted, was fairly easy. The sergeant did not talk much and had beady eyes and a somewhat crazed expression. I thought to myself, *I'll be glad when we get this guy out of our hands.*

In accordance with Bureau standard procedures, we handcuffed him with his hands behind his back and drove him to the FBI office to be fingerprinted before being confined. Once we got to the office, a slight glitch took place, which grew into a major problem. As I inserted the key into the handcuffs, the key-hole spring broke and the handcuffs would not open. My partner was a veteran agent, and he immediately said he would get a hacksaw to cut through exceptionally dense metal. The sergeant began snorting and his eyes widened. The cuffs were heating up as I was sawing and making abrasions on the wrists of the subject. Consequently, we started pouring water on the sergeant's wrists in an effort to limit the pain. Very little progress was being made to cut through the cuffs. In fact, the cuffs began to tighten on his wrists.

A simple arrest process that began at 6 p.m. in the evening was now going into 2 a.m. the next day. After hours of sawing, the cuffs finally came off, with the sergeant sweating profusely, burns on his wrists and on the verge of exploding into a rage. He was hurried off to confinement by 3 a.m. However, the long bureaucratic process of filling out Bureau reports for the destroyed government property (the handcuffs) began. That was almost more tortuous than sawing off the handcuffs! So much for an early dinner at home with the wife and kids.

Very seldom did I arrest someone without having at least one other agent with me. If I was confident that a subject would be at a particular location, I made a point of having another agent with me. Occasionally when I was alone, I would follow up on a lead and stumble upon a fugitive and make an arrest. This happened in the Spring of 1966 in West Philadelphia.

I was checking on a lead from a case agent from Chicago. The subject was wanted on an Unlawful Flight to Avoid Prosecution (UFAP) for passing worthless checks throughout the United States. Ninety percent of the time, for such leads from another field office, I would not personally confront the fugitive. But on this day, the fugitive answered the door of a small rowhouse. I identified myself and asked to come in. He offered me a seat and I began asking questions. I knew he was a scion of the family that owned international dry-cleaning franchises. He readily admitted to that. He was a twenty-five-year-old White male, good looking, with an engaging personality and a quick wit. He did not show signs of being nervous. He said he had been traveling around the US and Europe for two years with different young women, although he did not readily admit to any illegal activities. Finally, after an hour or so of denial and obfuscation, he admitted to passing the bad checks and the illegal use of the credit cards of the women.

I asked him why he got involved in such a spree, particularly since he did not need the money. Basically, he said he just enjoyed the adventure of it all, especially the excitement of eluding the authorities. After his admission, he did not show any signs of being distraught. In fact, he was smiling and seemed somewhat relieved that the adventure was over. He asked if I would allow him to go the restroom before going downtown to be incarcerated. I said "certainly" and stood outside the bathroom.

A couple of minutes went by. Suddenly, I said to myself "Holy shit! I shouldn't have left him out of my sight!"

I broke open the door just as he was beginning to slit his wrist. I took the razor from him, handcuffed him from behind, and took him downtown. I should have been with him. His disposition was such that he showed no outward signs of wanting to harm himself. That was a lesson learned.

A few weeks later I had to arrest a female fugitive who was a five-month's pregnant woman in her apartment. She made a similar request to relieve herself before taking her to my car. She wanted privacy, but I stood there watching her while she cussed me out and accusing me of being a voyeur. During the drive, I called the Field Office to get a female police officer from the Philadelphia P.D. to assist me with the booking of the woman. There were no female agents in the Bureau at the time. The policewoman could not have taken my place quick enough.

There were at least three cases I investigated when I thought I was going to be killed. One related to a fugitive I almost caught in North Philadelphia's Jungle one fall afternoon. I was by myself talking to a woman in a downstairs apartment of a rundown building. As we talked, I saw the flash of a Black man running out of an upstairs apartment and disappearing into another. The man was obviously the fugitive, so I ran up the stairs in hot pursuit. The man apparently jumped out of a second story apartment, because I saw him running through a back alley littered with garbage and broken furniture. I went back downstairs and told the lady on the first floor to call me if this man returned. To my surprise, she called in the late afternoon and said the man would be hiding in the basement of the apartment building around 6pm that evening.

I gathered three other members of the fugitive squad, including my supervisor Dick Rogge, all of whom were White, and we made the trek to the apartment in the predominately Black "Jungle" to apprehend the fugitive. Very few Whites were ever seen in that section of the city. Since I was the lead agent on the case, I recontacted the lady in the first-floor apartment, and she confirmed that the man was still in the basement and that there was only one entrance and exit to the basement.

I was in front of our team as we moved slowly down the stairs into the pitch-dark room. I had my Smith & Wesson revolver drawn and another agent held a large flashlight. Obviously, I would be the first target if the fugitive was armed. He was known to carry a firearm. On those stairs, my heart pounded, and the palms of my hands were sweating. I kept calling out to the guy to give up. I was waiting for the crack of the gun and wondered how I would feel when his bullet hit me. Those five minutes I experienced were the longest in my life.

 The manager of the apartment was wrong. The fugitive was not in the basement. I felt exhilarated because he was not there to shoot me! But on the other hand, I was extremely disappointed about not capturing him.

Nevertheless, I continued investigating cases alone in the area unless it was clear that a fugitive was at an identified residence. Such was the case when an informant pin-pointed the location of an armed and dangerous fugitive one late afternoon that summer. The only agent available to help me arrest the subject was a bookish accountant. I did not recall that he ever participated in such an assignment. Despite his lack of experience, I did not expect any problems because he was a very conscientious agent. I advised him of the subject's background and physical description as well as my plan of capturing him. The agent was excited about working with me.

My plan was to make the capture between 2 a.m. and 4 a.m. when the subject was more likely to be sleeping. When we arrived, I told the agent to go in the alley behind the residence in the event the subject attempted to escape out the back. I gave my partner time to position himself. Then I went to the second-floor apartment of the fugitive and knocked on the door, saying load and clear, "Open up--FBI!!" I yelled the order and knocked again, and instantly something hit the door hard from inside the room. I immediately kicked the door, and to my surprise the whole door fell down.

A Black, teenage boy was in the bed of the one-room apartment yelling, "Don't shoot! Don't shoot! He went out the window! He went out the window!"

By that time, I had my revolver out. I got a glimpse of a brown-skinned figure running across the tops of the connected rowhouses. I immediately went out the window running in the light of a full moon toward the figure. I had not been out the window more than a few feet when I heard an authoritative, familiar voice yell after the fugitive disappeared, "Stop or I'll shoot!" I recognized the voice as that of my partner. I stopped for a split second and yelled back, "You SOB, it's me! Put your G D gun away!" and then continued to run toward the direction of the escaping fugitive.

After running fifteen yards across the connected roofs, I came to an open window and climbed inside. I looked to my left and saw a Black man and woman standing in their night clothes in an open doorway. Their eyes and mouths were wide open with stunned expressions. As I pushed the door to open it wider, I asked if they'd seen a Black man in his undershorts. They shook their heads from side to side nervously saying "... no, no, no." I pushed the door open more and walked inside the apartment, making a quick survey of the room.

Then I went down the flight of stairs and met my partner as well as a couple of apartment residents walking up. I asked what they had seen, and they shook their heads. I suspected the fugitive was still in the building, and that the couple at the top of the stairway may not have told me the full story. I went back up the stairs pushing the door even wider, and then I noticed both were making side glances to their right without saying anything, and finally I got it. With my gun out, I looked behind the door, and sure enough—there was the fugitive in his boxer shorts with his hands holding his clothes over his privates!

I had been hitting him in the head and body each time I opened the door over the past ten minutes. I told him not to move. I had my partner take the clothes and handcuff him. I yelled, "We have to get out of here fast." The Black neighbors were beginning to wake up, most of whom had no respect for the authorities and were prepared to find an excuse to confront us.

With the fugitive in his skivvies, we ran past walls in the apartment scrawled with paint with statements like "Kill the pigs, "Power to the people," and "Off the honkies." We pushed the fugitive into the back seat of our car and sped off just as the sun was peeking over the roof tops of the dreary Jungle. The fugitive was fingerprinted and confined without further problems.

What I considered a routine AWOL case turned into one of my more dangerous assignments. I received a lead from an agent in the Boston Field Office about an eighteen-year-old Black man who moved to Philadelphia and did not respond to his 1-A draft classification which directed him to report to a Boston draft board. On numerous occasions, I attempted to reach the young man at the apartment address given to me. I left notes and my phone number at several of the residences in the neighborhood with no results. I did not find anyone who knew where he lived, and I transmitted reports of my efforts to Boston.

The case remained open in Philadelphia, with no new leads nor status reports coming from Boston for over two-and-a-half years. I was surprised to get a phone call one morning from a young man who sounded African American and said he had a note with my name and phone number on it asking about him. He said he wanted me to come by his apartment to talk. He did not sound hostile or angry, and I had no reason to have any trepidation about meeting with him. I did not immediately recall his name, but I said sure. We agreed to meet the next day.

When I arrived at his apartment in the Jungle, a young man opened the door dressed in US Army camouflage fatigues and invited me in. I immediately sensed that I had walked into a bee's nest. There were six young Blacks, ranging in age from eighteen to approximately twenty-three, all of whom were dressed in green camouflage battle gear. Two leaned against the wall of the room cleaning their fingernails with what looked like combat knives, approximately eight inches long. All had scowls on their faces.

The fellow who opened the door started talking. He said he had heard that I was looking for him for dodging the draft, and that he served more than a year fighting in Vietnam and ". . . wanted to know what the problem was." I informed him that I had not received information about him having served, and that I'd contact the FBI Field Office in Boston and find out why his case was not closed.

I expressed my appreciation to him having fought for the country, and I would make sure his case was immediately closed. He continued to talk, while one of the men moved behind me next to the door. I told him to move away from the door and he did not budge. The subject continued to talk, saying that all the men in the room had served in Vietnam, came back home, and were honorably discharged. However, none were able to find jobs, and all were living in poverty. To top it off, he found the note left by me stating I wanted to talk with him.

He was venting about the inequity of what he and his Black patriot friends were experiencing in Philadelphia. He wanted to know what I was going to do about it, beyond what I told him about closing his case. I considered his remark to be rhetorical. He knew I had no answer. He said that the only food he was getting was from an old Black man who utilized his welfare check to cook a potful of frozen chicken backs mixed with peas and rice to serve him and his Army veteran friends once a day.

I recalled the man he was describing, because I had talked with him two years before about this young man. And he had told me what he was doing for the unemployed young men in the neighborhood. He received no compensation for his humanitarianism. The subject felt that I, as a government agent, represented the cause of all the degradation and pain he was experiencing, despite having put his life on the line for America in Vietnam.

The justified anger, frustration, and hatred from the men enveloped the room. They wanted someone to pay for their horrific predicament, and that someone was me. I considered my life to be in danger and demanded again that the man behind me move away from the door. This time he complied with my order.

Simultaneously, I moved my right hand across my suit coat pushing it back so that all in the room could see the top of my service revolver. I then slowly backed out the door while sweeping the room with my eyes. As I was leaving, I said, "Thank you for bringing this matter to my attention. I apologize for the mix-up." I slammed the door, quickly made my way to my parked car, and drove off.

Driving back to my office, I was fuming. My anger was directed toward the case agent in Boston for not informing me of the status of the case. Also, I was angry about how those young patriots were being treated back home after defending their country. I did not see this as a unique situation, but obviously a pervasive problem, especially as it effects young men of color in the nation's

UNITED STATES DEPARTMENT OF JUSTICE

FEDERAL BUREAU OF INVESTIGATION

WASHINGTON, D.C. 20535

March 28, 1967

PERSONAL

Mr. Carver C. Gayton
Federal Bureau of Investigation
Philadelphia, Pennsylvania

Dear Mr. Gayton:

I want to commend you for the very creditable work you did in the investigation and apprehension of Identification Order Fugitive Linzo Covington, the subject of an Unlawful Flight to Avoid Confinement case.

You exercised much initiative in conducting a probing investigation to quickly identify and locate this badly wanted fugitive, despite the fact that his appearance was changed. Your noteworthy contributions to the arrest plans resulted in his apprehension without incident and I want you to know of my appreciation.

Sincerely yours,

J. Edgar Hoover

I received several letters of commendation from Director Hoover during my tenure with the Bureau including this one from March 28, 1967.

urban ghettoes. It was and is SHAMEFUL! My experience in that apartment was seared into my soul.

Although I had been recognized for participating in various arrests and for the quality of my work during my four years in the Bureau, there was one arrest that stood out during my last year. One citizen saw an FBI "Most Wanted Fugitive Identification Order" (IO) picture and summary of the crime at a local US post office in South Philadelphia. He/she recognized the subject and notified the Philadelphia Field Office. I was assigned the case. All IOs are distributed to post offices throughout the country and are the next level down from the well-known "Ten Most Wanted" list of the FBI.

Linzo Covington was serving 25 years in the North Carolina State Prison for robbery and aggravated assault in 1964 when he escaped with another prisoner "under a blaze of bullets" fired by prison guards. An "Unlawful Flight to Avoid Confinement" Federal warrant was issued as a result.

After I was assigned the case, I immediately conducted a series of interviews over a two-day period. I led a team of agents in organizing a plan to capture Covington. The investigation was capped by an agent posing as the Human Resource Director of a business where Covington had applied for a job. He was called to the office by the agent and told he got the job. He showed up at the office at the designated time where four agents were strategically situated. After he sat down, we converged on him and arrested him without incident. During my interview with him, he expressed surprise to be captured because he had gone to great efforts to change his appearance.

A few weeks after the arrest I received a letter of commendation dated March 28, 1967, marked "Personal" to Carver C. Gayton, Federal Bureau of Investigation, Philadelphia, Pennsylvania.

CHAPTER 13

National Security

I NEVER INTENDED TO STAY in the Bureau more than five to ten years. After finishing my master's degree in education administration at Temple University, my plan was to eventually move back to the West Coast. I had one semester to go before finishing the degree when I received a call from my FBI class counselor, Fred Fehl, whom I had not seen since graduation in the spring of 1964. It was now mid-1967.

Fred said that a former agent and good friend of his, Regis Carr, was now the Director of National Security Agency Special Security Programs at Lockheed Missiles and Space Programs in Sunnyvale, California. Regis was recruiting to build up his team of Special Security Representatives. Fred wanted to know if I was interested in talking with him. I told Fred that I had no plans to leave the Bureau but was willing to talk.[27]

In my talk with Regis, he explained that he had an elite team of former Secret Service and FBI agents working on Top Secret and Cryptographic National Security Agency projects in Sunnyvale. He had heard good things about me and wanted to know if I was interested in joining his team. I told him that the possibility of working and living in California intrigued me, but I could not give him an answer until I talked it over with my wife.

Mona Lombard Gayton (my first wife) and our children Carver Jr., Cynthia, and Craig.

Mona was very excited about the possibility of moving to California. Her older sister Leonella and her family lived in Palo Alto, just a few miles from Sunnyvale. Leonella's and her husband's three children were close in age to ours. Mona was very close to her sister and was ready to move the day I talked to her about the job offer. It was a done deal. I let Regis know of my decision and began preparing for the transition.

I let my supervisor Dick Rogge know of my plans and sent an official letter of resignation to Mr. Hoover.

Dick Rogge, a wonderful leader and great boss, eventually became the Special Agent in Charge (SAC) of the Los Angeles, California, Field Office. While there, he heard of my plans to possibly leave the Bureau and took the time to send me the following unsolicited note. I really appreciated the letter. I was only 28 years old and receiving that note from a legendary agent like Dick meant a great deal to me. Dated August 18, 1967, it said:

While you were not on my squad as many of the others, I nevertheless feel that you were a mighty valuable contribution and asset to the fast-moving, heavy-volume desk. Your enthusiasm and conscientiousness will not be forgotten, and if your family decided to make the Bureau a career, I don't think you will regret it. I fully feel that if you do remain with the Bureau, there will be administrative possibilities for you. I certainly thank you for ramrodding the numerous collections which were necessary for the various functions that had to be prepared for me during my stay in Philadelphia.

—Sincerely, Dick

The short time I was in the bureau changed me profoundly. I witnessed a side of life in America that I did not realize existed. What poor Blacks in particular were subjected to regarding poverty, crime, and struggling family lives within the ghettos of Washington, DC, Kansas City, and Philadelphia seemed almost overwhelming. The fact that any Black was able to rise above those circumstances was a miracle to me—and a tribute to the resilience of the race.

On the other hand, I also met a large cadre of Black intellectuals and professionals in the East, many of whom I had previously only read about. The large number, compared to Seattle, was awe inspiring! The fact that I was able to converse and relate to them without feeling intimidated gave me a feeling of accomplishment and the desire to set even higher standards for myself— professionally, culturally, and economically.

I also saw the opposite ends of the economic and social spectrum of Blacks were farther apart than I had observed in Seattle. That gulf, in my mind, was not healthy for Black culture and achievement. In many of the Black professionals and intellectuals I'd encountered in the East, I felt there was a lack of empathy and concern for their less-fortunate brethren.

All in all, I became a more enlightened person during my four years living in the East. It was the best informal life education I have ever received. I was forced to become more introspective about my life and who or what I desired to be. I am grateful that the Bureau gave that opportunity.

———

I drove my wife and three children in our 1964 Chevy Nova from Philadelphia to Palo Alto, California. We stayed with my wife's sister and her family for two weeks. We purchased a home in Mountain View, California, three miles from my office in Sunnyvale, where Lockheed Missiles and Space Company was located. My job as Security Representative for Special Security programs was fascinating. Our team

The stenographers from the Philadelphia FBI Field Office presented me with a humorous goodbye card when I departed for California.

was composed of eight representatives. Each worked on separate programs under the umbrella of the US National Security Agency.

Although we all had Cryptographic Security Clearances, we did not have "the need to know" clearances for each other's projects. The only person who had total knowledge of all the projects was our director, Regis Carr. Initially, my primary job was to do background checks for folks being brought into my project and to give briefing and debriefings of those being hired or leaving the project.

The project I worked on resulted from the exposure of the United States' U-2 spy plane flights over Russia by pilot Francis Gary Powers whose plane was shot down May 1, 1960. Much of the work previously done by the U-2s was transferred to "Spy in the Sky" to launch satellites to spy on enemy territory. A few months after I arrived, I had to escort rockets from Sunnyvale to Vandenberg Airforce Base in Lompoc, California, and sign them over to the Airforce at the launching pads. I would also have the task of taking top-secret documents and equipment on the turbo prop, four-engine Lockheed Hercules C-130 planes in flights to other parts of the country, officially turn them over to the proper authorities, and fly back to Sunnyvale. The only personnel on such flights were me, the pilot, and the co-pilot. I was never allowed to tell my wife the purpose of such flights or where I was going.

The secrecy surrounding my job at Lockheed was more all-encompassing than at my work with the Bureau. The danger of leaks regarding the very technical and sophisticated projects, as well as a deep fear of the Soviet Union intelligence network, kept several of my team members on edge and led to them looking forward to their lunch martinis. Periodic exposés of activities within top-secret projects of our team by the Aerospace Editor of *The San Jose Mercury News* certainly contributed to some of the tension.

The closest social relationship I had in Sunnyvale was with Gary Miller, a former US Secret Service agent who had been assigned to guard Vice President Hubert Humphrey for several years. Gary left the Secret Service to have a more normal family life. However, there was no question he missed his Secret Service job. Gary was a fun and interesting guy. We got into animated discussions about Martin Luther King, whom I supported, and his speaking out against the Vietnam War, among other political issues, as well as conversations about our families. The discussions were respectful because we truly liked each other. Gary was a blues music enthusiast, as was I. His favorite was the great Mississippi Delta blues icon, Jimmy Reed. He knew more about the history of the blues than any other White guy I had ever known.

Four years later, after both of us had left Lockheed and I was working as an administrator at the University of Washington, I got a call from him. He told me he had gone back into the Secret Service and was heading the team protecting President Nixon while the president was visiting Seattle. He just wanted to say "Hi." We didn't get a chance to see each other, but I have often thought of him.

I clearly understood why he excelled as a Secret Service agent. He was intelligent, had a great sense of humor, and was a truly dedicated public servant. The one thing I couldn't understand about Gary was how he could eat a jarful of pickled jalapenos in one sitting without breaking a sweat!

———

As I was settling into my job at Lockheed and my homelife in Mountainview, California, in the spring of 1968, I received a phone call from Joe Jones, a good friend and former teammate on the University of Washington's 1960 championship Rose Bowl team. He said I would be getting a call from Joe Kearney, the U of W athletic director. Jones recommended me to be the first Black, fulltime assistant coach in the history of the University of Washington. Joe Kearny's call was at the behest of Head Coach Jim Owens. The conversation with Joe would lead to another major career change. The surreptitious life I led for almost five years was rapidly coming to an end.

PART IV

RECONNECTING WITH COACH JIM OWENS

CHAPTER 14

Football Homecoming

IN EARLY 1968, demands were made by 14 Black U of W athletes because of alleged discriminatory practices within the Athletic Department. One of the demands was "the hiring of a Black coach or administrator." A *Sports Illustrated* article in the early summer claimed that discrimination existed in the Husky football program of Coach Owens—even in the Rose Bowl year of 1963. As a result of the charges, U of W President Charles Odegaard appointed the Hammer Commission to investigate the allegations. The findings of the commission led to the recommendation that a Black assistant football coach be hired. The recommendation was publicly supported by Coach Owens.

At the time, I was somewhat aware of the racial unrest that was taking place on campus, and obviously had some trepidation but I expressed interest because of my desire to come home after being away for five years, and because of the challenge of coaching the Huskies.

Never in my life have I felt so alone. That moment, however, emboldened me to maintain pride in myself and to move forward in ways that I believed would be in the best, long-term interest of the student athletes and the University.

Owens wore two hats, one as Athletic Director, and the other as Head Football Coach. Looking back, I should have questioned the convoluted approach of Joe making the initial contact with me about the assistant coach position rather than Coach Owens. I have my own assumptions but nothing more. The fact remains, I accepted the job offer after a great deal of discussion with friends and family.

But before I describe these years, I'd like to give an overall view of my prior experience with Coach Owens.

I was recruited to the University of Washington to play football by head coach Darrell Royal in 1956 and played freshman ball that year. In 1957, after Royal's departure to the University of Texas, Jim Owens was hired. Owens immediately initiated a rugged and disciplined approach to training and off-campus deportment that was unprecedented in the history of Husky football. Some players hated it; others, like me, welcomed the challenge.

At the beginning of our '57 season, during an August afternoon session of one of our "two-a-day" practices, Coach Owens became very angry and disappointed in the progress of our practice. The temperature was 90 degrees with a humidity level close to 90 percent. After an hour and a half of lackluster scrimmage, he had the team go through a series of continuous start and stop sprints for at least

U of W football coaches, 1968 (Gayton, front row, far right).

another two hours. We were allowed no water during the practice. Few of us remember exactly how long it lasted.

That practice session is now known as the infamous "Death March." By the end of the afternoon, I had lost close to 15 pounds. Many players fainted. At least six were taken to the hospital. And predictably, several of them quit the team. A very similar event, depicted in the book *The Junction Boys* by Jim Dent, took place at Texas A&M a few years earlier under Coach Bear Bryant where, coincidentally, Coach Owens served as an assistant.[28]

That one incident of the Death March was a primary contributor to the myth and legend of Jim Owens. In many ways I believe it was a metaphor of how he approached not only football but life. One had to "pay the price" to succeed. Many of us who endured the Death March considered our survival as a badge of courage and determination. Of those who participated, I was one of the five remaining players who became members of the 1960 Rose Bowl team.

Years later, one of Coach Owens's top assistants told me that Owens regretted how he conducted the Death March, but he never expressed his feelings to the players. Bear Bryant, on the other hand, apologized directly to team members for the "Junction Boys" incident at Texas A&M.

I was plagued with shoulder injuries my junior year and knee injuries my senior year, but I was able to play in the 1960 Rose Bowl with a knee that was at less than 50 percent of its normal strength. The personal pain and disappointment, however, were somewhat wiped away because it was the *first Rose Bowl ever won* by the University of Washington. That group of approximately 50 young men is regarded by many as the best football team in the history of the University. The other Blacks on the team included George Fleming, Ray Jackson, and Joe Jones; an extremely dedicated and gifted cadre of running backs.

The following season, I asked Coach Owens if I could be a graduate assistant coach for the team and he agreed. I became the first African American graduate assistant football coach in the university's history and contributed in that capacity to another successful Rose Bowl victory season. I was very grateful to Coach Owens for giving me that opportunity.

I mention all of the above accounts of my early connections with that great team and Jim Owens to indicate that I was a true believer in the Jim Owens approach to football. I was a blood and guts ball player and proud of it. *No one* could ever question my dedication and courage as a player. I will forever be bonded to that group of men—each and every player. The magic of that team will live on.

At the time I returned to the U of W in 1968, there was racial tension throughout the United States and particularly on college campuses. The "Black Power" movement was in full swing and was inflamed by the assassination of Dr. Martin Luther King, Jr., in April of that year. It was within that charged atmosphere that I moved to Seattle in August 1968 with my wife and three small children.[29]

The Black football players on the U of W campus were affected by the climate of the time, and obviously sensitive and on-guard because of allegations of race discrimination within the athletic department. However, none of them were actively involved in the racial politics taking place on campus or in the Seattle community while I was employed by the athletic department.

My duties as assistant football coach started immediately. My employment package also included the titles of Assistant Track Coach, Counselor, and

Assistant to Vice President for University Relations Bob Waldo. Despite the titles, the overwhelming amount of my time was devoted to the football team.

The next four months were extremely time consuming with coaching, individual and group counseling sessions with Black and White ball players, and recruitment activities. Working with the U of W Black Alumni Club was a priority. I was also a member of the club under the leadership of my close friend and fellow 1960 Rose Bowl teammate, Joe Jones. A wide variety of community events with the club and the athletes took place, which went a long way toward connecting the athletes with the local Black community. The club also played a major role in recruiting Black athletes from across the country. My typical day during my 15 months with the Athletic Department was from 7 a.m. to 1 a.m., seven days a week!

Although the football season ended with a disappointing 3-5-2 losing record, there were indicators that the racial situation was beginning to move in a positive direction. Harvy Blanks, the very talented and outspoken running back for the Huskies, was quoted as saying in a November 12, 1968, article in the *Seattle Post-Intelligencer* by Dave Dupree: "When things that got me down last year start getting me down now, I can go to Coach Gayton. He had a profound effect on me, the other Blacks and all the players. His presence is enough to assure us that if everything is not all right now, it will be pretty soon."[30]

Georg Meyers, Sports Editor of *The Seattle Times,* said in his April 3, 1969, column that of the 45 letters of intent to join the team signed that spring, 10 were from Black athletes. He went on to say, "It is mentionable, because a year ago this month national publications labeled Washington as a school whose Negro alumni advised Black athletes to shun." Meyers added, "Gayton ... shrugs off credit and delivers no lecture of the *startling* Washington success in recruiting among Negroes." [31]

Another indicator of positive change took place toward the end of spring drills in 1969. In a coaching staff meeting, several staff members complained that we were, as a staff, being too easy on the ball players. They said that the way we were carrying out our responsibilities as coaches was not in the tradition of "hard-nosed" Husky football. They went on to say that the Black players in particular were being coddled. I took issue with that perspective, because it was a direct reflection on the role that I was hired to perform, which was to counsel the Black athletes. To coach Owens's credit, he made it clear during the meeting that he firmly supported me and the job I was doing, and that the program was moving in the right direction. He said that he intended to stay the course.

The two coaches who had been the most vocal about these concerns left the program before the beginning of the 1969 season. I did not know whether they left on their own volition or were asked to leave.

I was flattered by the positive newspaper accounts of progress and the apparent firm commitment by Coach Owens to maintain the direction being taken to improve race relations in the athletic department. But during my months in the department, I never indicated that the racial climate was at a point where all involved could *relax* their efforts. Nevertheless, I was encouraged during my first year on the job that important progress was being made. I was enthusiastically looking forward to building on those successes.

The gnawing concern in the back of my mind was that my agreed-upon role of bridging the communications gap between the Black players and the coaching staff, on its face, reflected a dysfunction within the Athletic Department. I rationalized what I was doing by considering the role *temporary,* until a more trusting culture could be established within the department.

During the early summer of 1969, my dad had a stroke and became terminally ill. I then divided my time between checking on him in the hospital, working, and being with Mona and my kids.

CHAPTER 15

A Triggering Incident

THE POSITIVE LOCAL PRESS coverage concerning changes taking place in the football program was clouded by a September 1, 1969, article in *Sports Illustrated*. Reporter John Underwood wrote a two-part series on beleaguered college football coaches throughout the nation who faced rebellious players in general, but Blacks specifically. One of the programs highlighted was the University of Washington's. Underwood wrote: "Owens hired one of his former players, Carver Gayton, a Negro, to serve as coach and intermediary, and relinquished much of his direct authority over Black football players to Gayton. Gayton soon had more say than any four assistant coaches, Bud Wilkinson or Bear Bryant."

The thought of me having that kind of control over Coach Owens, of all people, was ludicrous! There was no indication, in the article, as to the source of the poisonous perspective. Clearly there was some mischief afoot from either disgruntled assistant coaches, downtown boosters, or both. There can be no doubt that the coach was livid after reading the statement.

Coach Owens and I did not discuss the article. One reason was because I did not read it or know about it until a month or so later.

In the meantime, I went to see my dad around the first week of September. He was awake but could not talk. I told him how I loved and appreciated him, and tears came streaming down his face. I had never seen him cry before, and I started to cry myself. I held his hand and told him I would continue to pray for him. Dad died on September 20th. I then began working with our family—especially my mom—to make arrangements for Dad's burial and funeral. I was an emotional wreck. I was not focused on football.

Taking plays from the coaches' box in 1969.

The football season began with two disastrous losses against Michigan and Michigan State universities. I was not present at either game. The entire *Sports Illustrated* article was a dog whistle to Owens to get tough or his job would be in jeopardy. I sincerely believe that the reporter's assertions helped set the stage for the traumatic events that took place toward the end of the season. Coach Owens would, indeed, make sure everyone knew who was in charge of the program. [32]

The football team continued its losing ways throughout the first two months of the 1969 season. Many of the players, both Black and White, became disgruntled and the coaches were frustrated as well. Late in the evening on October 29, I was asked by several Black football players to talk with them about a coach taking "unfair" disciplinary action against Landy Harrell, one of the Black running backs, during that afternoon's practice.

The discussion evolved to a point where a number of the players wanted to boycott the team. In essence, I explained to them that in my mind the incident as described to me did not justify a boycott. Many were not placated, and as a result, I felt that the intensity of the discussion warranted my passing on what transpired to Coach Owens. I talked it over with the coach that evening.

At the time, he seemed to take the information in stride, without any outward display of emotion one way or another. I, on the other hand, was very disappointed that I was not able to reach common ground with the players on the matter, as had been the case regarding so many similar situations over the previous two seasons. Anger, strain, and frustration—all were elements that led to the precipitous decision Coach Owens made the following afternoon.

The next afternoon, Thursday, October 30, after a team meeting convened by Coach Owens failed to indicate whether a boycott in fact was going to take place, a very angry, flushed-faced Coach Owens called a meeting of university officials. These included Assistant Attorney General Jim Wilson, Faculty Representative to the Pacific Coast Conference Harry Cross, Vice President of Student Affairs AI Ulbrickson, Jr. (as I recall), Athletic Director Joe Kearney, and several other officials of the University whom I cannot recall.

The coach commenced to describe the "crisis" and outlined what he intended to do to resolve it, which was basically to present a loyalty oath to each one of the 80 players. Considering how he led the meeting, it was clear he wanted to have witnesses for what he was about to do. It was by no means an information-gathering session.

I was in complete disbelief. I blurted out that it was ridiculous to have a written loyalty oath as Coach Owens initially proposed to do. I did not support a loyalty oath in any form. Harry Cross, the faculty representative and a School of Law professor, expressed the same opinion. Owens then said he would ask each player to respond orally to a loyalty oath. Then Owens left the meeting and proceeded to start the process on the field of Husky Stadium.

I was in complete shock. I had no prior knowledge of the subject of the meeting. From the expressions of most of the people in attendance, they were as surprised and befuddled by Coach Owens's actions as I was.

Coach Owens confronted each player on the team individually and demanded that they pledge 100 percent unconditional loyalty to him, the team, and the university. No other individuals were present to witness the one-on-one conversations. The upshot was the suspension of four Black athletes. This surprised, angered, and shocked me. The four suspended players were Harvy Blanks, Ralph Bayard, Gregg Alex, and Lamar Mills.

Coach Owens's action was not consistent with how I believed he had been attempting to deal with the Black athlete situation during my two-season tenure. The loyalty oath was ill-advised at best, and at worst, demeaning. In addition, the way the suspensions were carried out had the effect of undermining my relationship with the athletes. The fact that I was kept out of the loop regarding key decisions concerning their future status resulted in the communication lines between me and Coach Owens being so damaged that I could not carry out my role in the manner agreed upon when I first arrived. The four suspended athletes were among the most intelligent and reflective thinkers on the team. Three of them were also among the most *soft-spoken* up to the time they were asked to give a loyalty oath. I felt compelled to resign in protest of how the young men were suspended, but I held off.

The crisis led to an emergency meeting of the entire University of Washington Board of Regents and President Charles Odegaard. It took place November 2nd, the Sunday afternoon after the suspensions, and was held at a business building near Seattle University. The meeting was not disclosed to the press or the public.

Jim Owens and I were invited to give our individual perspectives on the events that led to the suspensions and any other information we felt was relevant to the matter. The focus of the session was on gathering facts. I do not recall any value judgments or conclusions being made by the regents during the meeting.[33] It was a very emotional meeting to say the least. As I recall, Coach Owens and I participated in the discussion for several hours.

Georg Meyers, the highly respected and insightful Sports Editor of *The Seattle Times*, in his November 2, 1969, column said Coach Owens's loyalty oath venture, ". . . reflected almost a suicidal impulse." He added that, "It is not inconceivable that some players with reservations as to Owens and his program felt constrained to pledge 100 percent." He went on to say: "It was an enterprise open to many avenues other than truthful expressions of total loyalty. There is no evidence that Owens said that anyone who faltered in the pledge would be sacked." Myers pointed out: "Owens suspended the four, and all were Black. It was not surprising that Black discrimination became the outcry." As Meyers implies, the oath did not instill loyalty to the university and the program. It engendered fear and devalued truthfulness. The whole process was built upon a disingenuous foundation."[34]

The following week, Bob Schloredt, the legendary football great and fellow teammate and coach, telephoned me and said he and his wife wanted to come by my house to talk with me and Mona. Obviously, my stand with the Black athletes had led to rumors that I would resign from the coaching staff, and I suspected that Bob wanted to talk about that real possibility.

When Bob arrived, he said he came on behalf of Coach Owens and implored me not to resign. I told him I was still thinking about it. Bob's wife started to cry, as did my wife. They hugged each other. They had grown very close during my two years in the Athletic Department. We all knew if I left, the friendship between us would never be the same. By the time Bob and his wife departed, it was clear that I would resign my position, although the words were never spoken. That meeting was one of the most heart-wrenching experiences of my lifetime.

Joe Kearney, the Athletic Director, anticipated I might resign. He called me into his office. He appeared distraught and said he would "promote" me to Assistant Athletic Director if I did not resign. He also confided in me that he would have fired Jim Owens over the suspensions but was fearful he in turn would have been fired as a result of pressure from influential downtown contributors to the University. Because of the downtown donors' strong support of Coach Owens, Joe added, "If our conversation becomes public, I will deny it ever took place."

On November 10th, all but Harvy Blanks were reinstated with the team after my brother Gary Gayton, an attorney, and his law partner Ron Neubauer, filed a suit against the university on behalf of the players. Coach Owens said he decided to ". . . review the suspensions because of indications there were misunderstandings on both sides." I announced my resignation the same day, citing the fact that Harvy Blanks remained suspended and that a "communication chasm" between me and the coach due to the suspensions had, in effect, "nullified" my role within the Athletic Department.

University administration and staff worried about backlash from downtown donors who powerfully supported Coach Owens. This was not an observation without significant merit. Don Hannula, a *Seattle Times* reporter, gave credence to the university administrators' fears in his December 14, 1969, article "The Longest Saturday." He said Coach Owens met with the very influential Husky Quarterback Club the day following the November 30th 57-14 defeat of the Huskies by UCLA which had been boycotted by all of the Black football players after the suspensions. While all of them played in key positions, the athletes and I remained in Seattle.

Hannula observed that "Coach Owens was wildly cheered by the group, including many previously asking for his head. When Owens was introduced the following weekend before the Stanford game, Husky stadium erupted with the biggest and most emotionally charged ovation of the season. Those two incidents surely proved to university officials who had any thoughts of firing

Coach Owens over the treatment of the Black athletes, that it would be an exercise in futility. Overnight, Coach Owens's power and influence became more formidable than ever."[35]

I entered the Husky field with Coach Owens before the Stanford game began. The thunderous applause for him nearly shook the rafters of the stadium. Never in my life have I felt so alone. That moment, however, emboldened me to maintain pride in myself and to move forward in ways that I believed would be in the best, long-term interest of the student athletes and the University.

Violence and threats resulted from the events. Tension, fear, and anger were pervasive within the Black and White communities of Seattle. The Black players were threatened by Whites who supported Coach Owens's decision. Coach Owens's teenage daughter was hit in the face near the family's home by an unknown assailant. I received letters, postcards, and phone calls from across the nation threatening my family and me. It was an unprecedented time in the history of the city and, for many on both sides of the issue, is still painful to discuss.

What was transpiring within the Husky football program was not unique to the University of Washington. Black grid boycotts took place that November at the Universities of Indiana, Minnesota, and Wyoming, among others. Some observers have made the point that the U of W situation influenced Black players at other schools to boycott. I consider that mere conjecture. The social and political climate across the country was ripe for the kind of upheavals that took place in college athletic programs.

What was unique about the U of W football program was that during the tenure of Jim Owens, documented racial issues flared up within his teams on a continuous basis from at least 1963 through 1971. I am not aware of any other major college program in the nation where such a pattern existed for so long. With such a record over a protracted period of time, clearly Coach Owens, for whatever reason, did not have the capability and/or commitment to work effectively and earnestly with Black athletes.

CHAPTER 16

The Truth Sometimes Hurts

PRESIDENT CHARLES ODEGAARD established what was called the University of Washington Human Rights Commission in April 1970 to investigate charges of racism within the Athletic Department. The commission was chaired by Professor Lavern Rieke of the U of W Law School and was composed of seven faculty members, 12 administrative staff, and eight University students. I was also a member of the commission.

As the commission was deliberating, racial conflict arose again within the football program. Although the 1970 season ended with an admirable 6-4 win-loss record, the best since Owens's 1966 season, four Black athletes resigned from the team. They stated, "The racial practices of the coaching staff have forced us to the point where we can no longer tolerate the playing conditions imposed upon us." The four included Mark Wheeler, Washington State "Back of the Year" from Seattle Prep, and All-Coast cornerback and future All-American Calvin Jones whom I'd recruited from Balboa High School in San Francisco in 1969.

These resignations resulted in 40 different equal rights and civil rights organizations announcing a boycott of University of Washington sports programs and stating they could no longer advise Black athletes to compete at the school. The organization was called The Coalition of Equal Opportunity Football.[36]

Firing the coach would have surely triggered pressure from powerful contributors and supporters to question the leadership of President Odegaard and quite possibly the leadership of the regents themselves.

This latest turn of events led Georg Meyers of *The Times* to make another cogent observation in his January 17, 1971, column. ". . . the administration—meaning [President] Odegaard and/or the regents—might fire Owens. That would be the most explosive course, the least palatable to administrators who believe 'cleaning house' is the only solution in the athletic department. The curbstone version of that contingency would be: It's Odegaard or Owens. And it might be. It all adds up to a gloomy prospect, that is because the truth sometimes hurts." [37] [38]

The Human Rights Commission appointed by President Odegaard issued its report in late January 1971.[39] Among its recommendations included the firing of Coach Owens and Athletic Director Joe Kearney, the hiring of another Black assistant coach, and the appointment of a Black as an assistant athletic director. The Board of Regents rejected the recommendations to fire Owens and Kearney.

As I implied previously, I doubt that the regents seriously considered the commission's recommendation to fire Coach Owens, regardless of the veracity of the Commission's findings. I suspect that in their view, the negative political implications of them supporting the commission on this matter were too great. Firing the coach would have surely triggered pressure from powerful contributors and supporters to question the leadership of President Odegaard and quite possibly the leadership of the regents themselves.

The politically expedient route they took worked. There was no public outcry against the regents' decision, except in the Black community. The other high-level recommendations supported by the regents included hiring Ray Jackson, my friend and 1960 Rose Bowl teammate, as coach, and appointing Don Smith, a former Seattle sportswriter and AT&T executive, as Assistant Athletic Director. Both Ray and Don are Black.

Calvin Jones, the star defensive back who quit the team at the end of the 1970 season, went to Long Beach State College and was preparing to play for Long Beach in the fall of 1971. Jones said later in an October 12, 1972, University of Washington *Daily* article, that he was convinced his decision to leave the university when he did was the right one. He pointed out that, "If it meant that Don Smith and Ray Jackson got hired, then maybe that was what it took to bring about change."

In the summer of 1971, the newly selected assistant athletic director, Smith, contacted Calvin Jones to advise him that Coach Owens wanted him back on the team "with no strings attached." Negotiations involving Smith, Owens, and my brother Gary, sealed the deal with Jones. Jones came back to the U of W to star for the Huskies as a first team All-American defensive back. He then moved on to the pro ranks where he also excelled as a standout defensive back, for the Denver Broncos.

The hiring of Smith and Jackson, and the subsequent return of Calvin Jones, went a long way toward easing the racial tensions within the football program. This new climate resulted in the University of Washington Information Services issuing the following press release on April 10, 1972:

> In view of positive steps that have taken place within the Department of Sports Programs at the University of Washington, the U. of W. Black Alumni Club [of which I was a founding member] is assuming a position of support to the department and in particular the Black administrator and black coaches in their pursuit of a fair and equitable sports program, Joe Jones, president of the club, announced Monday:
>
> • There is no doubt that the stand of the club and the Black community against the discriminatory policies of the Department of Sports Programs has led directly to the hiring of blacks in key positions within the department.

- *The black community of Seattle should be commended for its firm stand, in face of adversity from the majority community, against the discriminatory policies of the Department of Sports Programs. The resultant changes that took place are benefiting not only blacks, but all people genuinely concerned with human justice.*

- *The Black Alumni Club, in keeping with its objectives and goals, will continue to work with black students in a common drive toward dignity and pride. The club will continue to promote fund raising activities for black athletes and Educational Opportunity program students.*

- *The hope of the club and Black community is for the Department of Sports Programs to continue in a positive direction. The Club, as always, will assume a monitoring capacity and reserve the right to challenge inequities, if and when they occur.*

Whether justified or not, true consensus within the Black community that the athletic department had turned the corner for the better did not take place until the departure of Jim Owens in 1974.

PART V

MOVING FORWARD

CHAPTER 17

Affirmative Action

WHILE I WAS WORKING through the morass with the U of W Athletic Department and my issues with Coach Owens toward the end of 1969, I was also having conversations with Dr. Robert Waldo, vice president of University Relations and his top assistant Pepper Quigley. This was not unusual given my dual role as a coach for the Athletic Department and an assistant to Bob Waldo. After my resignation as assistant football coach, I continued full-time employment on upper campus with Dr. Waldo.

The emotional trauma surrounding my separation from the Athletic Department was eased considerably by the wonderful guidance and understanding of Bob and Pepper. Pepper was especially consoling. We had many sessions, drinking hot tea and talking over all aspects of the matter. He was an excellent listener. My wife Mona was also very supportive throughout the upheaval. She never questioned any of the actions I had taken.

. . . I was concerned that I might be jumping from the frying pan of the Athletic Department into the fire of academia.

During the last week of December 1969, I received a telephone call from Dr. John Hogness, MD, the newly appointed executive vice president of the University. He asked me to come to his office and offered me a new position as the Director of Affirmative Action Programs, beginning in January 1970.

President Lynden Johnson signed Executive Order 11246 on September 24, 1965. In essence, the order stipulates that all government contractors who do over $10,000 in government business are prohibited from discriminating in employment decisions on the basis of race, color, religion, sex, or national origin. It also requires contractors and subcontractors to take affirmative action to recruit, train, and hire the affected groups where they are underrepresented, and set goals and timetables relative to all areas of the employment process, which, in the case of universities and colleges, includes faculty and staff. My role was to establish the policies and procedures to help ensure success.

I was flattered that Dr. Hogness offered me the position. Although I was working within Bob Waldo's University Relations Office, it was clear in my mind that Dr. Hogness, President Odegaard, and Waldo had discussed and agreed upon offering me the affirmative action position. But I was concerned that I might be jumping from the frying pan of the Athletic Department into the fire of academia, especially since I was not a member of the essentially all-White, old boys' club. Nor was I a member of the academy as a tenured PhD. In other words, I lacked "legitimacy."

There were few job options for me at the time. After I talked over the situation with my wife, we rationalized that the job would give me the opportunity to continue my graduate studies at the university through its tuition support program, while also providing an important human rights contribution to the institution.

I accepted Dr. Hogness's offer and set out to lay the groundwork for the program. I was the first individual within higher education institutions in the State of Washington to hold such a position. Guidelines for such positions were provided by the US Department of Labor as well as the US Department of Education. Both agencies were extremely helpful, otherwise I was on my own.

Initially, my job, which was extremely important for the University as a whole, was to *understand* the concept of "affirmative action" and how it differed—yet complemented—the term "non-discrimination."

The Executive Order was, and continues to be, a necessary addendum to the Civil Rights Act of 1964. The Civil Rights Act focused primarily upon non-discrimination and color blindness, rather than taking affirmative steps to correct the systemic remnants of discriminatory acts of the past. One of the Order's primary objectives was to set goals and timetables university-wide to recruit, hire, and retain groups identified within the order.

From a policy point of view, most of the White-dominated faculty and staff at the U of W in 1970 had a difficult time grasping the intent of the order. Detractors of the order considered it to be contrary to the 1964 Civil Rights Act. For example, they saw setting goals that focused on race as a violation of the Act which they interpreted as emphasizing *color blindness*, e.g., *not* considering the race of a person when making a hiring or promotion decision. Some programs attempting to meet the requirements of the order, especially in the construction industries, allowed the establishment of "quotas." In other words, they set definitive numbers for job targets rather than more amorphous goals. Quotas are specifically disallowed under the order.[40]

Required reports to the government had to include targeted goals concerning training and employment, and had to identify individuals by their race and sex.

Carver, as U of W Director of Affirmative Action Programs, meeting with (left to right) Joe Jones, Joe Kearny, and Bill Hilliard

During the early years of my job, my office periodically made requests for such information from the other University offices. Many faculty members, in particular, refused to comply because they considered the requests to be *out of compliance* with what they considered the Civil Rights Act's emphasis on "color blindness."

Pockets of the University complied with the order, and there was a positive increase of minorities and women in faculty and staff positions. If staff managers and academic administrators did not buy into the policy, no progress would have been made. However, no real sanctions were applied against those department heads who failed to meet their goals. My office had no power to apply sanctions when warranted. In such situations, usually my office—or on rare occasions, the US. Department—would ask for a report on corrective steps to resolve the identified issue(s).

Examples of nationally recognized Black academics and administrators who joined the University of Washington from 1969 through the mid 1970's include: Dr. James Banks, Professor of Education; Jacob Lawrence, Professor Emeritus, College of Art; Dr. Samuel Kelly, Vice President of Minority Affairs;

Dr. Thaddeus Spratlen, Professor of Business Administration; David Llorens, Professor of English and former *Ebony* magazine executive.

On the personnel side, the record-keeping requirements of the Executive Order forced the university to computerize its database. A very beneficial spinoff from the affirmative action requirements was that the university's entire personnel record-keeping system was brought into the more efficient digital age.

One of the stipulations of the Executive Order was to initiate staff training to assist minorities and women in enhancing their skill levels in their assigned jobs, as well as provide opportunities for advancement into higher level jobs. No such training was offered for staff before the initiation of the Affirmative Action Program.

I hired a Black woman named Lue Rochelle Brim, a recent graduate from the University of Texas, to initiate a staff training program focused on minorities and women who were current employees. Obviously, I wanted her to work closely with the director of personnel to develop the classes. Over a two-year period, she had done such a terrific job that the director asked if Lue could work within his office as Director of Staff Training. I was honored to have her promoted into such a prestigious position. She was charged with developing training classes for all staff personnel. After many years, Brim retired as the training director and started a thriving private business as a training consultant.

In essence, the requirements of the Executive Order enhanced the quality of record keeping and training for the entire University. Staff training continues to be offered within the University.

By 1972, my office was primarily a policy development and record-keeping operation, with regular required reports being sent to the Department of Education within the US Department of Health, Education, and Welfare (HEW). Staff complaints concerning race or sex discrimination were handled by the University's Personnel Office. Faculty complaints were directed to the relevant academic departments and colleges, with the Faculty Senate having the ultimate authority if issues could not be resolved at the lower levels.

In 1972, the United States Congress passed Title IX, the federal civil rights law, which protects people from discrimination based on sex in education programs or activities that receive -federal financial assistance. The law applies to any institution receiving federal financial assistance from the Department of Education, including state and local educational agencies.

I was selected by Governor Evans to be the State of Washington United Nations Day Chair, a celebration commemorating the anniversary of the US entry into the United Nations.

Obviously, the law had a direct impact on state universities like the University of Washington. It emboldened the already influential women's movement on the U of W campus. As the Director of Affirmative Action Programs, my staff had the responsibility to develop the relevant policies to comply with Title IX.

I needed help in that regard. For my new direct report, Executive Vice President Philip Cartwright recommended a woman and recent MBA graduate from Harvard University to assist me. It became apparent to me after a while, as well as to Dr. Cartwright, that a separate affirmative action office for women would need to be established in the near future.

Sure enough, in 1975 I was asked by Dr. Cartwright to chair a search committee to seek a Director of Affirmative Action Programs for Women. The national search resulted in recommending Dr. Helen Remick, from the University of California, who had an excellent background in women's studies. Dr. Remick remained at the University of Washington for thirty years, ultimately retiring as a Vice Provost.

...the federal government's emphasis on the intent of "affirmative action" was diminishing and the euphemism "diversity", which was less of a lightning rod, became the label for anti-discrimination matters affecting faculty and staff on campus.

By the end of President Nixon's administration, it was clear that the federal government's emphasis on the intent of "affirmative action" was diminishing and the euphemism "diversity", which was less of a lightning rod, became the label for anti-discrimination matters affecting faculty and staff on campus. My office became even more of a record-keeping operation to meet the Order's requirements. I did continue to meet with faculty college and department heads to mediate minority faculty complaints and similarly did the same concerning staff discrimination matters.

The status of the university's affirmative action program was reflected in a December 1976 *Seattle Times* article entitled "U. W. Has Progress to Report in Minority Hiring." It pointed out that the university had heard nothing concerning its report on affirmative-action compliance from either the Office of Civil Rights or its parent agency, the Department of Health, Education and Welfare, since the report was submitted January 30th. A new annual report was due in less than 30 days. Both reports required a breakdown of the 15,000-person workforce by race, sex, and job classification.

Executive Vice President Cartwright was quoted as saying ". . . substantial progress had been made in the eight years since the university first began to aggressively recruit minorities and women in an attempt to end bias on the campus." He went on to point out that, "Budget cuts, however, have hampered severely efforts to get more minority and women faculty members. In most cases, the university is simply replacing retiring faculty and those resigning."

The same article quoted me:

The Director of Affirmative Action Programs for minorities said "Minorities make up 19 percent of staff and 6 percent of the university's affirmative action tenure-ladder rank faculty. The U of W's affirmative action program is entering a new phase, with major concerns being where minorities are employed in the university structure, and what happens to them once they are employed."

Statistics show most minorities still are concentrated within the low-paying job categories. Once hired, minorities continue to have problems. The number of minority staff discrimination complaints covering a broad range of matters continues to rise... Minority faculty have an inordinate amount of difficulty concerning tenure and promotion decisions... The staff entry-level salaries generally are lower than non-minority employees.

Dr. Cartwright countered my remarks by pointing out:

... a study shows that this latter discrepancy is due to years of experience, which minorities often lack. Part of the explanation for increased complaints is the existence of mechanisms, both in private industry and the university, to invite and redress grievances. My perspective on this situation is to create innovative affirmative action mechanisms to eliminate the discrepancies while celebrating the university's past accomplishments in minority employment.

At the end of my tenure in 1977, the university was not where it should have been regarding equal employment opportunities for minorities and women, but it was certainly better off on many levels than it had been in 1970.

My Activities and Accomplishments as U of W Director of Minority Affirmative Action Programs

A sampling of the activities and accomplishments of my office during my years as Director of Minority Affirmative Action Programs at the University include:

- Authored the following University documents:
  - Affirmative action and equal opportunity policy statements.
  - Purchasing Department's equal opportunity policy for vendors
  - Equal opportunity policy for the Staff Placement Center.
  - University's grievance procedure policy.
  - University's equal opportunity policy concerning services provided by the University to outside organizations and companies.
  - *A Guide to Lawful and Effective Employment Interviewing* is a reference for University Employees who have hiring authority. It contains information which assists hiring officials in conducting interviews in accordance with applicable equal opportunity employment /affirmative action laws and university personnel practices and procedures.
- Created University-wide staff training office. The activities of the office included offering five management training courses, general educational development tests, career counseling, and on-the-job training programs for university employees.

- Created affirmative action seminars for university vice-presidents, deans, directors, and department chairpersons. The seminars were held twice a year to provide awareness of current laws, regulations, and programs relative to equal opportunity. Nationally renowned speakers in the field of equal opportunity were featured at each of the seminars.
- Created the University's affirmative Action newsletter, published nine times a year and disseminated throughout the campus and the nation.
- Initiated the establishment of the University's affirmative action computer system to provide data concerning the University's minority and women employees.
- Initiated the creation of the University of Washington Human Rights Commission and several ad hoc affirmative action committees for faculty and non-academic staff.

Although there were the expected bumps along the road concerning the implementation of the University's affirmative action program, it's important to recognize that all of the above achievements could not have been accomplished without the cooperation and support of the President's Office (including the Provost's Office), the Staff Personnel Office, and the Faculty Senate, as well as the Deans of the various colleges.

CHAPTER 18

Unchartered Times

BEGINNING IN 1972, I was accepted into the University's Department of Public Administration's Master's Degree Program. While working with the FBI in Philadelphia, I started taking graduate courses in education administration at Temple University. When I left the Bureau for my new job at Lockheed Missiles and Space Company, I took graduate courses

Ms. Chamberlin, my Madrona Elementary School kindergarten teacher, surprised me with a picture taken years earlier, in 1942, of me and my family dog Sarge on the school playfield. Sarge was giving me a bit of trouble.

in political science at San Jose State University with the intention of rounding out my academic base. I felt that the MPA would provide a greater variety of job options in the field of higher education. Working on the U of W campus made it especially convenient for me to continue my graduate studies.

At home, Mona encouraged me to get more involved with our children's activities and suggested I join the Parent Teacher's Association (PTA) at Harrison Elementary School where our two sons, Clark and Craig, were enrolled. Louise Mckinney, a family friend and wife of the well-known

Reverend Samuel McKinney, was the principal of the school. I was one of the few fathers who attended the meetings. Probably for that reason, I was asked to be the president of the group. When my wife had made the offhanded suggestion that I should get involved with our children's lives by joining the PTA, neither of us could predict the impact it would have on our family.

I enjoyed the meetings and attempted to do the best job I could. Evidently, I did too good of a job. In early 1973 after a year in the role, I was contacted by Philip Swain, the president of the Seattle School Board. He asked if I would be interested in being appointed to the board. I remembered Phil from when he joined the board in 1961. He had visited Garfield High School when I began teaching there.

I was flattered by his offer. I told him I would be willing to serve for the remaining months of the term of Al Cowles, the board president, who was resigning to take a new job in Washington, DC, as vice president of the American Arbitration Association. Phil said his offer could only be made if I agreed to run for the office in the coming fall election. I told him I would talk it over with my wife.

I considered the offer an opportunity for career advancement and a contribution to the community. My wife agreed and I accepted Phil's offer. After completing Al's term, I ran for office and was unchallenged. With a campaign team chaired by my brother Gary, along with heavyweight committee members from Seattle such as Rev. Samuel McKinney, Larry Gossett, Jerry Grinstein, Judge Charles Z. Smith, Arthur Buerk, Joe Jones, and Freddie Mae Gautier, no one was brave enough to challenge me.

In the fall of 1973, I was at the downtown Plymouth Congregational Church giving a campaign speech regarding my candidacy to retain my seat on the Seattle School Board. At the end of remarks, I was approached by a diminutive, gray-haired, White lady.

She said, "Hello Carver, I'm Miss Chamberlin."

Ms. Chamberlin was my wonderful kindergarten teacher at Madrona Elementary School in the early 1940s. I was astonished. I had not seen her for over twenty-five years and did not recognize her. I said, "Miss Chamberlin, it's so wonderful seeing you. You should know that you were one of my very favorite teachers!"

She thanked me and said, "I've had a scrap book for many years. And in the process of rearranging it, I came across some pictures I took of you *before you enrolled* at Madrona. I thought since you are running for the School Board, this would be a good time to give them to you."

I opened the envelope she gave me, and there were four glossy 4" by 5" pictures of me with our family dog, Sarge! I had no recollection at all of the photographs having been taken. I was no more than four years old at the time. But since my family lived only a block away from the school grounds, I would take Sarge with me from time to time to play. I was overwhelmed by her thoughtfulness.

Ms. Chamberlin wished me well for the campaign and made a point of mentioning that I was one of her favorite students.

I did not have the opportunity to talk with her again. Less than a year later, she passed away.

My most significant role while on the school board related to protecting Garfield High School from being closed due to the opinion of the Washington State Office of Superintendent of Public Instruction. The Office held that it was a segregated school with a student enrollment which was 90 percent Black. But strangely enough, no such opinion was put forth for schools in the state with enrollments of *90 percent White.*

Being the only graduate of the iconic school on the board of directors, I took issue with the State's opinion. I told the board that every effort had to be made for Garfield to remain open without conflicting with state or Federal civil rights law. My colleagues agreed, as did Loren Troxell, the Seattle Public Schools district's superintendent. Superintendent Troxell then assigned Assistant Superintendent Dr. Hal Reasby to look into the matter and work with a committee of board members. The committee comprised of Phil Swain as chair along with me and Patt Sutton. Reasby knew of Booker T. Washington High School in Tulsa, Oklahoma, which had a similar student enrollment make-up as Garfield, and that the Tulsa School District decided to desegregate Booker T. Washington by making it a "magnet School." As such, it no longer had a home neighborhood from which students were accepted. Students instead had to apply for admission and were drawn from across the district.

Dr. Reasby and our small committee visited the school in Tulsa in the latter part of 1973. We were impressed with what we saw. We agreed that the Tulsa model would be an excellent fit for Garfield. At the regular school meeting of Wednesday, June 12, 1974, Phil Swain presented a "Desegregation-Resolution" which stated in essence that:

Garfield High School shall be desegregated with the beginning of the 1975-
76 school year. Desegregation shall be accomplished by the elimination of all

transfers granted to students who would normally graduate from high school after June 1975, who are not participating in the Voluntary Racial Transfer Program, and who are residents of the Garfield attendance area; by adjusting the Garfield attendance area boundaries; and by the development at Garfield of "Exemplary" academic and occupational programs designed to attract students from the entire district . . .

On a broad scope, the Garfield "Exemplary" i.e. "magnet school" experiment has become a resounding success. According to the year 2000 *U.S. News and World Report* National Ratings, Garfield—with its 57 percent minority enrollment, and 30 percent economically disadvantaged students—ranked 11th in the State of Washington. It was also number one of 23 high schools in the Seattle Public Schools district. Despite the high ratings, the district continues to realize that Garfield still had equity challenges. For example, Black students were a relatively small percentage of students enrolled in and graduating from Advanced Placement courses.

While on the school board, I worked full time at the University and completed my MPA degree. I was then accepted into the Department of Political Science doctoral program while raising three young children, with most of that burden being placed on my wife. My commitments outside of the family had a negative impact on my marriage and led to the necessity of marriage counseling. Mona and I met with a psychologist as well as a psychiatrist. The sessions led to us concluding that it would be best, for the family, for us to separate. The final blow to me came after several sessions with the psychiatrist. He said, "How in the world did you two ever get together?" The emotional distance between us was so broad that neither of us was able to respond to his fundamental questions with cogent answers.

The psychiatrist made the situation even more painful for me by accusing me of "looking at the world with rose-colored glasses" by even *attempting* to work on a Doctor of Philosophy degree, implying that the challenge was too great for me to handle. At the time, I was the only African American enrolled in the Political Science Department at the University of Washington working toward a PhD degree. I considered his remark as "dog whistle," really meaning "Who do you think you are as a Black man, thinking you can complete a PhD degree from an elite research university?"

Nevertheless, the session solidified my thoughts to end my marriage. It was one of the most heart-wrenching decisions I have made in my life. On June 5, 1975,

I announced that I would not run for the school board again because of "personal reasons."

The visit with the psychiatrist also cast some doubt in my mind about pursuing the degree. I thought maybe I was expecting too much of myself. When I entered the program, I never gave a second thought to being the only Black enrolled or that it could work against me.

I set up a meeting with my faculty advisor, Dr. George Shipman. I told him that I might have too much on my

I was given a drawing as a gift when I left the Seattle School Board in 1975.

plate and that I was thinking of dropping out of the program. Dr. Shipman said I was doing well in my course work and that I had all of the skillsets to be an excellent professor. He went on to say that it would be a mistake for me to drop out. That was all I needed to hear. I kept moving forward and never looked back. I'll always be indebted to Dr. Shipman.

I successfully defended my dissertation: *Federal Funding and its Impact on the University*, in 1976. My thesis investigated the effects of federal funding on the development of higher education. Utilizing Parsonian Functional Analysis, I sought to identify the societal role of universities as a part of a conglomeration of interrelated and interdependent parts. Put another way, Parson's focus is on how individuals' actions are organized through their roles in social institutions in ways that contribute to society's basic functional requirements. Understanding the basic elements of this esoteric premise has helped me better understand any organization I've participated in—from football teams to massive conglomerates like the University of Washington and The Boeing Company.

The divorce was also finalized in the summer of 1976. I was not sure what my next career step would be. I knew I wanted to step down from my role as Director of Minority Affirmative Action Programs but given my focus on completing my doctorate along with all that was involved in my divorce, the last thing I had in mind was looking for a new job.

Fortuitously, toward the end of the summer I received a phone call from Dr. Dael Wolfle, a member of my dissertation "Reading Committee." He said he wanted to set up a meeting and talk about a possible job opportunity for me. Dr Wolfle was one of my favorite professors. He had distinguished himself over the years as the first Executive Secretary of the American Association for the Advancement of Science. (In 1979, he would receive the University's Alumnus Summa Laude Dignitas award.)

During our meeting, he asked if I'd be interested in applying for a position as assistant professor at Florida State University in Tallahassee, Florida. He told me his first job out of graduate school had been as an assistant professor in FSU's psychology department, and he had had a positive experience teaching there. He had information from a colleague that a relatively new public administration department had been established at FSU and Wolfe considered me an excellent candidate for the job.

I told him I was flattered that a man of his national academic stature would recommend me for the position. I said I was interested because of the respect I had for him and his judgement. The only trepidation I had was I did not know much about FSU, nor the deep South. Dr. Wolfle sent a wonderful letter of introduction to the chairman of the department. I was invited to make a presentation at a department colloquium comprised of faculty members and graduate students.

I made my presentation in the early winter of 1977 and soon after was asked to become an assistant professor beginning the coming fall.

The first week of August, my two sons and I packed our bags in Seattle and began a leisurely trip in my two-door Chevy Camero sedan to Tallahassee, Florida. Since the fall term of FSU didn't begin until the middle of September, I had no definite plan on when to arrive. I drove south from Seattle on coastal Highway 1. From Los Angeles, we went east on Highway 10 through Nevada and all points beyond.

The weather was perfect all the way to Tallahassee. I would average driving 400 miles a day, stopping at scenic or interesting spots along the way. The places we stopped to eat were the usual drive-ins. As the sun began to set each day, we would find a cheap motel to rest for the night.

A special stop was at the spectacular Grand Canyon. To my son Craig's lifelong regret, he missed out on viewing the site due to an upset stomach. He would become aggravated when I would show family members a photo of him sticking his head out of the door of the car anticipating throwing up his lunch.

On August 16th, we heard on the radio a news report on the passing of Elvis Presley. We were entering the city limits of Memphis, Tennessee, that afternoon and drove by Graceland, Elvis's mansion, as the mourning crowds began to arrive. We stopped for a few minutes across the street from the gate and took a few pictures and then we continued on our way.

We turned south toward Mississippi on Interstate Highway 55. The plan was to stop at a couple of places in Yazoo County where John T. Gayton, (aka J. T.) my paternal grandfather, was born and raised.

First, we stopped at the Yazoo County Courthouse in Yazoo City. At the time, there were no other people in the building besides one White employee, White me, and my two young sons. I found a variety of marriage licenses and land deeds, etc., related to my grandfather. I asked the clerk for help. As she provided the documents, I began reading them and making copies of information that, up to that time, was not known by my family.

For example, I had not known that J. T.'s father, David, was a "sharecropper," a tenant farmer who gives part of each crop as rent and usually is subjected to perpetual debt. David worked for a landowner who was probably his *slave master* before the end of slavery in 1865. My dad and my grandfather often called people (Black or White) they did not respect "sharecroppers" knowing full well that David had been a sharecropper. I had no idea of the meaning of the word until I was a young adult.

After we had been at the courthouse about 15 minutes, five strapping White men came walking through the building. It was evident to me that the clerk had made a few phone calls. They were looking around, with no clear indication of a purpose for being there. That was all that I needed. They were suspicious of us Black Yankees visiting their town, and we were not welcome. I gathered my boys together, got in the car, and drove off.

I also visited the African Methodist Episcopal Church in Yazoo City. I thought the pastor of the Church would have some knowledge of the family since they were long-time members. The pastor's wife came to the door, but she only opened it a few inches and was very brusque with me. The clerk's suspicion and fear of me—a stranger in town—evident at the County Courthouse, was now demonstrated by the Black pastor's wife.

She said she had never heard of the family and suggested I go into some of the hills surrounding the town where there was a scattering of small Black churches. This was common in the rural South. Slave masters did not encourage religious gatherings of slaves. As a result, Blacks would meet secretly away from the masters' homes. Thus, small Black churches in the hills are a remnant of slavery in the South.

As a Black man, I had considerable trepidation about going into the Deep South, especially in Mississippi, and I certainly was not going into the rural hills of that part of the country asking questions. I had never been in the Deep South before.

My visit to the small town of Yazoo City gave me an uneasy feeling of the rural South that remained with me during my residency in Florida.

Continuing south, we were on our way to New Orleans. After we arrived, we toured the French Quarter, stopped for a while, and had wonderful creole beignets, tea, and chicory-flavored coffee. From there we drove to the suburbs of New Orleans, to Algiers, Louisiana, to visit the home of my sons' Creole cousins. They were very hospitable, although at times I had difficulty understanding their Creole patois. Leaving Louisiana on Interstate Highway 10, we drove through Alabama and the Florida Panhandle and arrived in Tallahassee.

The boys and I stayed overnight in a Tallahassee motel while the condominium I had leased was being prepared. The next morning, I drove the boys up the Thomasville Highway and on to Interstate 75 to the Atlanta, Georgia, airport for their trip back to their home with their mother in Seattle. After seeing them fly off, I drove back to Tallahassee with tears in my eyes.

That road trip with my 12- and 14-year-old sons was one of the most memorable, yet melancholy, experiences of my life. The leisurely, 3000-mile car trip from Seattle to Tallahassee drew me closer to them. I didn't know when I would see them again. Before I had been offered the teaching position at FSU, I told Mona that I was willing to raise Cynthia, Clark, and Craig at our house in Seattle. Her lawyer talked her out of that. Looking back, Mona and I agreed that that probably would have been the best scenario emotionally and financially for our family.

The future was a blank slate. How to fill it in was a complete mystery to me.

CHAPTER 19

Florida State University

ON MY WAY BACK to Tallahassee from the airport, I crossed the Georgia-Florida state line and stopped at a gas station. I looked across the street while my car was being serviced and saw a white, palatial building surrounded by a huge field. I asked the attendant what it was, and he described it as an old plantation. The field was utilized during the fall and winter for hunters shooting quail and ducks. He went on to say more descriptively that the owner and hunters ". . . were a bunch of Yankees from up north who don't give a hoot about keeping up the building or the property." The derisive use of the term *Yankee* made it clear how he felt about Northerners. I soon found out that his outlook was not unique among Whites in the Panhandle of northern Florida.

I bought a local newspaper before I arrived at my new residence. The headline read "KKK [Ku Klux Klan] Marches on City Hall." A picture of the hooded demonstrators accompanied the headline. The Klan was protesting the induction of the city's first African American mayor. Tallahassee had a "weak mayor" system whereby the city council members rotate serving as mayor after a predetermined number of years. A city manager actually runs the city's day-to-day business.

I buried my head in my hands and shook my head in dismay. I walked across the street from the condo to a restaurant with the intention of winding down and treating myself to a sandwich and a glass of wine. I was especially interested in the wine.

I should have noticed the large number of pick-up trucks in the parking lot with Confederate flags pasted to their rear windows. That should have been a clue as to what was ahead of me. Immediately after I walked in the door, I was confronted by a short, stocky, middle-aged White man, with what I noticed was a sleepy or blind eye. He looked up directly into my face and said with his heavy southern drawl, "What are you! Mexican? Cuban?" I didn't wait for the inevitable "N" word.

I snapped, "I'm American!"

He responded, "You need to know that I'm a redneck from Wakulla County and proud of it." I had no idea of the significance of Wakulla County and did not want to find out. As I was slowly backing out the door, a crowd of men whom I assumed were his friends were gathering behind him.

He continued, "Where are you from?"

I said, "I'm from Washington."

He responded, "Washington, DC?"

As I continued to back away, I said, "No, the State of Washington."

He murmured, "Let me think . . . the State of Washington . . . the State of Washington. The only thing I know about the State of Washington is the great All-American, one-eyed quarterback from the University of Washington from years ago."

I immediately blurted out, "I played with him in the 1960 Rose Bowl! His name is Bob Schloredt!"

The red neck yelled out, "Yep! Hot damn! That's who it is! Bob Schloredt!"

He grabbed me around my shoulder and yelled again, "Let me buy you a drink! You played ball with Bob Schloredt—the greatest one-eyed quarterback in college football history! Man, o' man!"

We had some small talk, and I drank a couple glasses of wine with him and then left. As I walked back to my condo, I shook my head. What were the odds of me being 3,000 miles away from Seattle and meeting a one-eyed redneck who obviously could identify with and admire my one-eyed friend Bob—the only person he knew of from the State of Washington?!

Years later I told Bob about the incident, and we laughed about it. I told him, "Man, just knowing you may have, literally, saved my life!"

A few days later, on a warm sunny afternoon, I was walking through the FSU campus to get a feel for my new surroundings when I heard some rumblings that at first sounded like thunder. The noise got louder and louder, and I became concerned. I turned toward the sound and was shocked to see a group of young White men on horseback dressed in Confederate uniforms! They were waving sabers and screaming what I considered to be the high-pitched rebel yell battle cry.

I was not in their immediate pathway, but as a Black person I feared for my life. As they rode off into the distance, I asked a nearby White man, "What in the hell was that?"

He matter-of-factly replied, "Oh, a group of frat guys get together and do that as a prank at least once a year." He explained that he did not believe it was prohibited by the university.

I sat down on a nearby bench with my heart racing. I thought to myself, *What in the hell have I got myself into, living in this part of the world?*

Fortunately, I found out there were other aspects of my Florida State experience that were not negative. For example, the concept of "Southern Hospitality" is refreshing, comforting, and quintessentially Southern. I got a real sense of Southern hospitality just shopping at the stores in Tallahassee. The first time I shopped at a Winn Dixie market I bought a loaf of bread, and the checker cheerfully said, "Y'all come back! Ya hear?" Impressed with her sincerity, I replied, "My goodness, thank you so much! I certainly will make it a point to come back! Bless you!" The checker stared back at me quizzically. Checkers at stores in Seattle never said such things to me when I bought items. I was thrilled to get a smile.

I soon found out that the checkers at all the stores in Tallahassee said the exact same thing to customers. "Y'all come back! Ya hear?" I wasn't special after all. That fact took a bit of the luster off the greeting; nevertheless, I still consider it a nice gesture.

Most folks from Tallahassee also say, "Yes, ma'am" or "Yes sir" or "Ms. Mary" or "Mr. Bob" when addressing adults. Such salutations connote respect for one another and create a pleasant atmosphere within a community.

During my free time, when not conducting a class or doing research, I would wind down by jogging a few miles every day. I would often see another jogger who was close to my age, and we began to talk. He was friendly and we had common interests in music and politics. I learned that he was a professor of history at FSU whose office was in the same building as mine. His name was Peter Ripley.

After about a month I asked him, "Pete, I know you are a professor of US History, but what are your specific areas of interest and research?"

He said, "Most of my publications and research relate to slavery in the United States and the Abolitionist movement against slavery, as well as the Civil War."

His response piqued my interest. I said, "That's interesting. My great-grandfather was an escaped slave who was active in the Abolitionist movement, but you probably wouldn't know anything about him. But his story is interesting family lore."

He said "Give me a try. What's his name?"

I blurted out, "Lewis Garrard Clarke!"

Pete got excited saying, "Carver! I have all sorts of information on Lewis Clarke!" He said he was working on a team of researchers headed by Dr. John Blassingame of Yale University. It was called The Frederick Douglass Papers Project. A primary focus of the project was on Black abolitionists like Clarke.

I was dumbstruck. I asked Pete if I could get copies of the material he had on Clarke. He said of course. He invited me to have dinner with him and his wife. At the end of dinner, he handed me a large cardboard box filled with copies of documents, letters, newspaper articles et al., related to Clarke's life. I was astounded.

I did not have the time to delve deeply into the details of all the papers he gave me. However, from thumbing through the material, it was clear that Clarke's story was far more important than just an interesting experience of one of our family's ancestors. The material covered his entire life, not just what was revealed in his 1842 biography, *Narrative of the Sufferings of Lewis Clarke, During Captivity of More than Twenty-Five Years* which only told of his experiences as a slave. Clarke was in fact an important leader in the abolitionist movement throughout the 1840s and 1850s. He was a well-known speaker on the subject of slavery and human rights through the years until his death in 1897.

My mother, Clarke's granddaughter, was not aware of this fact, nor was my respected mentor at the University of Washington, Dr. Thomas Pressly, a scholar of the slavery and Antebellum years in America.

Dr. Ripley was one of only a handful of scholars in America who knew such detail about Clarke's life. I concluded that my coming to Florida, 3,000 miles from my home, to teach at Florida State University, and meeting Peter Ripley, and him providing me with the treasure trove of documentation of Clarke's life was *more* than serendipity. It was *unfathomable!* In my mind, my coming to Florida was predestined.

My happenstance meeting with Peter Ripley was a transformative experience for me. Its full impact did not come into fruition until nearly forty years later when I researched and wrote my biography of Clarke *When Owing a Shilling Costs a Dollar, The Saga of Lewis G. Clarke, Born a "White Slave".*

———

I began contemplating seeking tenure in a permanent position as associate professor after teaching graduate seminars in organizational theory and public personnel management for one year at FSU. I enjoyed teaching the classes and had adjusted to the slow-moving Southern lifestyle in Tallahassee. The town was not far from Atlanta, where I could experience a more invigorating cultural and social ambiance. I figured achieving tenure would take approximately four years.

Cynthia, Clark, and Craig visiting me in the summer of 1978.

I would have no problem at all living in Tallahassee for that period of time.

In early 1979, I was approached by a colleague of mine, a professor in the Political Science Department. He asked if I would consider being on an investigative team of faculty members to assist the nation of Libya in improving its public personnel system. The team would be supported by a grant from the Arab League. [41] The team would utilize the Yugoslavian government's personnel system as a model, which was accepted and desired by the League. At this time, the Yugoslavian nation was still intact, behind the Iron Curtain, and under the control of President Tito. Yugoslavia was considered to have a relatively efficient public personnel system until its breakup in the early 1990s.

It was projected that the research effort would take approximately two years, and that the research results would essentially guarantee that I would be promoted to the tenured position of associate professor. Accepting the offer, I reserved a flight to Dubrovnik, Croatia, Yugoslavia, where the first meeting of the team was to take place with Yugoslavian and Libyan researchers and officials.

Soon after I made the plane reservations, I received a telephone call from one of my long-time mentors from Seattle, Phil Swain. It had been a while since we served on the Seattle School Board together in the mid-1970s. Phil had been employed as an executive with The Boeing Company for many years and said he was planning on retiring as Corporate Director of Educational Relations and Training. He went on to say "… there is an excellent possibility you could take my place if you would consider taking on a temporary position created by the company, reporting to me as Manager of Corporate Education Relations." The offer was too good to refuse. Although the two years in Tallahassee were rewarding professionally and socially, I felt guilty to be so far away from the children. The Boeing offer was especially important as I would be back home, close to my children where I could reconnect with them. And I would be considerably better off financially. I immediately accepted his offer. I contacted my investigative team leader for the Libyan project, told him of my decision, and then cancelled my plane reservation to Dubrovnik.

On my drive home from Tallahassee, I stopped in Washinton, DC, to see my daughter Cynthia and her cousin Stacey Lombard (Mona's niece) at Howard University, my mother's ala mater. Cynthia had graduated from Holy Names High School in the spring of 1979 and was now at Howard on a scholarship. I had attended her graduation with my mother and was so proud of my daughter.

It was a fun get together in DC, but I could see in her eyes she was somewhat sad. I assumed her sadness was related to the divorce. I was also able to get together with my brother Gary while in DC. He'd recently taken a job as a special assistant with US Transportation Secretary Brock Adams. Gary was having a ball in his new role.

My homecoming allowed me to be in Seattle at least during my two boys' final years of high school. Clark (Carver Jr.), an accomplished young musician and artist at Garfield High School was going into his junior year. The youngest, Craig, was entering freshman year at The Northwest School. I was somewhat concerned about how much time I'd be able to spend with them. Mona had established a new relationship and remarried. I did not want to give any indication of disrupting her new situation, but I made it clear to the boys I would always be available if they needed me.

Virginia Clark Gayton at Cynthia's graduation.
Cynthia was one of her grandmother's true favorites.

Going home also meant a significant change in the relationship I had with a woman I had been seeing off and on in Seattle since my separation from Mona. Patricia was a programmer for the computer system required for my Affirmative Action reports at the University of Washington. We'd grown close before my move to Florida. My time away from made me conclude I was not emotionally prepared to remarry, and I felt it was imperative for me to tell her face-to-face of my decision to break off the relationship. It would be a heart-wrenching period in both of our lives.

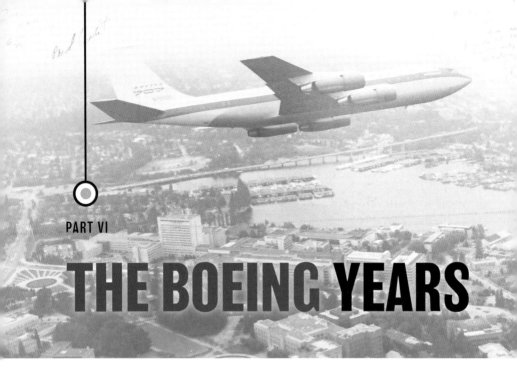

PART VI

THE BOEING YEARS

CHAPTER 20

Introduction to The Boeing Company

THE FACT THAT PHIL SWAIN, my mentor, asked me to come on board with The Boeing Company in the fall of 1979 as one of the first African American managers to work in the corporate offices was an honor in itself. I had admired Phil from afar before we worked together on the Seattle School Board. He had taken the lead in initiating a voluntary racial integration program for middle school children within the district as well as other significant issues. He did these things while working as a Boeing executive. What Phil did within and outside of The Boeing Company provided a model for me to emulate.

An obvious benefit of working for Boeing was that I would be employed by the most successful aerospace company in the world. Boeing was the number

I pledged to "provide funding models of programs with different funding approaches, tied to measurable goals; work to improve the culture of Boeing constituents and encourage support for the district."

---

one commercial aircraft company internationally, the number one exporter. Boeing hired more employees in the State of Washington than any other public or private entity.

Boeing manufactured the B-17 bomber that had helped change the course of World War II. Their Boeing 707 became the very first successful commercial jet airliner. The company also made military aircraft, helicopters, and missiles, and was the top National Aeronautics and Space Administration (NASA) contractor, et al.

The divisions I would be working with regarding training and education programs included the Boeing Defense and Space Group, the Boeing Commercial Airplanes Group (BCAG), and Boeing Computer Services. These divisions covered communities and cities throughout the State of Washington. Many Boeing operations had been established in other states: Philadelphia, Pennsylvania; the Wichita, Kansas area; the Portland, Oregon area; and Huntsville, Alabama. In a new managers class I attended, one marketing executive summed up his pride in working for such a great corporation by saying, "It's sure better than making match books, isn't it?!"

Being part of such a successful and powerful corporation offered me welcome challenges as well as opportunities. My years at the University of Washington and

Florida State University as an administrator and academician were wonderful experiences. I enjoyed conversations and debates with my colleagues on theoretical issues. But while I wrestled with theoretical analyses in academia, I always wondered, *how can these analyses bring a positive impact for our citizens and communities—especially for our diverse and economically deprived populations?*

At Boeing, I looked forward to working with a sense of urgency about outcomes! What Boeing had to offer with its talent, prestige, and culture was a better fit for my personality and my hopes for contributing to society. My challenge: How could key players within The Boeing Company partner with key players *outside* the company to make a positive impact in the field of education?

What kind of "company culture" did I find in Boeing when I came on board? Well, I saw several. The engineers had a "facts and data" culture. The marketing folks had a "pump 'em up" culture. And the machinists—blue collar workers— were the "direct, no-nonsense" folks. The challenge for me was to help facilitate the bringing together of those cultures to achieve a common mission and goals.

It's difficult for me to define the Corporate Offices culture other than to say it was an amalgamation of all the other ones. When I first arrived there in 1979, I was too much in awe of my surroundings to make any analytical assessment of its culture.

My office space was located in what was called "Mahogany Row." These were office spaces of former senior executives of the corporation who were now retired and were serving as consultants for Boeing. In other words, I was surrounded by *aerospace industry icons* on a regular basis!

Those I would see and talk with from time to time included the likes of Bill Allen, a lawyer and president of the company from 1945 to 1968, who famously "bet the company" when he authorized construction of the Boeing 367-80, which served as the prototype for the 707 jet airliners. I also connected with aerospace engineers/scientists Ed Wells and George Schairer who were the designers of the B17 Flying Fortress, the Boeing 707, and the 747. Ed Wells and George Schairer were considered geniuses and Renaissance men who were well versed on a wide variety of subjects.

CEO and Chairman of the Board Thornton Wilson would often refer to Schairer as "Chief Scientist" of the Company. Schairer would touch base with me from time to time, requesting that I advise representatives of Cornish College about our college donation policies. He was a member of the Board of Trustees of Cornish College, a performing arts institution. Interestingly, he never talked with me about our key engineering colleges or universities, which related more to his academic training.

I'd sit with some of these amazing gentlemen from time to time when I had lunch in the open-seating, corporate executive dining room. Very seldom did I talk. I was enthralled by their conversations. Each man had broad interests; none were one dimensional as scientists. I was fascinated. What a gift it was to me as a young manager/executive to hear those conversations!

Mal Stamper, president of The Boeing Company, decided to eliminate the exclusive executive dining room in the mid-1980s in an effort to be more egalitarian. Instead, he encouraged executives to have lunch in the general employees dining hall and mingle with all Boeing employees.

I agreed with the concept of what Mal was doing. However, his decision led to most executives leaving the Boeing facilities to have lunch at restaurants in the surrounding neighborhood. Sadly, the unique experiences I had had with those giants of the past ceased. I felt it was unfortunate that other young executives missed what I'd been exposed to.

During my first eight years with Boeing, I did not have a close relationship with the CEO and Chairman of the Board Thornton Arnold Wilson—also known as "T" Wilson. However, the experiences I had with him left me with deep and positive impressions. He created a welcoming environment for me during my early years.

One example took place in 1984 when Corporate Director of Public Relations Pete Bush retired. A going away reception for Pete was arranged, comprised of corporate executives.

I entered the room and was standing near "T" when I overheard him saying to Pete, "You and I are the only Goddamned Democrats in the entire room!"

I tapped "T" on the shoulder and said, " 'T', I'm the other Democrat!"

Without missing a beat, he said, "Damn it, Gayton—with you being a Black man in America, you *better* be a Democrat!" I fell out laughing.

"T" went on to say, "Gayton, you should know I went to an Historically Black College in Jefferson City, Missouri, for a year before I went on to Iowa State University. It was called Lincoln Jr. College." I'm not sure of the veracity

The Boeing Company CEO and Chairman "T" Wilson, Vice President Stan Little, and I were invited to attend a luncheon at the home of U of W President Dr. Gerberding each year. We were joined for this luncheon by Boeing President Frank Shrontz: (left to right) Little, me, Shrontz, Gerberding, and Wilson, circa 1985.

of his remark, but it was clear to me that he was attempting to make me feel comfortable within the all-White corporate environment. And I appreciated what he was doing.

At least once a year, from 1982 on, "T", Stan Little, and I were invited to a luncheon meeting with University of Washington President Bill Gerberding at the presidential mansion, also known as the "Walker-Ames Mansion." Our objective was to discuss the status of various University of Washington professorships and chairs funded by Boeing that were primarily within the colleges of engineering and business. I was included because of my role as Corporate Director of Training and Educational Relations (and later on as Director of College and University Relations).

We'd travel to and from the meetings in a Boeing van. I was surprised and flattered by how candidly "T" would talk with Stan about matters while I was present—like the maneuverings of some of his executive team in attempting to position themselves to make their mark within the company. He evidently trusted me. Which he should have. "T" did not talk about such situations in a mean way. In fact, he seemed humored by them.

These meetings took place until "T" retired in 1988. The dry wits of "T" and Bill were the highlights of the luncheons that I remember. A major takeaway for me was that I was accepted as a trusted confidant of these very powerful men.

———

As is the case in most jobs, all was not smooth sailing during my tenure at Boeing. You may wonder how I functioned during most of those years as the only Black executive assigned to the corporate offices. Having experienced being the only Black in previous roles, I knew how to navigate these environments. I learned not to challenge every racial slight, but I made sure that my integrity and respect as a Black man remained intact.

For example, one slight I did not confront was related to my "contributions" budget when I had included a donation of nearly $1 million for a math and science teachers academy for a predominantly Black high school. One colleague shared feedback he had heard from a high-level human resources manager: "Gayton is pouring money down a sh** hole. The school doesn't deserve it." I did not challenge the HR Director. I felt he was jealous of the fact that I was able to control so much money. I did not want to waste my energy. That project received acclaim throughout the state.

Obviously, there were slights I had to confront directly. One took place soon after I had been promoted to the executive payroll. One day I received a call from Terry Bergeson, the executive director of the Washington State Commission on Student Learning, whom I had known for many years, even before my employment at Boeing. She and I were scheduled to meet about an education matter. Then she received a call from an executive within Boeing's Government Relations office directing her to cancel the meeting. The executive was relatively new at Boeing and had previously worked within Governor Booth Gardner's office regarding education matters.

Dr. Bergeson did not know what to do. She was perturbed by the request and didn't want to get involved with any political infighting with the corporate offices of the company.

I was livid! I thanked her and said I would touch base with her later. I attempted to gather my thoughts. I walked down to the executive's office, entered the room, and closed his door behind me. I told him what had transpired. I pointed my finger at him and spoke in a slow measured voice, "Do not do that sort of thing again. If you do, you are in line for a rude awakening." Then I walked out.

Later that morning I received a phone call from one of the company's senior vice-presidents with whom I had a very businesslike relationship. In essence, he said, "What were you doing threatening the executive?" I explained that I did not physically threaten him, and I reiterated what I said. I pointed out that I did not swear at him, but there was no question I was angry.

He responded, "You did not have to swear for him to feel threatened. He could be threatened by the expression on your face." I chuckled and shook my head. His statement was a dog whistle to any Black person. The "expression" *was* my Black face.

I followed up by saying "Hey, 99 percent of the time I'm here at Boeing, I maintain my composure. This circumstance was an exception."

He shot back, "What I'm concerned about is that 1%." I laughed out loud, and I could hear him laughing as well. That ended the conversation. At that point I thought the ordeal was over. However, late that afternoon I was called into a conference room to meet with three other corporate vice-presidents to give them my side of the confrontation. Interestingly, my direct report, Senior Vice President Larry McKean, was not one of the three. I considered that a positive sign that he had my back on the matter and understood my anger.

It is interesting that while almost the entire top floor of the corporate executives was in an uproar over what had transpired, I was very calm. I had no fear. I had a sense of relief and solitude.

There were no further repercussions against me. The executive who tried to undermine me with Dr. Bergeson apologized for his actions several months later. He said he was going through a divorce and as a result was having some out-of-character emotional episodes.

I could mention other embedded racist incidents I endured, but that would take away from the successes I experienced with the broad array of folks I worked with to accomplish so much in the fields of education and training within and outside the bounds of the company.

CHAPTER 21

Cogswell College North

ONE OF MY MAJOR ASSIGNMENTS when I arrived at The Boeing Company was to be the administrator of a Seattle extension program that offered a four-year degree in engineering technology. At the time, Boeing accepted employees with two general classifications of engineering degrees. The four-year Bachelor of Science in Engineering (BSE) program taught higher-level mathematics and science and placed a heavy emphasis on theory. The BSE degree yields traditional research engineers and relates to invention and design work.

The other, the Bachelor of Science in Engineering Technology (BSET), is focused on practical application. At Boeing, this degree is needed for the actual building work.

Employees with either of these degrees could advance their careers to higher paying jobs within the company. However, schools where one could earn a BSET degree were hard to find. Before 1979, there were *none* in the Puget Sound area of the State of Washington where Boeing had most of its facilities. How could Boeing help prepare the trained workforce it needed?

Boeing's engineering community obviously felt that the dearth of BSET degree programs was a considerable problem for the company's future. They identified a BSET degree program taught at Cogswell College in San Francisco, California, as the program that Boeing wanted for its skilled, hands-on technologists.

The Boeing Company President Mal Stamper (seated, center) Cogswell College officials, and me at a Partnership meeting in 1979.

Cogswell College, founded in 1887, became a technical institute in 1932. It is a nonprofit and independent learning institution that stresses a hands-on approach to technology. Students were taught that "Bench time" is just as important as "book time."

Malcolm Stamper, president of The Boeing Company, initiated a partnership with Cogswell College. He signed a financial agreement with Cogswell to develop and implement an extension college in Washington state. The new extension school, Cogswell College North, was set up on the campus of Shoreline Community College in the North Seattle area.

Cogswell North could provide educational opportunities that served the technological needs of the company. Since The Boeing Company was already committed to subsidizing the continuing education of its employees, it made perfect sense for us to set up the right classes where employees could take advantage of them. Additionally, Cogswell North offered evening classes that were otherwise not available for either type of baccalaureate degree within the Seattle area.

President Stamper selected me to be the Boeing administrator of the extension program. My primary roles were to fulfill our financial commitments to Cogswell, publicize the program, and to ensure that an effective communication channel was established between me and the Cogswell leadership team.

The fact that Boeing went outside Washington state to establish the educational opportunities provided by Cogswell College caused considerable consternation in Olympia, the state capitol. When Senator Barney Goltz, chairman of the Senate Higher Education Committee, became aware of this, legislators wanted to know why Washington's own higher education institutions couldn't produce graduates that met the skill needs of the state's largest employer. Good question!

Senator Goltz asked of Bud Coffey, the Boeing corporate senior vice president of Government Relations, that a Boeing representative come to a meeting in Olympia and testify about this. I was tapped by Bud to go. Deans from the engineering departments of the University of Washington and Washington State University were also requested to attend.

The hearing took place in early January 1980. The testimonies from each of the major research institutions essentially said that, as research institutions, they did not have an interest in providing the types of applied engineering courses offered by Cogswell College.

In my testimony, I made clear that Boeing had no intention of criticizing the State of Washington's higher education programs. Boeing had no desire to have the research institutions move away from their research missions. In fact, we were pleased with them. However, Boeing developed the opportunity to work with Cogswell because the college provided the kind of courses that met the technical needs of the company.

From my point of view, the hearing ended the concern of Senator Goltz, but in my mind, Cogswell's presence in Washington was an *invitation* to the community colleges to see the possibility of broadening their educational missions.

Initially, Cogswell College operated on the Shoreline Community College campus, but soon after I arrived at Boeing it moved to facilities in Bellevue. After a few years, the college then moved to a larger facility in Everett. In total, Cogswell operated in the State of Washington from 1979 through 2006, offering a variety of technical and business courses.

Over the years, enrollment averaged about 300 students—most of whom were Boeing employees who had their tuition reimbursed by the company. Boeing oversight of the program came from my office until my departure in 1997.

I strongly believe that Cogswell North's presence had a major impact on expanding the technical course offerings of the community colleges in the state. Cogswell filled a vacuum for the educational requirements of current and prospective employees of Boeing as well as suppliers. Some community colleges seized this opportunity to fill the recruitment needs of the manufacturing industry within the Puget Sound Area. In particular, these schools were the Seattle Community Colleges, Bellevue Community College, and Renton Technical College. They began offering evening courses directed toward Applied (technology) Baccalaureate degrees in the sciences—and at a lower cost than Cogswell. This ultimately nullified the need to maintain Cogswell College North in the State of Washington. The best news was that The Boeing Company's need for technology education was being served!

These four-year baccalaureate degrees offered in the community colleges created an opportunity for the State Board of Community and Technical Colleges to allow the community colleges to *change their name* to "college." This gave those institutions a boost in prestige, as well as a clearer definition of their academic offerings. This label distinguishes the difference between research institutions, such as the University of Washington and Washington State University, and the applied academic offerings of the community colleges.

Clearly, The Boeing Company's unilateral action of bringing Cogswell College into the Puget Sound area, inadvertently changed the academic framework of the community colleges. The Boeing Company and Cogswell College, in partnership with the community colleges, produced a win-win cooperation between business and education that endures to this day.

On May 19, 1980, Walt Evans, a *Seattle Times* columnist, wrote an article about me entitled "A Lot of Life: From Football to Varied Careers, Gayton Has Filled Years with Action." Walt interviewed me over lunch at the Broadway Restaurant in Capitol Hill. We covered my life from my football days at Garfield High School and the University of Washington, to my years in the FBI, to my arrival at The Boeing Company in 1979. It was a very flattering account in which Walt basically welcomed me back to Seattle.

A few days after this article was published, I received a phone call from one of my former students. Four years earlier, while working on my doctorate degree, I'd been a graduate teaching assistant in the U of W Political Science Department. I remembered this woman as an outstanding student. I also recalled a short meeting that we'd had in my office to clarify an assignment. As we talked on the phone, we mutually agreed that it would be fun to get together for a cup of coffee sometime.

One thing led to another, and we began dating. I enjoyed her company because she was bright, attractive, and one of the few folks who laughed at my jokes. We had many dates over the next four years and a few vacation trips together. All in all, I cared about her very much. When I escorted her to U of W Alumni events or to a "T" Wilson reception at his home, my friends always had very positive comments about her style and grace. I was proud to be with her. But alas, I felt that neither one of us was ready to tie the knot, and we went our separate ways after four very memorable years.

CHAPTER 22

Early Childhood Education

ONE ISSUE CAME TO NATIONAL attention in the late '70s that gave me the chance to participate in some of the most exciting work I've ever done.

There was a perception rising among US industry and government leaders that our country was losing its preeminence in commerce, industry, science, and technological innovation. This was definitely a serious concern. These leaders were saying that we were being overtaken by competitors in nations such as Japan and Germany. That perspective was expressed in the publication "A Nation at Risk: The Imperative for Educational Reform; a Report to the US Secretary of Education" by the National Commission on Excellence in Education, dated April 1983.

The "Nation at Risk" report acknowledged that there were many reasons why the US was less competitive, but only one was the focus of the report: improving the educational institutions of the nation. Essentially, its conclusion was that the educational foundations of our society were being eroded by a rising tide of mediocrity that threatened the future of the nation and its citizens. The report concluded:

If an unfriendly power had attempted to impose on America the mediocre educational performance that exists today, we might well have viewed it as an act of war. As it stands, we have allowed this to happen to ourselves. We have even squandered the gains in student achievement made in the wake of the Sputnik challenge.

The charge of the commission was to provide practical recommendations for educational improvement within our schools and colleges.

A year before the "Nation at Risk" report came out, Governor Spellman of Washington state started action on these same concerns. He created The Temporary Committee on Educational Policies, Structure, and Management in 1982. The charge was to conduct a review of Washington's public school system, including both the common school system and the colleges and universities. The fifteen-member committee included individuals such as Chairman Fred Haley, the owner of Brown and Haley; Betty Jane Narver, community activist; John McGregor, the Eastern Washington agri-business mogul; President Emeritus Charles Odegaard of the University of Washington; Allison Cowles Sulzberger of the famous publishing family; and then there was me.

I represented Boeing and was the only person of color. It was one of the most prestigious and impressive boards/committees I served on during my career. I was asked by Corporate Vice President Stan Little to serve on the committee.

According to Governor Spellman, "The purpose of the Governor's committee was to address a mounting concern that state-supported education did not measure up to legitimate expectations of effectiveness and quality." I was especially interested in our discussions concerning early childhood/pre-kindergarten education and the positive impact on children of color. The concept really had its debut during President Johnson's administration's War on Poverty and its Head Start Program during the late 1960s. Longitudinal studies reflected the long-term positive impacts on Black children.

There were two Black women who introduced me to the early childhood education movement. Louise McKinney, principal of the Martin Luther King Early Childhood Center in Seattle, and Dorothy Hollingsworth, director of the City of Seattle's Head Start program and a Seattle School Board member. I was aware of the Head Start program when it was first initiated during the administration of President Johnson in the late 1960s. Both women were pioneers in promoting and implementing the concept. Their model influenced my discussions with the committee concerning education reform.

We presented the final report of our committee to the state legislature and the governor in January of 1985. Although the entire report was important, I felt that the section on "Addressing Particular Student Needs" was the most significant because it prioritized "Early Childhood, Pre-Kindergarten Education."

I was especially pleased. The Governor's committee had encouraged entities from business, education, and government to come together on a specific priority. That partnership—in one form or another—has not only been sustained but built upon over the years.

Prior to 1983, The Boeing Company's involvement in public school kindergarten through twelfth grade programs was virtually non-existent. But while the Spellman committee was underway, Boeing became involved in a second, closely related effort. The Boeing Company's position on K-12 education changed dramatically in 1983 during the advent of the Washington Roundtable. This group focused on pre-college issues and problems. The Roundtable, a privately funded entity at the time, was comprised of CEOs of thirty-one of the largest business firms in the state. Their primary concern was the economic stability of the state. In 1983, they established an Education Committee chaired by "T" Wilson who, in turn, appointed a Working Committee on Education made up of executives from member companies. The Working Committee's task was to determine the major issues confronting K-12 education within the state and then present its findings and recommendations to the Roundtable.

At the beginning of the Working Committee's study, "T" advised us Boeing members of the committee. He wanted us to look specifically into the kinds of things The Boeing Company could do to enhance its relationship with the public schools. "T's" directive represented the beginning of what became a company-wide involvement in broad-based programs to assist public schools. I was designated by "T" to chair an internal Management Advisory Committee on Education of just Boeing executives entirely separate from the Roundtable. It was comprised of four, division-level vice presidents. When the corporate-wide initiative was launched by "T", he pulled me aside and said "Gayton, let's show the education community what they have to do within the next three years to turn things around and then move on to other things." I laughed heartily, considering "T's" remarks as tongue in cheek. But Boeing continued its deep involvement in K-12 education matters for my remaining fourteen years with the corporation.

I want to share the story of my experience with the separate working committee "T" had established within the Roundtable. The committee ultimately included non-Boeing members from other corporations. There was no question, however, that "T" wanted the Boeing members to take the lead on the necessary work needed for the team. It was led by Harry Goldie, executive vice president of the Boeing Aerospace Division. Several engineering managers from other Boeing divisions were also part of the team. I was responsible for staff support as director of Educational Relations and Training. Our Boeing contingent provided most of the research information for the Roundtable Education Committee chaired by "T".

One of the first tasks Harry identified was to create a "war room" in one of the corporate office spaces. We gathered data about K-12 issues and posted them up on the walls of the room. This resulted in a blackboard covered with a list, in non-prioritized order, of over 200 issues!

Then we gathered data on each issue, sometimes inviting experts from the education community to explain things we weren't familiar with. I added "early childhood education/Head Start" to the list of 200. Initially, it was near the bottom of the list because it was unfamiliar to the other team members.

At the time our internal Boeing team was doing its research, the Governor's state-wide Temporary Committee on Educational Policies, Structure and Management was finishing up its historic report. The Temporary Committee, as well as the Roundtable, were delving into the *same fundamental issues* concerning K-12 education. (The Boeing Company and the Roundtable were two of the granting organizations supporting the Temporary Committee's study.)

Staff members of both committees worked closely together from the inception of the Roundtable in 1983. During the Temporary Committee's deliberations, I advised that Louise McKinney and Dorothy Hollingsworth be interviewed by both groups. None of the other committee members knew of either of these exceptional educators, nor had they heard of "early childhood education." Goldie asked, "What is 'Early Childhood Education'? Is the term some sort of 'education-ese'? Only known among educators?" Nevertheless, he was open to hearing from both women.

Mrs. McKinney provided background information on Head Start. Essentially, the program aims to provide comprehensive early childhood education, health, nutrition, and parent involvement services to low-income children of color and their families. The program's services and resources are designed to foster stable family relationships, enhance children's physical and emotional well-being, and establish an environment that helps kids to develop strong cognitive skills.

The Perry Project Longitudinal Study Findings

The 20-year longitudinal study of the Perry Project compared the preschool group to a non-preschool group. In following these children from the age of 7 through age 27, researchers found striking differences between the two groups:

Incidences of crime: Only 7% of adults who had participated in the Perry program had been arrested five or more times compared with 35% of those who had not participated in the preschool program. Of those in the preschool program, 7% had been arrested for drug related offences compared to 25% of those in the no-program group.

Economic Status Earnings: Adults in the program group were four times more likely (29%) to earn $2,000 or more per month than were adults in the no-program group (7%). Almost three times as many (36%) owned their own homes compared to those in the no-program group (13%). More than two times as many owned a second car (program group, 30%; no- program group, 13%). As adults, 59% of those in the program group

had received welfare assistance, or other social service at some time, compared to 80% of those in the no-program group.

Educational Attainment: In the program group, 71% graduated from regular adult high schools or received General Educational Development (GED) certification, compared with 54% of those in the no-program group.

Cost benefit analysis: A distinct aspect of the Perry study was its economic cost-benefit analysis. The analysis weighs the cost of the preschool program against the economic benefits resulting from the program-higher earnings, and reduced incidences of crime, welfare assistance, and special education services. Looking at all the statistics from participants at age 27, the analysis found that every public dollar spent on the program saved $7.16 in tax dollars. This $7.16 figure has become the most often cited statistic from the study. The analysis conveys the value of the activities in terms that the business community understands.

The program's creator and first director, Jule Sugarman, originally conceived of it as a catch-up summer school program. He wanted to teach low-income children, in a few weeks, what they needed to know to start elementary school. The Federal Head Start Act of 1981 expanded the Program.

When Mrs. McKinney gave a presentation to the Boeing working committee, she shared her overview of a study called the Perry Preschool Project in the Ypsilanti School District, in Ypsilanti, Michigan. This study, initiated in the early 1960s, is now regarded as landmark research that establishes the human and financial value of high-quality pre-school education. The study showed that for those who participated in the program there was a significant reduction in arrests and drug related offenses, greater economic status earnings achieved, and a higher level of education attained. Also, a cost analysis found that every public dollar spent on the program saved $7.16 in tax dollars.

After our working group studied the 200-plus education issues reflected in our "war room," we concluded that the Early Childhood Education issue justified being at the top of the list! Two things drove our decision. First, this educational issue had a longitudinal study to back up its conclusions. Second, the positive cost-benefit analysis not only made economic sense, but it was free of political bias. Since most of our committee members were engineers, they could appreciate the "facts and data" outcomes reflected in the Perry report.

I was extremely pleased with the decision. The team could see the positive, broad, economic, social, and political impact that a quality, national early childhood education program could have on the citizenry of the nation. In business terms, the Roundtable could saw the program as a wise investment for the entire economy in partnership with the education community. The engineers in our group were amazed by the science behind the Perry preschool study. It resulted in them having much more respect for educators as a whole.

I also was very proud that that I had a role in introducing two African American women, who happened to be national leaders in early childhood education, to our team. There was mutual respect for all involved.

The working group met regularly over a period of 18 months and conducted 280 interviews with educators and officials of educational organizations. Members of the Committee also visited nearly one-quarter of the state's school districts!

Richard Page, the initial president of the Roundtable, was quoted in the December 5, 1984, issue of *Education Week*. He said that the education discussions among a variety of groups from the public and private sectors represents "…a major dialogue for the first time among the educators themselves with the public…" within the State of Washington.

After approximately three months of meetings, I found out all was not smooth sailing within the Boeing committee. I was not aware of any problems until "T" asked for a meeting with the Harry Goldie team, which included me as the primary staff support member and two engineering managers Goldie had selected. During the meeting, Goldie blurted out a non-sequitur to "T" that Gayton was spending too much time working on other community obligations.

I was shocked. Goldie never mentioned his concern to me. I immediately shot back that I continued to fulfill my responsibilities concerning the Roundtable Working Committee as well as the obligations I had on behalf of Boeing within the community. I went on to say that Goldie's concerns had never been mentioned to me before. "T's" response was interesting. He merely smiled and went on to the next agenda item. "T" never asked me about that episode. I assumed that he was satisfied with my response to Goldie. Obviously, my trust in Goldie dissolved. However, my commitment to make the committee's work successful never waned.

The research and conclusions of our Boeing-led Working Committee of the Roundtable were discussed with the oversight Roundtable Education Committee led by "T" Wilson. The Education Committee agreed with the conclusions of the Harry Goldie team. This information was shared with the Roundtable as a whole, as well as Governor Spellman's Temporary Committee on Educational Policies, Structure and Management. We also presented to a grassroots group in the state called Citizens Education Center Northwest.

The stand of these various groups on the issue of Early Childhood Education reflected a business/public sector collaboration on a transformative scale that is seldom seen locally or nationally—especially in today's political climate.

All of the parties involved had Early Childhood Education as a priority going into the 1985-87 biennium legislative session, with positive results. The Roundtable's position in 1989 was as follows:

As a priority matter, the Roundtable favors the rapid expansion of the State's present program to serve all at-risk children. At the same time, a cooperative effort should begin with early childhood care and education providers to explore ways to create extended day programs for children served by the state's early childhood programs and for young at-risk school-aged children. The objective should be to provide these programs on a universal basis for all at-risk children as rapidly as possible.

As of 2021, "Early Learning" remains as one of the top three areas of emphasis for the Education Foundation of the Washington Roundtable.

The ground-breaking work of the Washington Roundtable Education Committee, of which I provided the key staff role, also influenced the National Business Roundtable, which continues to have early childhood Education as a national education priority. Between 1989 and 1990, I was asked to make three presentations to their "Business Roundtable Corporate Involvement Seminars" about Washington Roundtable Education Committee activities with specific emphasis on our Early Learning efforts. It's apparent that our work had an impact.

It is interesting to note that in their May 2003 "Corporate Voices" report, the National Roundtable stated:

Over the past two decades business leaders have invested time, expertise, and resources in efforts to improve K-12 education in the United States. What we have learned leads us to conclude that America's continuing efforts to improve education and develop a world class workforce will be hampered without a federal and state commitment to early childhood education for 3- and 4-year-old children.

In essence, the National Roundtable was saying: We're on the right track. But if we expect to have a competitive world-class workforce, we—the business community—need to make sure our federal and state partners expand access to high-quality early learning programs.

After my Boeing role with the Washington Roundtable, I had the opportunity to take my experience to a new level. Norman Rice was elected Mayor of Seattle in 1990. He called to ask me a favor. Would I work with his team to organize what he called the Seattle Education Summit?

The point of the Summit was to bring a sense of community back to Seattle around the issue of education. Rice felt that the community had become further divided on public school education since June of 1989 when voters had passed an anti-busing initiative. The challenge was how to bring every neighborhood together on the issues of quality and diverse education. Thus, the idea of organizing a citywide education summit.

The mayor asked me to represent Boeing as part of the city's organizing efforts. I readily agreed. Having known and respected Norm for many years, I considered his request an honor.

Organizing such a summit was going to take an enormous amount effort and brain power. The mayor's office pulled together a planning group of 60 stakeholders from throughout the community, led by co-chairs Ancil Payne, CEO of King TV, and Dr. Constance Rice. The planning and logistics for the Summit were a huge challenge but the Rice team made it work.

Soon after the initial community meetings, Summit organizers and Rice's staff gathered in a room with walls covered with lists. The reports from the sites were prepared for the citywide summit meetings in May. Patterns became clear fairly quickly. There were five priorities determined as the result of the meetings:

1. Enhance the learning environment for students and teachers.
2. Involve the community in school-based decision making and make schools community gathering sites.
3. Make every child safe, healthy, and ready to learn.
4. Recognize and celebrate cultural diversity in schools.
5. Enhance basic education funding.

After the April meetings, I was asked by Mayor Rice to be the Working Group Chair for the number one issue, "Better learning environment." My co-chair was John Morefield, the very bright and innovative principal of Hawthorne Elementary School. Others on my forty-member Task Force included such luminaries as James Washington, Jr., famous sculptor; Dee Dickinson, iconic educator; Larry Matsuda, community leader, Dr. Robert Gary, legendary coach and teacher; and Bernie Whitebear, iconic state-wide activist.

My Working Group meetings had open discussions around the broad area of "Enhancing the learning environment of the schools." I encouraged discussion and discerned a common thread around early learning. At that point, I talked about my involvement with the Washington Roundtable as well as Governor Spellman's Temporary Committee. I related the conclusions of both groups concerning Early Learning and the research that supported these programs. The consensus of the meeting was that our number one priority would be early childhood education.

Phase 2 of the Summit was held on May 5 and 6, 1990. This phase represented a chance to pull all the brainstorming together, prioritize solutions, gain consensus, and adopt a plan. Two thousand citizens gathered to hear the conclusions of all five Working Groups. I presented the conclusions from ours.

After all the Working Group chairs spoke, Mayor Rice and his team decided that the theme for the entire Summit would be "Safe, Healthy, and Ready to Learn."

To meet that vison, funding was needed. This required a fourth phase, with the Rice team proposing a tax levy called the Families and Education Levy (FEL) on June 16. This levy would fulfill the recommendations from the outstanding Summit. The $57.4 million levy would include five elements, in priority order:

1. Early childhood development for children 5 years old and younger
2. School-based family services
3. Comprehensive health care
4. Out-of-school activities
5. Educational enhancement

Beyond the Families and Education Levy, the Seattle Education Summit established an Implementation Accountability Agreement to provide an ongoing way of monitoring and coordinating the initiatives of the Working Groups. The preamble of the agreement reads:

We, the people who live and work in Seattle, hereby reaffirm our personal commitment to creating a truly excellent education system which meets the needs of every child in our community.

The accountability group, chaired by Bob Watt, the Mayor's chief of staff, had 32 signatories, of which I was one, representing The Boeing Company. The list was headed by Mayor Rice. Others included former Governor of Washington Dan Evans, State House Committee on Appropriations Chair Gary Locke, President of the Seattle Education Alliance John Mangles, Superintendent of Schools Bill Kendrick, Dean of the U of W College of Education Allen Glenn, President of the Seattle Education Association John Carl Davis, U of W among other leaders in the education, business, government, and nonprofit sectors.

Each signatory of the agreement pledged to answer the question "What are you accountable for?" I pledged to "provide funding models of programs with different funding approaches, tied to measurable goals; work to improve the culture [re: education needs] of Boeing constituents and encourage support for the district." Basically, I expressed a succinct description of my job at Boeing. In my mind it was beyond a job. It was a whole-hearted personal commitment.

Also on June 16, all the signatories of the Accountability Agreement made an announcement:

A Comprehensive Early Childhood Education Pilot would be initiated immediately. Its objective was to pilot a full-day, school-based early childhood education program. It would blend funds from the city's Head Start program, the state's Early Childhood Education Assistance Program (ECEAP), and city childcare resources and services into one program at an elementary school. The school district would provide school staff support. The program would promote integration of children from all income backgrounds.

I considered this special announcement of the pilot program by Mayor Rice and his team as a direct acknowledgment of the Working Group I had chaired. Our singular recommendation was early childhood education development of children five-years-old and younger. My team and I were extremely proud!

The levy was passed in November of 1990 with a 57 percent approval vote. The levy was approved again in 1997, 2005, 2011, and 2018. It now provides over $200 million dollars over seven years in additional resources for the schools.

The leadership, vision, and organizational skills of Mayor Rice and his team which led to the passage of the Families and Education Levy was unprecedented in the annals of Seattle political history. The backdrop of that achievement was the work of many different groups: The Washington Roundtable Education Committee, The Roundtable Working Group, and the Washington State Temporary Committee on Educational Policies, Structure and Management. The Summit processes recognized that the common thread binding those groups together was the priority of early childhood education.

As the representative of The Boeing Company, I had the opportunity to ride that train all the way through to some great conclusions! I was proud to serve in a leadership role within each of these groups, including the Summit.

There is no question that the Summit was an unbridled success. Successive Families and Education Levies have easily passed over the years. However, after the Summit, Mayor Rice was prescient in saying that "some changes would take place...right away. But many changes will take time..."

Unfortunately, there's no clear evidence that a critical mass of students, especially poor children of color, have benefited from the goals of the Summit. Nevertheless, the Summit and the other committee efforts gave us a major positive takeaway. The private and public sectors, as well as responsible conservative and progressive political entities, were all able to find common ground in the long-range benefits of early childhood education.

As reflected in a May 2020 editorial in the *New York Times*:

The most viable escape from poverty is a good education beginning at an early age. In 1965, the Federal government started a program for lower-income children called Head Start. Darren Walker, who rose from poverty in Louisiana to head the Ford Foundation, has credited his escape from poverty to signing up for the program's first cohort. A growing body of research backs him up. Yet federal investment remains paltry. Head Start is available to only 11 percent of kids below the age of 3, and 36 percent of those ages 3 to five.

I'm assuming those figures are also relevant to Seattle's situation. Nevertheless, there's a gleam of *enlightened self-interest* that bodes well for resolution of other important issues that currently divide the nation. But we need to go beyond proven pilot programs and agree upon well-meaning policies and legislation. Now, we need to muster the necessary human and financial resources to meet overall goals. I never have been a champion of "unfunded mandates."

The Boeing Company continues to place early childhood education at the top of its list of education issues. The company's 2024 website stated:

Our education efforts take a holistic approach to prepare the next generation for success in the 21st century. We take the long view that early learning is essential to giving all students a strong and equal start in life. Boeing helps early learners in their formative years by supporting efforts to improve early caregivers' preparation and to drive awareness of early education's importance.

In spring of 1985, at the same time as my role in the Roundtable Education Committee began winding down, I was selected as president of the University of Washington Alumni Association. It was a distinct honor, especially since I was the first African American and person of color to be so recognized in the association's one-hundred-year history.

At the end of my term in 1986, the board of the association asked me and a guest of my choice to be goodwill ambassadors on a 12-day cruise in a show of appreciation. This would be a reenactment of the route the ill-fated *Titanic* had taken in 1912. Other invited guests included movie stars/entertainers from a bygone era, such as Virginia Mayo, Cornell Wilde, Herb Jeffries, and Helen O'Connell. Robin Beckham, a very bright and vivacious woman, was my guest. She fit in well with the personalities onboard. Robin became known in her own right in the TV broadcasting business in Pittsburg and Savannah as a talk-show host.

The cruise began in South Hampton, England, and eventually docked in New York City. Mingling among those stars, and the great musical entertainment, made the cruise an experience of a lifetime.

CHAPTER 23

Captivated

Our first date, 1988.

IN APRIL OF 1988, I was asked by Mal Stamper, president of The Boeing Company, to attend a national conference of the National Action Council for Minorities in Engineering (NACME) in Houston, Texas. Mal was a member of its board of trustees, but unable to attend. He wanted me to represent him because the primary mission of the organization is to increase the number of underrepresented minorities in engineering and computer science—a theme under the purview of my office. Though it was a last-minute request, I agreed to adjust my schedule and attend the three-day conference. (I could read an org chart.)

I arrived at the hotel in Houston late in the afternoon on a Thursday. As with all such conferences, a reception was held that night and Boeing was one of the sponsors. I entered the reception room and recognized a few people from past such conferences. However, I strode past them because I couldn't help but see the profile of a striking Black woman in a green silk dress!

I was immediately drawn to her. I am not a forward person, but I walked over and tapped her on the shoulder. She looked around—and then looked down—and said, "Oh! There you are!" She was over six feet tall and I'm five-feet-ten with my shoes on.

I replied, "I just wanted to introduce myself." Which I did. She said her name was Carmen Walker. I went on to say, "I hope you don't mind my being so forward. I tend to introduce myself at conferences like this to get to know the attendees." I lied! That was the first time I had done anything like that. We exchanged niceties.

There was another reception hour after the next day of meetings. When I entered the room, I saw Carmen. She walked over to me with another woman and said to her friend, "This is the Carver guy I was mentioning."

Then to me, she said, "Carver, this is one of my best friends, Kathy, a schoolmate of mine when we attended Clemson University."

We started talking and laughing. We all clicked together. I suggested that we go to the hotel restaurant and have dinner and said that I would buy.

The dinner was one of the most enjoyable evenings I had ever experienced. Both women were very intelligent and extremely humorous and engaging. Carmen told me that she worked for the Duke Power Company in Charlotte, North Carolina, as a manager in their Human Resources division. She had also been asked to come to the conference at the last minute by the director of her department.

Our dinner lasted at least two hours. Although both women were very attractive, I was fixated on Carmen's unique beauty. After we parted the restaurant, I went to my room and immediately telephoned her room. I asked that we have lunch together on the last day of the conference. The lunch was great, and I let her know that I'd make it a point to stay in touch with her.

After I got back home to Seattle, I found an invitation in the mail from Jackie Goldfarb, the wife of a longtime friend, Michael Goldfarb. It was an invitation to his fiftieth birthday party at their new home in Medina, Washington, walking distance from the Bill Gates, Jr's., compound. I immediately thought that the May party would be a great time for me to invite Carmen as my date to meet some of my Seattle friends. Thankfully, Carmen agreed!

Carmen flew up to Seattle and stayed at my home in the Magnolia district. On the evening of Michael's party, a long limousine arrived to pick us up. Joe Diamond, the legendary Seattle parking-lot magnate, and his wife were the other couple in the limo. Champagne was served and we drove off to the party.

As I recall, there were about twenty couples at the party. Carmen had no problem whatsoever connecting with everyone there. By the end of the evening, I swear, she was addressing nearly everyone by their first name. I was amazed. So were the other guests.

Carmen and I were married December 31, 1988.

The only problem with that evening was that Carmen probably thought I partied that way all the time. Wrong!

Carmen blew me away that evening. I was truly smitten.

The next thing I knew I was flying down to Charlotte to see her and some of her friends. Then we drove to Anderson, South Carolina, in her sleek red Corvette to meet her parents and the rest of her family. Her mother and father were truly wonderful, salt-of-the-earth people. They didn't display any pretense whatsoever and welcomed me with their Southern hospitality.

Contrary to my basic personality of not making knee-jerk decisions, I was seriously thinking of asking her to marry me. I hesitated when she told me the story of her leaving Anderson to enter Clemson University. She had cried in the arms of her mother and father on the porch of their home!

I asked her, "How far away is Clemson from Anderson?"

She said, "Fifteen miles."

Here I am, thinking of taking her 3,000 miles away to Seattle when she was crying about 15 miles?! I felt I had no chance whatsoever of taking her away to Seattle.

And there was another hurdle I had to clear. When I did ask Carmen to marry me, she said, "You first have to ask my father for his approval."

Here I am, an older guy who'd been divorced; Carmen and I were mature adults. Why did I have to jump through *that* hoop? But I promised that I would go through the

My son Craig was my best man.

ritual. Carmen set up a dinner at an old mansion in Anderson with her parents where I planned to ask for her hand.

I was on pins and needles. What if he said no? As dinner progressed, I finally launched a long, impassioned plea for his permission. While I was talking, he did not look up as he continued to eat his fried chicken.

Then in between bites, without looking up, he finally said, "Carmen is a grown woman. She's old enough to make her own decisions. Could you please pass the salt?"

What an anti-climax!

Six months later, with my son Craig as best man, Carmen, the city of Anderson's first Black Beauty Queen, and I became husband and wife. Craig got to know Carmen better than Cynthia and Clark because he was living in Seattle when I met her. He was the only sibling in Seattle at the time and he connected well with Carmen. I was proud to have him by my side. As of 2024, 36 years later, I still love her with all my heart and soul. Marrying her transformed my life and made me a better person in incalculable ways.

∽

CHAPTER 24:

Family Matters

WHEN I FIRST JOINED The Boeing Company, Cynthia was attending Howard University, the alma mater of her grandmother, Virginia Clark Gayton. She then transferred to George Washington University where she graduated with a BA in International Relations. She came back to Seattle from time to time in the 1980s, primarily during the holiday seasons, to visit with me and other family members. While in DC, most of her communications with me and my mother were through her beautifully written letters, which we both saved over the years.

Cynthia held a variety of jobs for a few years and decided to enter George Mason Law School where she graduated in 1995 with her JD Degree in Intellectual Property. She became a member of the Virginia Bar as well as the District of Columbia Bar. This was the beginning of a long and fruitful career as an attorney and a highly regarded academic.

Clark considered himself a "New Yorker," moving there in 1984 after graduating from the prestigious Berklee College of Music in Boston on a full scholarship. In New York, he began performing and recording as a professional musician—playing trombone, cornet, tuba, and keyboards! Clark performed with some of the finest musicians in the world, including the likes of Lionel Hampton Band, the Duke Ellington Orchestra, Ray Charles, the Quincy Jones Orchestra, and Nancy Wilson.

Although Cynthia and Clark had not been able to visit Seattle often since they left high school to live back East, the kids (especially Cynthia) and I talk often on the phone and never miss calling on holidays and birthdays. It's still not enough!

Craig received his BA degree in Sociology at the University of Washington in the spring of 1988. He enjoyed the subject matter but had no burning desire to become a sociologist. He was dating a young lady who attended a community college and was majoring in nursing. She enjoyed the health sciences and nudged Craig in that direction. Craig took courses in biology, physics, and chemistry. This was a great surprise to his mother and me. He had never demonstrated an interest in these areas during his K-12 years. Because of his dyslexia, we did not have high expectations of him academically in any area. Out of nowhere, Craig started getting As and Bs in the science- and math-related courses he was taking in community colleges, which he needed for his new interest: entry into dental school.

Ultimately, he was accepted into dental schools at the University of California in San Francisco and at Howard University in Washington, DC. There was a caveat for entry into Cal. He needed another chemistry class before he could be accepted. He had no problem taking the class except that it would delay his entry for one year, whereas he could enter Howard immediately. Craig said he did not want to wait a year because he was getting too old. (Too old at 29? Yikes!)

Craig decided to have his tuition paid for at Howard by applying for the US Army Health Professions Scholarship Program. The application was approved. He entered the program in 1994. He had to commit to serve in the Army for two to six years after receiving his DDS with the rank of captain.

I did not give much thought to being twenty years older than Carmen. She was very mature and wise. I felt that our personalities meshed. The adage that "age is just a number" is a reality with us. She would never be another "mother figure" to my three children, but she could become more like an "older sister" to them over time.

Carmen and I wanted at least one child together. I was somewhat concerned about how my older children would feel about having a half brother or sister. Considering Carmen's age and that she had never had a child but wanted to, I assumed that Cynthia, Clark, and Craig expected us to have at least one child.

Clark Gayton graduating from the Berklee College of Music in Boston in 1984.

Craig Gayton graduating from Howard Dental School in 1995 with his best friend Randy Wilkens at his side 1995.

The Gayton Clan, 1982.

On December 5th, 1990, two years after Carmen and I were married, Chandler Walker Gayton was born in Seattle. Chan was healthy and there were no complications during the delivery. Craig, who was taking post graduate courses, took time to welcome his young brother into the world. He came to Carmen's room less than an hour after the delivery.

The doctor, Craig, and I were giving each other high-fives and dancing. Carmen looked wonderful after the operation. But I could see her getting a bit peeved. She finally said, "You guys are having way too much fun!" She was halfway kidding. Carmen and I really appreciated Craig being in the room with us. Naturally, it created a lifetime bond between him and Chan.

At the time of Chan's birth, Cynthia and Clark had been living on the East coast for years. I would see them from time to time on holidays. But the thing that kept me connected with them were the loving letters and cards I received from them and the long telephone conversations I continue to have remind me of how special they are.

Whenever Cynthia, Clark, Craig, and Chandler got together, the older ones recognized that I treated Chan differently from the way I treated them when they were growing up. They said I was less strict with Chandler than I was with them. When I think about it, I tend to agree. I treat my older kids the way my dad treated me. I can't remember him ever treating me in a mean way. I never remember my father saying he loved me. But I knew by his example that he did.

I have expressed myself in a more caring way with Chan than with my older children. I've noticed with Chandler that it was easier telling him that I love him. Recognizing this frailty, I try to tell my older kids that I love them. The fact remains: I truly love all my children.

One thing is certain: they have been more outspoken and direct with me than I ever was with my father. I never confronted or challenged him. I felt that doing so would be disrespectful. However, I do not feel that my kids are disrespectful when they challenge me. I'm often learning from them, but I must admit, sometimes their comments give me a twinge of pain. When that happens, I try to ease the pain with a joke. The pain goes up a notch when they shoot back with, "Aw, Dad—not that old joke again!" In all circumstances, the pain ultimately goes away.

CHAPTER 25

Tech Prep/Applied Academics

BY 1990, THE EFFORTS of my office to involve The Boeing Company in developing new K-12 programs were bearing fruit. As a result, the company made a "Contributions Projection" for K-12 programs that totaled nearly $20 million in cash and in-kind contributions over the next five years. The company's commitment and involvement in pre-college programs, with significant emphasis on students of color, endures to this day.

In 1991, I was promoted to the executive pay grade level with a new title: Corporate Director of the Office of College and University Relations (CURO). My job was to manage and coordinate all external college relations programs and maintain cognizance of all university relations activities. I reported to Larry McKean, Corporate Senior Vice President of Human Resources.

Although my direct line of interface was with Larry, I also connected regularly with five other corporate senior vice presidents: Executive Vice President Doug Biegle, Bud Coffey for Government Relations, Deane Cruze for Operations, Bert Welliver for Engineering, as well as Harold Carr for Public Relations. Connecting with so many senior VPs did not box me in at all. In fact, it gave me considerable flexibility. With all of my responsibilities, they all knew that I could not, ordinarily, be available at a moment's notice.

Here are some of the broad areas I began to address:

- Improving the corporation's college intern and scholarship programs
- Developing an effective minority and female recruitment program
- Correlating research within company goals and objectives to determine how well the processes were working
- Streamlining recruitment processes of students to meet the needs of the company more effectively
- Collecting and sharing company-wide research results
- Directing funds to colleges and universities that more directly benefit the company
- Developing a database on university programs and activities

All of these initiatives grew out of one simple fact: Boeing needed an appropriately trained workforce. Therefore, Boeing needed to have ongoing relationships with all levels of the education system if the college and university programs were to be effective. The ultimate goal we were attempting to achieve was a seamless pathway between K-12 programs and colleges and universities.

We started pulling together a corporate-wide Committee of College and University Relations, which I chaired. I went to our division engineering organizations (Boeing Commercial Airplanes, Boeing Computer Services, and Boeing Defense & Space) to find people for my committee. I paired most of the committee members with institutions they had graduated from, so they already had familiarity, experience, and connections with the colleges.

The schools we reached out to were Boeing's primary sources for the hiring of future employees. My committee members' role was to advise faculty members about the kinds of courses and research that were relevant to companies like Boeing and their schools where possible Boeing funding would have the most impact.

A similar committee was eventually established with members from Boeing business division organizations. We asked those members to reach out to universities where we recruited most of our business majors.

Both committees had members who represented Historically Black Colleges and Universities (HBCUs) as well as research institutions like Stanford, Massachusetts Institute of Technology, Cal Tech, and the University of Washington. All of these schools were relevant to the needs of the company.

These Boeing committee members, whom we referred to as "focal points," would meet on a regular basis with their counterparts at the universities they represented to exchange information, emphasize best practices, and identify areas that needed improvement. I chaired regular meetings with the focal points. I learned a lot about the company and the various universities through my role as the organizer/leader of the committees. Not being an engineering expert, I did a great deal of listening, while also knowing when it was necessary to speak up.

I was excited about the establishment of the committees. And the committee members felt the same. Their committee work took them out of their day-to-day roles within their divisions; it connected them with the outside education world, and it was stimulating. Committee members and their counterparts in education learned from each other. Each benefited in the long run. Boeing could build better products, and the universities could provide more relevant courses and research. A great example of win-win!

Soon after my promotion, I had an interesting conversation in the corporate offices with Dean Cruze, who had been recently promoted to the position of senior vice president of operations. He congratulated me on what my office was doing concerning higher education matters, but he had a point of view that he wanted to discuss with me. I braced myself. Dean was a very likeable guy, but he never minced his words. I really appreciated this.

Over the years, Boeing had expended a lot of money in the engineering programs at four-year research universities like the University of Washington. Dean questioned the direction of the company in what he considered to be this inordinate investment of money. He emphatically pointed out that it takes relatively few research engineers to design a new jetliner; but it takes literally *thousands* of technicians and technologists to build it! (Technicians are usually defined as those with two-year applied Associate of Arts degrees from two-year community or technical colleges. Technologists are considered those with applied four-year Bachelor of Science in Engineering Technology degrees [BSET] from colleges like Cogswell College North.)

Dean went on to say that the *technicians* needed to be more highly skilled because of the rapid changes in technology.

Lester Thurow, the esteemed economist from M.I.T., was on the same page as Dean. He pointed out that America does well in educating the top 25 percent

...what's the use of having someone invent new products if others can't produce them? Consequently, the real route to success is to also educate the majority of the population who will be the producers.

of the labor force, the group that will invent the new products of tomorrow. But what's the use of having someone invent new products if others can't produce them? Consequently, the real route to success is to also educate the majority of the population who will be the producers.

Dean's enlightened comments also fit within the company's concept of "design-build." This means that the research engineers understand and work more closely with the technologists, *and vice versa*. He correctly pointed out that new age technicians do not necessarily require a four-year degree like those offered at a research institution like the University of Washington. I told him I agreed with his insightful comments and that I was aware of a new education program called "applied academics." This was something that we, as a company, could possibly build upon. Dean energized me!

During my years of working within the K-12 arena, I met often with the training manager focal points throughout all the divisions at Boeing. I was introduced to the training managers by my assistant director, Bob McKenzie. Bob was a former Navy fighter pilot, and he had an exemplary background as training manager for the Boeing Aerospace Division for many years. Bob had done the yeoman's work on organizing the committees.

Bob introduced me to Gene Dight, who took Bob's place as training manager for the Aerospace Division. Gene also served as the company's business representative on the King County Vocational Advisory Committee.

I was especially interested in a program that Gene mentioned to me. Gene related a concept called "applied academics" which focused on upgrading traditional vocational education. In these upgrades for future technical workers, emphasis is placed on needing to negotiate conflicts, work with rapidly changing technology, and communicate clearly. Additionally, the new workforce needed to be technically skilled and computer literate, with a grounding in traditional courses in social sciences and humanities in order to participate as active team players.

The applied courses were taken at the high school level (grades 9 through 12). These were Applied Physics, Principles of Technology, Applied Communication, and Applied Mathematics. These courses were designed to give high school students the groundwork they needed to pursue two-year associate of arts (AA) technical programs at community colleges. The courses had been developed by a nationwide consortium of vocational education agencies. With the help of our education and training managers—and especially Gene Dight—Boeing began encouraging schools to adopt this type of curriculum.

Research by the consortium indicated that over 60 percent of students involved in applied academics planned to continue their education after high school. That figure was much higher than the national norm for traditional high school vocational students.

The information Gene gave me regarding applied course work related directly to what Dean Cruze and I had talked about. The challenge, in my mind, was this: How can we get significant numbers of students to take these applied courses that will benefit high-tech companies like ours?

I wanted to encourage participation in the applied academics curricula. So, beginning in 1990, my office (CURO) recommended—and was granted—a $300,000 pool to pay up to 60 percent of the costs of teaching the curricula. The maximum we could grant per school was $30,000. As a result of our efforts, approximately 100 schools in Washington state began teaching at least one applied academic course.

As a supplement to the applied academics campaign by Boeing, we initiated a "teacher intern" program. Teachers could apply for paid internships at Boeing in school districts where our applied academics initiative was established. During a six-week period in the summer, ten teachers worked in technical areas of the company and were paid $3,000 each. To strengthen their grasp of science and mathematics, the teachers were required to do a ten-day "walkthrough" of the applied academics curricula toward the end of their internships and provide written reports about what they learned from their experiences and how they were to incorporate their knowledge within the applied academic curricula they were teaching at their home school.

The overall administration of this pilot effort was the responsibility of my office. But we worked very closely with the respective division training managers implementing the program. It was truly an interactive team effort. There was a great deal of excitement among the Training Managers to be at the front end of this innovative and much-needed program. They felt they were helping to make science and math more meaningful and relevant for young students.

Word of our applied academics program began to spread throughout the country. The Center for Occupational Research and Development (CORD) out of Waco, Texas, contacted me. Dan Hull, CEO of CORD, suggested that we meet. As the result of the Boeing initiatives, CORD began to see a substantial increase in the sales of their materials—especially throughout the State of Washington. Dan Hull wanted to find out about our educational initiatives which were impacting their sales.

CORD published books and teaching materials. They produced contextual learning publications on applied mathematics, principles of technology (applied physics), applied mathematics, and applied communications. Basically, these were all STEM-related (Science, Technology, Engineering & Mathematics) materials focusing on solving real world problems. I invited Dan to come to Boeing to meet with me and our division training managers. In that meeting, Dan mentioned an educational process called "Two-Plus-Two," or "Tech Prep," which dovetailed the last two years of high school with the two-year community and technical college. Students would graduate high school with an Associates of Arts degree (AA) at the end of the senior year. Given the technology interests of Boeing and other manufacturing companies in the state, I felt that Tech Prep would be a natural fit with the applied academic initiatives of the company and our education community partners.

The Two-Plus-Two/Tech Prep concept was originally conceived and promoted by Dale Parnell, president of the American Association of Community and Junior Colleges. In his book *The Neglected Majority*, published in 1985, Parnell directed our attention to the nation's high school students who were not

(Left to right) Boeing Commercial Airplanes Training Manager Rick Lengyel, President of the American Association of Community Colleges Dale Parnell, me, and Bruce Gissing, executive vice president of Boeing Commercial Airplanes, the division where most Tech Prep students, school teachers, advisors, and training managers participated in the program.

heading to traditional colleges. The book explored ideas of connecting education to career pathways and integrated learning. Parnell contended that special needs and talented students deplete most public-school resources, including teachers' time and energy. As a result, kids in the middle quartiles typically receive minimal attention. Often, they end up with an unfocused education that doesn't prepare them for either college or work. As a result, many of these students become lost within the system.[42]

Dr. Parnell's book provided the framework for what he called the Tech Prep associate degree that would build a stronger relationship between high school and the community college providing a basis for today's career and technical students to be successful in highly skilled and in-demand jobs.

Dan Hull introduced me to Dale Parnell in the late 1980s. My relationship with Dale continued over the years until his passing in 2017.

There were clear positive results of the initiatives led by my office concerning Tech Prep coupled with the applied academic course enhancement activities. As a result, I recommended to my superiors that we expand our efforts to include "articulation," i.e., partnership grants/funds to schools and colleges who provided the best proposals to the company. This recommendation was wholeheartedly approved.

During this first phase from 1990-1993, a pilot program was initiated whereby the company provided a total of over $3 million in funding to various high schools and community colleges in the state who pledged to work together to establish applied academic programs and develop articulation agreements. Specifically, the funds were utilized as follows:

- Through an application process, seed grants were given to 60 high schools throughout the state to implement applied academic courses in applied physics, applied mathematics, and applied communications.
- Articulation grants were awarded to community and technical colleges to develop Tech Prep curricula in partnership with high schools that would allow high school juniors and seniors to take courses for credit toward an associate in arts degree.
- Boeing continued its six-week summer high school teacher internship program, providing applied academics teachers experience in the manufacturing workplace environment that could be taken back to the classroom.

I held many discussions about Tech Prep with Earl Hale, the executive director of the Washington State Board of Community Colleges. We also met with Bill Selby, vice president of Boeing Commercial Airplanes in Renton, who also served on that board. I met with Bill often about the program, which he strongly endorsed. He and I, as well as Earl, met with the state Legislature in early 1991. This led to the approval of the Community and Technical College Act. This statute accomplished two things: It established the requirements for a two-year, postsecondary "technical degree" and merged the state's existing technical and community college systems.

This decision had special significance to me. It acknowledged the efforts of my role with The Boeing Company concerning Cogswell College. It also reflected my office's emphasis on bolstering the rigor of technical education. And it showed how Boeing's effort was having a systemic impact on postsecondary education. Great things!

Historically, "vocational education" had been seen as a dumping ground for those students who could not succeed in traditional colleges (academic curricula). This merger now brought greater prestige to the concept of vocational/technical education. This merger also stressed the industry's need for technical employees with a strong applied academic base and the ability to work within increasingly complex and competitive manufacturing organizations.

The fruit of all these efforts was a new, two-year AA degree in manufacturing technology, approved by the state based upon the Tech Prep concept. As the program developed, it was assumed that students would remain in their respective high schools while taking the courses. This was not an ironclad requirement for receiving the grant. (The current Washington state-wide Running Start Program where 11th and 12th grade high school students take two-year associate degree classes at community and technical colleges is based upon the Boeing model. The only difference is that the Tech Prep classes would be held at the high schools.)

A second phase of the Tech Prep program was initiated by my office toward the end of 1992. We formalized a partnership called the Manufacturing Technology Advisory Group. Boeing team leaders worked along with education representatives from other industries, including Hewlett Packard, Simpson Timber Company, and the Eldec Corporation. We also included State leaders from labor and education. The purpose of the committee was to support the development of a manufacturing education program for Washington State's existing and future workforce. MTAG's priorities directly related to Washington state's new Community and Technical College Act. Here are the things we focused on:

- Identifying basic manufacturing entry level skills
- Soliciting involvement of other manufacturing firms in the State
- Advising secondary schools and community and technical colleges on a core curriculum that responds to industry's needs
- Determining methods of measuring students' attainment of competencies
- Developing a recommended process by which industry becomes involved effectively in Tech Prep

In 1994, the work of MTAG was enhanced by a National Science Foundation grant of $500,000 to help the group to move forward. Receiving such an award from such a prestigious organization gave us enormous credibility—not only in the State of Washington, but nationally.

A third phase of the company's Tech Prep program began in 1993. We initiated a paid summer internship program *for students* who were enrolled in the Manufacturing Technology Program. This internship provided the students with three progressive summer sessions, beginning after their 11th grade.

They were introduced to career opportunities in manufacturing, taught basic factory skills, and advised on selecting specialty fields within manufacturing. The sessions were coordinated with high schools and colleges to ensure that the instruction complemented the students' academic courses.

Because of labor laws and Boeing labor union agreements, no one under the age 16 was allowed to work on the factory floors. That was a hurdle we had to get over. But I was able to receive approval from our corporate legal counsel to allow these internship students in. I also worked with the International Association of Manufacturing (IAM) as well as the Seattle Professional Engineering Employees Association (SPEEA) to get their approval and support of the program. After I explained to them the intent and details, each union became an enthusiastic supporter of the internships.

In the summer of 1993, we had twenty-five student interns. The number reached 300 in 1997. At the same time, the company continued the teacher internships for secondary and two-year colleges that had started in the first phase of the program. Boeing's investment in internships over the following five years exceeded $3.5 million.

Students benefited from work-based experiences coupled with a strong applied academic curriculum. Our student internship pilot program clearly demonstrated that focused, on-the-job experience can open up new and relevant worlds to students. One student's comment expressed the feelings of many, when he said, "I learned more math during my four-week internship than four years in school."

Students who took the applied technology/Tech Prep classes as well as at least one summer internship program were being hired *directly after graduation*. Why? Because Boeing manufacturing supervisors were exuberant about their skill levels! This was the first time in 35 years that Boeing was hiring students directly out of high school.

With Boeing's continuous learning imperative for employees, these new young hires were encouraged to continue their learning. Through the company's tuition reimbursement program, employees can take classes for free if they're enrolled in accredited post-secondary institutions.

I remember a conversation I had with Alan Mulally, then the senior vice president for Airplane Development in the Boeing Commercial Airplanes Group (BCAG). In 1995, he had promoted the overarching theme for the entire corporation as simply "Working Together." He basically meant not letting the cultures of the various divisions (groups) hinder the needs of the whole; and at the same time, utilizing the various cultural perspectives to continuously improve the company's products and services.

In mid-1995, I met with Alan and several other division/group executives to discuss corporate-wide college recruitment policy while the company was experiencing an economic slowdown. Alan clarified, in a direct but respectful way, how he saw my corporate role in developing the new policy. He said, "Gayton, remember. It's the profit centers who pay for your corporate salaries."

By "profit centers," he meant the Commercial Airplanes Group, the Boeing Defense and Space Group, and Boeing Computer Services. Basically, he was saying not to run off making policies from on high without talking things over with the divisions first. In other words, "Working Together." I could not agree with him more.

Alan Mulally served as President of the Boeing Commercial Airplane Group (BCAG) from 1998-2005 and later went on to lead the Ford Motor Company as CEO from 2006-2014.

In June of 1995, I was asked to represent the company in Washington, DC, before the US Senate Sub-Committee on Education chaired by Senator Jim Jeffords of Vermont. They had asked a variety of innovative education leaders from across the country to testify and I was one of them. My testimony focused on our Boeing Tech Prep program.

Afterwards, Bill Baranger, the senior vice president of Congressional Affairs for The Boeing Company, made these comments to me in a letter:

The Committee staff felt that your presentation on the Boeing Tech Prep program was excellent. They said that it contributed significantly to the overall success of the hearings by illustrating business's role in vocational education. Feedback from Senator Jeffords and Senator Gorton was also very positive.

I cannot emphasize enough that the
evolution of the education programs that
were implemented throughout the Boeing
Corporation required incredible collaboration.
We had buy-in and support at all levels
within the company.

After the hearing, Washington's Senator Gorton sought me out and expressed his congratulations for my remarks.

Senator Edward Kennedy was also at the hearing. A month or so later, I was asked to give a presentation on our education programs for a panel held at the John F. Kennedy Library and Museum in Boston. I was the only panel member from outside the State of Massachusetts. Senator Kennedy thanked me afterwards.

I cannot emphasize enough that the evolution of the education programs that were implemented throughout The Boeing Company required incredible collaboration. We had buy-in and support at all levels within the company. We also had the buy-in of the surrounding communities of the company profit centers. This included education and labor leaders as well as buyers and suppliers. As the Corporate Director of Education Relations and Training, I couldn't just wave a magic wand and expect all of these programs to automatically happen! Their success depended on the dedication and commitment of scores of Boeing employees from throughout the company.

Tech Prep has evolved within the State of Washington since that early 1990 pilot funded and coordinated by The Boeing Company. It and Running Start have become essential, broad-based elements of the rubric of "Career Technical Education" (CTE), what used to be called "vocational education." The Washington State Office of Public Instruction (OSPI) recently issued a

Looking Back:
Essential Outcomes of Tech Prep

IN HINDSIGHT, I see a number of essential outcomes that resulted from our Tech Prep efforts:

- Close communication was developed between educators and the private sector. Programs that the education community develops should reflect the basic kinds of skills and attitudes that employers expect.

- There was wide involvement of all players. The Boeing team was very pleased to see high school teachers, two- and four-year college instructors, state vocational staff, union representatives, and private trade schools, all sitting down together to design programs. This epitomizes, to me, the essence of what true education should be about: teaching and learning together.

- Academic and vocational faculty discovered mutual needs and concerns. Each area began to learn much from one another and found that students responded positively as subject matter was reinforced across disciplines.

- Equivalent credit was awarded for equivalent outcomes. I was enthusiastic about representing The Boeing Company on a special state legislative taskforce. This taskforce recommended that certain vocational course work, approved by local districts, be accepted as the academic equivalent to core requirements for entry into the state's university system. The Higher Education Coordinating Board of Washington reviewed and approved this recommendation. As a result, students began to enroll more freely into many of the high school vocational courses knowing that this would not close the doors to their achieving a baccalaureate degree. Fundamentally, it was about opening doors for more pathways to higher education but maintaining quality in the process.

- New coursework was developed, instead of old ones being warmed over. Tech Prep (Two-Plus-Two) requires instructors to examine, totally, the content of what they teach. It may require replacing old content with new, even adding new courses. The process requires community and technical colleges to review seriously what is taught in high school so that students' precious time is not spent going over ground that they've already covered. Truly competency-based approaches began to be developed. If students were sent to a community college with a portfolio of skills already mastered, they would not have to take a test to prove what they already knew.

report about the numbers of students involved in all these programs. As of 2018, 24,000 students were taking Tech Prep/CTE dual-credit courses. Additionally, 10,400 students were taking Running Start professional/technical courses, and over 100,000 students were taking CTE/applied academic courses. The Running Start program had over 27,000 students, in-total, taking both professional/technical courses as well as traditional courses like English and social sciences. In 2022, Governor Jay Inslee signed legislation making College in the High School classes free. The law went into effect in 2023. Within the first year of the dual credit courses, enrollment increased by 10,000 students. The new legislation supporting underrepresented students was 30 years in the wait, but better late than never.

Of all the activity during these years devoted to building Tech Prep, one event stands out to me as an exceptionally proud moment. During the first phase of implementing our Tech Prep program, our model began to receive national—and even international—recognition. As a result, in May of 1992, I was asked to speak to the European Communities [replaced by the European Union in 1993] /United States Conference. It was held in Noordwijk, The Netherlands, on June 25th and 26th. The conference was organized on behalf of the European Communities, composed of 34 nations, in cooperation with the United States Department of Education. The topic of the conference was "Schools and Industry: Partners for a Quality Education."

This meeting grew out of the Transatlantic Declaration on relations between the European Community and the United States, signed in November 1990 by President Bush and President Jacques Delors. The partnership was based upon continuous efforts to strengthen cooperation in various fields. Those included education and culture as well as academic and youth exchanges. It was agreed that the topic of their first exchange would focus on partnership between education and industry. This would be followed with a wider effort to have a series of joint events of mutual interest.

At the time, I was serving as a board member of CEO Dan Hull's Center for Occupational Research and Development (CORD) which had as its primary role publishing applied academic textbooks for schools and colleges. Also on that board was Betsy Brand, assistant secretary of the Vocational and Adult Education Division of the US Department of Education. Betsy knew of the educational programs being initiated under my leadership at Boeing. As the primary US organizer of the conference, she felt The Boeing Company program would be a good business representative for the theme of the conference.

Boeing executives felt I should accept Betsy's invitation to speak at the conference for two reasons. First, to have an international platform to share what we were doing concerning vocational education. Second, to speak about some of the factors that made it difficult for Boeing to be competitive against the European giant jet airliner company, Airbus Industries, that received significant government subsidies. Such subsidies placed The Boeing Company in a disadvantaged position.

Dean Thornton, the president of the Boeing Commercial Airplane Company, helped me develop my speech. The first part related to the competitive disadvantage issue. The remainder focused on our Tech Prep program. The feedback I received from the speech was extremely positive.

For Boeing to allow me to make that speech, as the only US corporation on the two-day agenda, was a once-in-a-lifetime opportunity. There I was, looking out into this huge auditorium with scores of representatives from around the world! They were all listening through their headphones from interpreters. Remembering this experience still gives me an immense rush of pride.

CHAPTER 26

Learnings from the Boeing Years

LOOKING BACK ON MY 19 YEARS with The Boeing Company, I must say I was very fortunate to have worked in leadership roles with the foremost aerospace company in the world. Being human, I did not achieve complete success in all my endeavors within The Boeing Company. However, I feel very proud of the accomplishments of the teams I led over my two decades. The education projects assigned at the company bore fruit over the years because of the outstanding folks I worked with in the company as well as leaders throughout the state in the private and public sectors. I was very proud of how the company committed to relationships with the external education communities. It's about working together and understanding the roles of the key players. It's about working within the framework of continuous quality improvement.

Much of the internal training role of my office was guided by my staff—especially Bob Mckenzie, my assistant director. His long history in training and his special relationship with the various division training managers was invaluable. He understood that our corporate role was not to direct the divisions but to work with division managers to come up with agreed upon and effective policies within the best interests of our employees and our customers, stockholders, and our community.

There were two individuals who tied the loose ends together in the Educational Relations and Training Office and subsequently, the College and University Relations Office for nearly fifteen years. They were my administrative assistants Kathy Wyatt and Barbara Overman. Both were university graduates with Baccalaureate degrees who excelled in writing, computer skills, and people skills. It was because of them that our entire office was admired and respected. I was indeed fortunate to have them as my colleagues!

Many accolades came from our work—too many to list here. But as I wound down my years at Boeing, two recognitions deserve mentioning. In 1995, the prestigious National Employment Management Association presented Larry Mckean, the company's senior vice president for Human Resources and my boss, the Pericles Award. This award is presented each year to the most innovative and effective human resource program in the nation. Larry received it for our school-to-career program. That was followed up in 1997 with the National Alliance of Business (NAB) recognizing the company as having the best school-to-work program in the nation.

I was overwhelmed with pride about the two human resource recognitions. I was especially pleased that I had a leadership role for each. I do not recall any similar recognitions for a human resources program for the entire company during my nearly twenty years at Boeing.

I announced my retirement from Boeing when Governor Gary Locke asked me to join his executive cabinet as commissioner of the Washington State Employment Security Department. When the word spread, I received a wonderful gift. On behalf of Boeing Corporate employees, my boss Larry McKean gave me a large, framed photograph of the 1954 prototype Boeing 707 jet airliner flying over the University of Washington campus. That plane changed the course of the aerospace industry. The photo was signed by both University of Washington President Richard McCormick and Boeing CEO Phil Condit. Each wrote a message expressing their best wishes for a job well done. The picture was especially moving in that it represented over 40 years of my close relationship with two institutions that transformed my life in so many positive ways. As it is said: a picture is worth a thousand words.

The programs I was leading were recognized in
The Boeing Company's May/June 1990 issue of Managers.

A framed and signed photograph of the Boeing 707, the company's jetliner that
changed the course of history, flying over the University of Washington was a special
and meaningful retirement gift.

Management Take-aways for Life

WHILE I WAS AT BOEING, a number of key principles and concepts were ingrained into my management style. I consider them important. They transferred to other positions I held—in government, in community-based organizations, and in my private life

Large System Integration

One day I was walking in front of the Boeing Corporate Offices with Company President Mal Stamper. The sunny sky was clear. Suddenly we heard the roar of a gleaming 747 jet airliner landing at Boeing Field. Stamper pointed to the huge jet and said, "Carver, that beautiful plane was designed and built by thousands of employees working together. There is not one person who would know how to put that plane together alone. It is the ultimate example of 'large system integration.' Think about it. What a miraculous achievement!" That statement made me think of large systems in general, whether in manufacturing, government, education, etc. I firmly believe that employees need to be on the same page to meet broad goals of a system. In doing so, they must know the importance and relevance of their individual roles.

Continuous Quality Improvement

All employees, especially leadership, should embrace the concept of continuous improvement of their job assignments. When I first arrived at Boeing, the leadership felt there was a malaise within pockets of the company.

The malaise was an attitude among too many workers called "If it ain't broke, don't fix it." Boeing leadership felt that our competitors in the US and Europe were more diligent on improving their products and reducing costs. I had an excellent administrative assistant who took shorthand and typed all of our communications. In the late 1980s, all corporate offices received a directive stating that our communications had to be on the Windows software for personal computers. When I told my administrative assistant, she became indignant. "I've been an excellent executive secretary for many years, and I'm not going to change." I agreed that for the most part, she did an excellent job. I also said I'd arrange for her to take computer courses. She refused. I had no choice but to have her transferred to another job within the company at the same pay level that was not affected by the directive. A year or so later, all the company divisions had to follow the directive. Because of the impact of technology within large organizations, the "If it ain't broke, don't fix it" mantra went out of style. Continuous improvement and being open to adapt to rapid change *was* the new culture.

Breaking Down Communication Barriers

Within large corporations like Boeing, there are usually many organizational units. These units have their own cultures and narrow interests. If these "silos" of interest are not broken down, they can often work to the detriment of building a product like the Boeing 747 jetliner. For example, Boeing works within the concept of design-build between the engineering and manufacturing units of the Boeing Commercial Airplane Division. Breaking down the communication silos within the division makes sure that there are representatives of the manufacturing unit working with the engineering design or research unit. This collaboration makes it easier and less costly for the manufacturing unit to build the airplane. Before the design-build concept was initiated, the tendency was to figuratively "toss the design over the fence" between design and manufacturing units, with individuals going back and forth for explanations before manufacturing could understand the design. Design-build breaks down the communication silos. My office also had to work within this concept to provide the best training possible for building aircraft. Knowing how to deal with the silo factor helped me immensely in working with other large organizations after leaving Boeing.

Working in Teams
Working within teams has been a common thread over my lifetime. It began during my years playing and coaching football in high school and college. My time at Boeing reinforced my commitment to teamwork and brought profound understanding of it. Remember Mal Stamper's words

about thousands of employees working together to build the 747? That plane is fundamentally a flying celebration of teamwork. Aristotle said, "The whole is greater than the sum of its parts." This continues to hold true for me.

The Need for a Diverse Workforce
In the late 1990s, Boeing identified diversity as one of its core business values. "Our people will reflect our geographic diversity." In those days, the position of most Fortune 500 companies was: "We will not discriminate on the basis of race, creed, sex or national origin." That's fine, but Boeing made the point that the success of its business depended on having diverse points of view from different races, cultures, sexes, creeds, etc., in order to continuously improve its products and ultimately increase shareholder value.

Leading with Principles
The successful Boeing leaders led with the principles of integrity, respect, and empathy. In my mind, the value of these principles is summed up in a conversation I had with my friend Quincy Jones, the great music producer. "Carver, if anyone disrespects you as a human being, you need to respond with these words: 'Not one drop of my self-worth depends on your acceptance of me.'" Having pride in oneself is fundamental. Treating people the way you want to be treated goes a long way in life.

PART VII

A QUANTUM LEAP INTO A NEW WORLD

CHAPTER 27

Washington State Employment Security Department

TO MY SURPRISE, on December 16, 1996, The Boeing Company announced it planned to acquire its long-time rival McDonald Douglas Aircraft Corporation. Soon after the announcement, rumors began to take place throughout the company that part of the deal was to relocate the Boeing Corporate Offices from Seattle to Chicago. If that was to come into fruition, I had no interest in making that transition. I was a longtime Seattleite with established roots in the city.

Off and on over the years, I had lived in Washinton, DC; Kansas City, Missouri; the San Francisco Bay area; and Tallahassee, Florida. While all of these places had unique and good qualities, I was always drawn back to my hometown.

It's clear that when the public and private sectors come together in an understanding and commitment to common values we hold for our society, we all rise up!

My extended family was in the city. Most of my longtime friends were here, as well as my social network. The moderate weather was to my liking and the physical surroundings of the city are the most striking in the country. Also, the education system in the Seattle Metropolitan area from K-16 was second to none in the nation at the time.

I had to consider my age in determining whether to move and pull up stakes in Seattle. Nearing 60 and close to retirement, the thought of moving to Chicago to start a new life was simply out of the question.

Probably the driving factor behind not moving to Chicago related to Carmen. She had established the beginning of a very successful real estate brokers practice in the Puget Sound area. It would not have been practical, professionally or financially, for her to come with me to Chicago. It would be to the detriment of our entire family.

Gary Locke, whom I had known for many years, was elected governor of the state in November 1996. Toward the end of December, he telephoned me and asked for permission to talk with Phil Condit, CEO of The Boeing Company. He wanted to talk about possibly hiring me as Commissioner of Washington State Employment Security Department (ESD). I said sure. Phil gave his approval.

Gary said he admired the work I had been doing on behalf of Boeing concerning education reform. He wanted that kind of skill set and perspective incorporated into ESD's programs. I told him I was flattered and interested in his proposal, and I needed to talk with a few people, especially my family, before I could give him an answer.

Carmen was in complete agreement about not moving to Chicago. Her only concern was about me driving back and forth to Olympia every day. I said I could handle it.

I called Phil's office a few days later and said I wanted to talk before I made any decision. I wanted to get a sense of what direction Corporate Headquarters was going in. How would we be impacted in light of the merger with McDonald Douglass? Phil came right to the point. He said it was too early to tell and he really did not know. More precisely, he did not extend any encouragement as to my future status. At the time, I felt he was giving me a brush-off. But looking back, I realize he probably did not know what the reconfiguration would look like so early after the merger announcement. It wasn't until September 4, 2001, that Boeing announced that Corporate Headquarters was moving to Chicago.

Phil's response certainly made me lean more toward Gary's offer. Gary needed my answer by the end of the year.

During my years with the company, I led the external education reform interests of The Boeing Company. I also led the internal restructuring of its policy direction in the education and training programs. This work gave me a feeling of satisfaction and accomplishment. As a result of my work, Boeing received a considerable amount of national and local recognition.

At the age of 58, I had no major new projects on my plate requiring my special attention. I felt prepared for a new challenge. Working for Governor Locke could fit the bill. Up until that point, I never had the experience of managing a large organization. The Employment Security Department had over 2500 employees, a budget of $500 million, and a trust fund of $1.6 billion!

Soon after I verbally accepted Governor Locke's offer, I received a telephone call from Steve Hill, Weyerhaeuser's Human Resources vice president and a member of Governor Locke's transition team. I'd known Steve since the early 1980s when he and I worked together on the Washington State Roundtable Working Committee for Education Reform. He had hired Carmen as a Human Resources Representative after our marriage. She relocated from Charlotte, North Carolina, to Seattle. Understandably, I had a great deal of respect for Steve.

Our conversation began with Steve congratulating me on my appointment. He said the Governor would appreciate having me select Cindy Zehnder as my Deputy Commissioner. She was serving as International Representative to the Teamsters Union from the Pacific Northwest. Steve described her impressive background. My response was that I had no idea who Cindy was, and that the selection of my right-hand person would likely be the most important decision of my tenure as ESD Commissioner. I told him I'd certainly consider his suggestion. Steve said, "Carver—you really have no options. What I'm saying comes directly from the Governor."

I had never been placed in such a position in all my years as a manager or executive. I told Steve I would get back with him within twenty-four hours.

I seriously considered turning down the appointment at that point. My concern had nothing to do with Cindy because I had never met her before. But the whole scenario made me think ". . . welcome to the new world of hard-nosed government politics!" I certainly felt uneasy about it.

I talked with a few people who knew Cindy. All had nothing but positive comments about her intelligence, political acumen, and connections with key movers and shakers throughout the state capital. The feedback I received convinced me that hiring her could be a win-win for me and the department. I called Steve back the next day and told him I would stay on board, but I had to talk with Cindy posthaste.

I had taught and written about organizational and general systems theory, but I had never put any of that theory into practice on a large scale. I felt it would be fun and a challenge to do that as the commissioner of ESD. The chance to run a large organization, plus my great respect and admiration for Governor Locke, convinced me to accept his offer.

I got together with Cindy that same week. I was, and continue to be, extremely impressed with Cindy Zehnder! I am grateful she was somewhat "foisted" upon me. It would have been extremely difficult for the ESD to achieve all that we did without Cindy's leadership, advice, and guidance—all of which was intertwined with a wonderful sense of humor.

I received my official letter of appointment from the Governor on March 1, 1997. My letter of response to him stated in part: "You can rest assured knowing that I will do my utmost to serve you and the citizens of the State to the best of my abilities. There are many challenges within the Employment Security Department, and I am looking forward to meeting them head on. I am in the process of building a leadership team that I am convinced will make a significant impact within the next two to four years."

Initially, Governor Locke wanted me to focus on the relevant education reform issues I had been working on at The Boeing Company. But after I joined the governor's executive team, President Bill Clinton set some major national policy in motion for welfare reform. He called it "the Welfare to Work Partnership." In line with this, Governor Locke created an initiative called "Work-First," anticipating the federal dollars that would eventually come through our ESD agency. The Clinton's guidelines would later become law with the Workforce Investment Act (WIA) of 1998.

The essence of the "Welfare to Work" was to stop allowing welfare checks and unemployment checks to be seen as "ends in themselves" for poor people. Part of the thrust was to help get the poor off welfare and to reduce the number of citizens receiving unemployment checks. But just as important was to help citizens develop the proper skills to get well-paying jobs, assisting themselves as well as businesses.

The idea of Work-First was to enlist employers who would commit to hiring welfare recipients through one-stop networks. Such systems would prioritize quality service delivery *amongst and between* each state agency involved in the one-stop network.

The theme of Work-First was adopted by all of the state agencies who would need to partner on this. They included the Employment Security Department (ESD), the Department of Social and Health Services (DSHS) the Washington State Board for Community and Technical Colleges, and the Department of Labor and Industries (L&I). We would also be partnering with representatives of the business community.

DSHS had the responsibility of providing welfare checks for the poor. The Employment Security Department provided unemployment to those eligible citizens. Labor and Industries regulated and enforced labor standards for the state, the community and technical colleges provided the training in sync with the business community's needs.

All of these entities needed to work together in order for the Work-First concept to work effectively. This meant establishing ongoing communication and cooperation among entities where *none* had existed before. We would need to "break down the silos," remove barriers, and build communication between them. For example, community colleges would need to make sure the training classes they offer were relevant to the current skill needs of businesses. Businesses would need to communicate with DSHS what educational requirements the welfare recipients needed to acquire jobs.

The common interest of key agencies and businesses was to get folks off welfare with family-wage jobs, which would enhance the economy, without having welfare checks and unemployment checks as ends in themselves. To do that, they would have to work together.

Governor Locke's direction was to establish Work-First as a temporary cash-assistance program. The goal was to help low-income families stabilize their lives so they could go to work and take better care of their families. We would help low-income families become self-sufficient by providing training and support services necessary for parents to get jobs, keep jobs, and move up the career ladder.

Within the context of Work-First, I thought carefully about the next four years. What was my vision? What goals should I set? My aspirations were as follows:

- All ESD employees will have a clear sense of their role in the agency and how it fits within the long-range mission and goals of the agency.
- Major stakeholders will have a clear understanding of their roles and responsibilities regarding the provision of jobs for the people of the State, and Employment Security will be regarded as the leader in facilitating the definition of those roles.
- The Employment Security Department will be regarded by the people of the State as truly the "Employment Agency" rather than the "unemployment agency."
- The concepts of "Team" and "Continuous Quality Improvement" will be fundamental characteristics of ESD in perception and reality.
- The Employment Security Department will be regarded as the

fundamental state entity for ensuring that welfare recipients, dislocated workers, disadvantaged youth, and job seekers generally, gain livable-wage jobs.

- All Employment Security Department managers will be regarded as leaders, facilitators, and team builders within and outside the agency in meeting the agency's mission and objectives.
- The Employment Security Department will become recognized among the top five Employment Security Departments in the nation in terms of quality of service and meeting customer needs.

There was hard work ahead to deliver on this vision and these goals. The Governor encouraged me to work, initially, with the agency leaders to break down silos so Work-First had a chance of succeeding. I understood what Governor Locke was referring to. Over my years with The Boeing Company, it was clear that *truly integrated systems were essential* to produce the best products and services. My intent was to encourage directors of the agencies to work in partnership to ensure the success of the program. From our initial conversations, I gathered that although the agencies had worked together at times over the years, true ongoing partnerships were not achieved.

I got a good feel for the partnership challenge when I met with Lyle Quasim, the highly respected secretary of the Department of Social and Health Services (DSHS). Prior to our March 1997 meeting, I only knew of Lyle through newspaper accounts. Lyle came across as very bright and engaging. I was especially impressed with his sharp wit. Although Lyle accepted the fact that it was imperative our agencies work together on the Governor's Work-First plan, he wanted to make sure I knew where ESD and I fit within the hierarchy of the Governor's executive cabinet.

First, he gave me a bit of background of DSHS. Then he went to a blackboard and drew a big chalk circle. He said words to this effect: "Carver, this circle represents me and DSHS in terms of budget and employees."

Then he drew a small, barely visible sliver. He was smiling and started to giggle as he said, "*This* represents you and your department." I fell out laughing.

I responded, "Lyle, I get the message. You're the 'main man.' I'm well aware of your point."[42]

I just knew, moving forward, that I was going to enjoy working with Lyle. His candor, sense of humor, and willingness to work as partners were crucial factors toward making my stay in Olympia enjoyable and challenging. I set up similar meetings with the other key agency directors. All the meetings were enjoyable and positive, but none were as off-the-wall and zany as my meeting with Lyle.

Along with Cindy Zehnder, I inherited an excellent leadership team. I received little, if any, push back from my division leaders. There was some wariness of my background as a former corporate executive, and the fact that I lacked an in-depth understanding of Olympia's political culture.

Chief of Staff Cindy Zehnder and me at ESD.

During one of my first executive team meetings, I asked about the importance of a program dictated to ESD from the State House of Representatives. I said that I did not consider the program as a top priority within my view of our agency's mission and vision.

One of my division directors exclaimed in disbelief, "But Commissioner—this is an 'unfunded mandate from the House'!" His emphasis was on the word "mandate."

I replied, "What you've stated is an *oxymoron*. If it is unfunded by the House, I do not consider it a 'mandate'."

There was a muffled gasp that rippled through the group. They viewed my statement as borderline insubordination.

I was pulled aside by one of my aides who advised that the mandate meant that we would have to find the dollars somehow or other within our budget. I cannot recall how the issue was ultimately resolved, but my perspective did not change. As an agency, we had to do everything possible to ensure that future "mandates" had the revenue source that did not reduce the agency's approved budget.

Another time, I had a meeting with one of my department heads and asked a variety of questions about one of her reports. I noticed she was becoming more and more peeved. I wasn't being critical of her or the report; I just wanted to have a clearer understanding. Finally, she blurted out, "I have been an administrator within ESD for *twenty years*, and no commissioner has ever questioned me the way you have!"

I was taken aback. She went on to express her loyalty to the agency as well as her competency.

Then I explained that I had no doubts about her competency, and I appreciated her years of service. I pointed out that my questioning was my style and not meant to be a personal attack. By the time the meeting was over, she had settled down. We ended up having a wonderful working relationship.

Reflecting on that conversation, I concluded the corporate/engineering culture and environment at Boeing had probably influenced how I was interacting with her. I was employed at Boeing for almost 20 years and most of my meetings were with current or former engineers. The questions would fly fast and furious! That would be the engineers' style—with no intent to embarrass any of the participants. They did not have interest in frills. They "wanted facts and data." That phrase was drilled into my mind while making presentations at Boeing.

I had been advised never to give out a report to a group of engineers before starting a meeting. Why? Because engineers will tend to read through it during the presentation and ask questions—which limits the speaker from being able to convey crucial points.

The meeting with my new department head made me realize ESD had its own culture. I needed to understand it and then strike a balance between my Boeing style of communicating and ESD's.

———

One of the primary reasons Governor Locke hired me was for my experience as a corporate executive at The Boeing Company. Knowing this, I wanted to incorporate a systemwide improvement model within ESD based upon the broad management principles I learned at Boeing. Essentially, they were:

- Establish a clear vision and mission focus for serving the citizens of the State of Washington.
- Incorporate a management system based on the concept of continuous quality improvement (CQI).
- Quality must be an attitude and behavior that permeates the entire organization.

- Deploy policy through effective performance management throughout the organization: Align the efforts of every individual and group with agency goals and objectives and establish criteria for measuring progress.

These initiatives created a framework for positive change in the workplace. Our Senior Leadership Team was led by me and included Cindy Zehnder and five other senior managers. Beginning in the spring of 1997, we agreed with previous ESD leadership that the agency needed to achieve results by having effective teams throughout the organization. However, the new direction required that we incorporate the concept of *continuous quality improvement* within those teams.

I came across many excellent leaders in the training units of the company during my time at Boeing. The most effective leaders were implementing "process improvement training" within their respective divisions (e.g., Boeing Commercial Airplanes, Boeing Defense and Space, etc.). At the Boeing Commercial group in Renton, I was impressed with an outstanding training instructor named Harry Lawson, whom I worked with for several months. Remembering Harry, I came up with the idea of having him work with ESD's Senior Leadership Team. As a Boeing "loaned executive" Harry could take responsibility to set up the framework for our process improvement system. My team enthusiastically supported this suggestion.

The next major challenge for me was to get Harry, and his direct reports within the company, to buy-in on the brainstorm. My former colleagues within Boeing's Corporate Government Relations Office also had to be on board.

As I talked with Harry, he got excited about the possibility of having a role in working with us. He realized that the final decision would require the approval of upper management within his division as well as the company's corporate offices. Fortunately, I was able to get approval on all levels! When I told the Senior Leadership Team, they were very supportive.

Harry organized the Process Improvement Management System (PIMS). This was the vehicle that implemented the legislation and policies relative to Work-First and the One-Stop delivery networks. In November of 1997, Harry set up five agency-level process improvement teams. They all received training on the intricacies and expectations of PIMS.

Meeting with Governor Gary Locke, (left to right) Department of Social and Health Services Secretary Lyle Quasim, and Washington State Board of Community Colleges Executive Director Earl Hale.

Part of the implementation of PIMS was an employment survey. This was conducted in the fall of 1998 after our teams had been functioning for eight or nine months. The point of the survey was for our team to study the results and determine how well our management teams were performing.

The positive results of the survey were confirmed by me and Cindy Zehnder as we traveled through the state in the early winter of 1998. We made two separate, several-day trips to visit our staff at sites in the field. At each site, I had face-to-face contacts with staff, which helped me understand their realities and their answers to our survey.

The previous ESD Commissioner conducted an employee survey in 1993. As a follow-up, we compared those 1993 results with our own survey results. It was good to find substantial improvement in the areas of empowering staff and supporting teams. In fact, the responses indicated that our greatest progress was made in teams and empowering self-direction within the team concept.

Our 1998 survey reflected that 70% percent of the respondents agreed with the statement: "I have authority to make improvements to my work processes." Compare this with only 54% in the 1993 survey. Big improvements came in several areas. Seventy-seven percent of the respondents agreed that they had the information they needed to do their jobs well.

A significant concern was that only 37% of our employees were well informed about what was going on *in ESD as a whole*. We also needed to find out why some of our employees continued to give relatively low ratings to issues involving fairness—such as discipline, employee complaints, and promotions.

Fundamentally, my take-away regarding "continuous quality improvement," was that the department needed to continue emphasizing team development and performance management efforts. And at the same time, we needed to take the necessary corrective actions.

I was especially impressed with the employees' openness to the findings of the survey and their pride in being part of an organization willing to learn where it falls short—and so ready to improve!

The findings also gave me a heads-up on what I personally needed to continue to emphasize as commissioner. I had to build upon traditional communication vehicles, such as employee newsletters, and connect better with management on all levels. I also realized, throughout my winter visits to sites, I was more effective when having *unstructured* discussions with employees, by being an aggressive listener, rather than surrounding myself with an entourage from Olympia during the visits.

There were also indicators the new Work-First program was making progress. Twelve months after its implementation, hundreds of ESD Work-First staff had assisted more than 34,600 people in taking a step toward getting off welfare by getting a job. Incredibly, that was more than 70 percent above the number for the prior year!

Put another way, ESD staff helped 14,000 more people and their families take a step toward success. Obviously, we did not do this alone. It took the willingness of ESD staff and DSHS, and myriad other organizations, to move away from their traditional silos, think creatively, and work cooperatively within a broad team environment. It also required an unprecedented partnership with the private sector, one in which all ultimately benefit. Offices throughout the state shared in this success, with performances that outstripped our ambitious goals.

There is another story to tell as well. It's the story of how *government bureaucracies can change*. It was evidence of a renewed sense of public service where service comes first. This was just a snapshot in history, but the message it tells me is this: It's clear that when the public and private sectors come together in an understanding and commitment to common values we hold for our society, we all rise up!

The Work-First story reminded me of a conversation I had with a private-sector executive whose company was doing some sub-contract work for ESD. His company was doing exactly what was prescribed in the contract, which pleased me. He also had a likable personality. Toward the end of our conversation, he said, "I know you were with The Boeing Company for many years." He wondered how I could adjust to working within what he considered to be a *non-productive* government environment. He asked, "Don't you get frustrated?"

I had heard such inferences from private sector folks for many years, but none were as blunt and direct as his. I felt very comfortable telling him that all organizations—whether public or private— have their share of talented and untalented employees. But more to his point, I said, "I have the good fortune of working within an agency that has extremely talented people. The majority of whom have skillsets that could benefit any private business. And the citizens of this state are mighty fortunate that such individuals chose to work in this agency, to help make the state better off for everyone."

I told him that I went into government as an FBI agent, especially inspired by the words of President John F. Kennedy in 1960, when he said, "Ask not what your country can do for you, ask what you can do for your country."

I went on to say, "And I think those words inspired a whole generation of folks. . . people who felt that there is no higher calling in this country than public service. So, I work within an organization of fellow employees who, for the most part, still believe in that calling."

————

During 1998, there were clear indications that the cooperative relationships with our cabinet-level partners—such as the Department of Labor and Industries (L&I), Department of Revenue, Information Services—were making progress in connecting with citizens *online*. The new "Access Washington" website provided citizens easy access to government information services around the clock over the internet. Prior to the emergence of the internet, the key state agencies responsible for Work-First offered their services exclusively through physical sites. As Cindy Zender and I made our fall tours of ESD sites in 1997 and 1998, employees were supportive of greater use of the internet for the services we offered. This information was passed on by me to the Access Washington Cabinet Sub-Committee.

The Access Washington Cabinet Sub-Committee was chaired by Governor Locke's excellent chief of staff, Joe Dear. Governor Locke was elated by the progress being made by the sub-committee. As he pointed out, "People can find jobs online through WORK Job Service. Businesses can file and pay taxes electronically. Homeowners can find out whether contractors making home improvements are registered and bonded. Kids can come home from school and get help with their homework at 'Just for Kids'."

ESD's Labor Market and Economic Analysis page was also within Access Washington. It provided a wide variety of labor market information to help businesses, government agencies, and the general public make informed decisions.

ESD's Labor Market Information provided career data, including projections of fastest growing jobs. It also provided economic data, such as employment, unemployment, and wage information used by employers, planners, economists, and job seekers across the state. The page also featured economic analysis, and special reports and publications that focus on trends in the labor market.

The ESD team was especially proud that our labor market information home page within Access Washington won a distinction. It was awarded first place in the nation by the Interstate Conference of Employment Security Agencies for electronic dissemination of labor market information. We were in good company with Access Washington, winner of the Digital State Award from the Progress and Freedom Foundation in both 1997 and 1998. Washington led the nation in the use of information technology to deliver services to citizens and improve government operations.[43]

The success of the ESD Process Improvement Measurement System (PIMS) initiatives was abundantly clear by the end of 1998. That year, the only state agency to submit more quality improvement initiatives to the Office of the Governor had *seven times* as many employees! The Governor's Office selected initiatives that could be applied to other agencies and were of public and media interest. These initiatives were published in the quarterly booklet, "Governing for Results," which was distributed by the Governor's Office in February of 1999.

Employment Security submitted 63 of its best ideas through December of 1998. The Department of Social and Health Services submitted 80, just five other agencies submitted more than 30 initiatives. A total of 26 agencies, both large and small, forwarded their best quality efforts. In a 1998 "Progress Report" on the state's efforts to make government work better, Governor Locke cited these results through December 1998: $22.5 million in costs saved and 172,000 staff hours saved—with more than $6.8 million in revenue generated.

The governor specifically cited some major Work-First successes, including 24.3 percent caseload reductions, more than 55,000 welfare recipients with jobs, and a doubling of the percentage of people on assistance who were employed. The results of ESD's initiatives alone accounted for nearly $1 million in savings. About half of ESD's initiatives submitted to the Governor's Office were published in "Governing for Results." This was a true reflection of the excellent work of many teams focusing on achieving measurable quality results.

ESD continued to make progress towards its Process Improvement efforts as indicated in February of 1999, by receiving the Governor's Quality Award for Service and Quality. The recognition was a harbinger for the agency's common goal for 1999: "The Year We Make It Happen."

When there are clear indications of a program being successful, others notice the leaders who brought that success. Outside organizations may entice such leaders to come do the same in their own organizations. Such was the case with Cindy Zehnder. Her talent was noticed by Speaker of the Washington State House of Representatives Frank Chopp. He hired her away from ESD in March of 1999 to become his chief clerk. To be hired into such a prestigious and powerful position was indeed a high compliment not only to Cindy but also the ESD.

In her farewell, Cindy pointed out,

"I am leaving not because I want to leave you, but because I have an opportunity to carry out our work into another arena that I just simply could not walk away from. I want to assure you that I have complete confidence and know that you are going to be very successful in where you are taking the agency. Carver and the Senior Leadership Team are a terrific group of people. You guys are doing everything right. When I come back next year to visit you, I will see remarkable things happening—because that's what you are capable of. Thank you very much, your work is very dear to my heart."

CHAPTER 28

Getting Out in Front of the Federal Workforce Investment Act

THE FEDERAL WORKFORCE INVESTMENT ACT (WIA) was introduced in Congress in April 1998 and was passed that summer. WIA initiated a coordinated federal aid program for vocational education, adult education, job training, and unemployment insurance. ESD's future was determined by this law's passage.

As I mentioned earlier, Governor Locke began his tenure in 1997 and, in anticipation of the WIA's passage, he emphasized bringing statewide workforce partners together into "one-stop" networks to better meet employment needs. The primary challenge was to bring the agencies together both physically and technologically. In my mind, this was similar to Boeing's integrated team/system concept. By the time WIA was actually passed, all of the major elements of the law were operating within the state, and we had gone beyond its requirements in many respects.

The public labor exchange, job training, labor market information, and unemployment insurance are all referenced in Title 1 of the Workforce Investment Act. These were already under the purview of ESD so ESD's level of interest in the law was extremely high. One of ESD's primary functions was to bring together individuals seeking employment and employers seeking skilled workers. ESD did this through statewide and local workforce investment systems to increase employment, retention, and earnings of participants, as well as occupational skill levels.

All of these efforts were intended to result in improved quality of the workforce, reduced welfare dependency, and enhanced productivity and competitiveness of our nation as a whole. ESD became the WIA grant recipient with oversight and monitoring for implementing the Act's intentions. ESD's major challenge was to continue improvement upon what we had already initiated.

The scope of the Act necessitated a strong systemic approach in dealing with the employment needs of the next century. Governor Locke appointed me to chair a committee to not only fulfill the requirements of WIA, but, in my mind, to make our "one-stop" system a model for the nation. The committee was comprised of department chief executives from the Washington State Labor Council, the Department of Social and Health Services, the Washington State Board of Community and Technical Colleges, and the Association of Washington Businesses.

The committee began meeting regularly during the latter part of 1998. The meetings were intense and concerned proposed and agreed upon changes in the PIMS processes needed to accommodate WIA. Much of what was discussed related to costs, protecting turf, and our willingness to change long-standing processes. Additionally, my Leadership Team members and I had virtual telephone and face-to-face meetings with ESD employees and partners. We also had superb support from the ESD staff as well as from the staff of the committee's agency partners.

As a result of the hard work of all involved, I made the following announcement in the June 1999 issue of the *Washington State Employment Security Department Labor Market Information Review*:

> *This summer Employment Security and its workforce partners launched a new venture called "WorkSource" to meet the employment needs of the next century. After an in-depth study by a marketing subcontractor, the committee felt that "WorkSource" covered all the bases of the partners involved, the primary emphasis being on jobs and work.*
>
> • *Ten WorkSource Centers in key locations opened, coupled with our new Telecenters' capabilities to process unemployment insurance claims by*

phone. These mark the start of the most monumental changes in the 60-year history of the Employment Security system.

- *Affiliate WorkSource sites, called WorkSource Connections, will be linked to the system, and self-service stations will be electronically linked to the system as well.*

- *As a result of the move from ESD Job Service Centers to Telecenters, people who need unemployment claims no longer had to stand in line at agency sites; they could file by telephone or the internet.*

WorkSource wasn't just a repackaging of resources and crowding local partners into one physical location. It was a dramatic change in the way we provide employment training services for employers and job seekers.

Employment Security's enhanced infrastructure was augmenting the resources from our partners in business, labor, private industry council, community, and technical colleges, DSHS and Workforce Training and Education, and Education Coordinating Board and the Governor's office.

The foundation being built together is unsurpassed by any state in the nation and positions us to meet the challenges of the next century.

With the major structural changes within ESD (i.e. WorkSource) having been complete and the Work-First welfare program working on all cylinders, I considered the major objectives of my term as Commissioner had been achieved. I was especially pleased with a *Seattle Times* editorial of December 27, 1999, entitled, "Welfare Reform: Let's Party Like it's 1999." The editorial began:

Right now, at the turn of the millennium, is an ideal time to be an upper-level bureaucrat.

Caseloads are down nearly 40% since 1997 and Federal welfare money will keep pouring in at high levels until 2002. Work-First advisors have the temporary political and economic freedom to try, well, almost anything.

One of the best parts of [Governor] Locke's strategy is the least costly. A $500,000 marketing plan will let residents know that food stamps, childcare subsidies and state health insurance do not count as welfare which has a five-year lifetime limit. A similar marketing plan for the Earned Income Tax Credit helped low-income families in this state take an extra $29 million back from Uncle Sam in 1998.

At the invitation of the International Association of Machinists, Secretary of Labor Alexis Herman and I visited their training center in Renton along with several Boeing training managers and IMA officials in December of 1999.

The editorial pointed out that there were challenges ahead, and thousands of parents were not close to finding jobs or decent childcare, and that certainly more work needed to be done. "But the good news is this: Washington recently scored first in the nation in job placements and work success, even while investing an extra $200 million of welfare savings in public education. Caseloads have plummeted 44% from 96,000 to 58,600. . . the unprecedented momentum is working. Party on!"

Over the four years of my tenure, the Employment Security Department experienced revolutionary changes which ultimately benefited Washington's citizens. That made me feel proud. That was why I had wanted to join Governor Locke's team. Of course, I could not do it alone. I gained enormous appreciation and admiration for the public servants of the ESD. The personal relationships of our employees were challenged because of restructuring dictated by WorkSource, but to the great credit of the ESD team, we became stronger than ever after the changes. As a whole, the agency bought into the

Carmen and I attended a fundraising event held at the Sheraton Hotel and were asked if we'd like a photo with the Mandelas. We were honored. It was a moment I will always remember.

concept of "continuous quality improvement" and the accompanying goals. It embraced the remarks President Clinton made at the time: ". . . public service is not a destination but a process."

Soon after the November 2000 election of Governor Locke to his second term, I received a telephone call from him asking that I stay within his cabinet as Commissioner of the Employment Security Department. I told him I was honored and pleased that he wanted me to stay on board, but I had not planned on remaining in my position. I referred to the initial conversation we'd had in 1997 when he asked me to serve, and I had committed to one term only. There was another important factor for me to consider. My youngest son was matriculating into middle school. He needed his father at home more often. I was driving back and forth between Seattle and Olympia daily, leaving at 6 a.m. and returning at 8 p.m. I hadn't been a coffee drinker before working in Olympia. Now, I cannot begin the day without my java. Governor Locke understood my family concerns, especially regarding my need to bond more with my son. I could tell by his tone that he was disappointed with my response. I assured him that I had the greatest respect for him and that it was a distinct honor for me to serve under his outstanding leadership.

I felt that our team had accomplished all, if not more, of the goals we set out to reach in early 1997. In spite of the fact that continuous quality improvement and "corporate memory" needed to be sustained, I decided not to stay on the Governor's Cabinet as Commissioner of ESD. In the November 17, 2000, official state press release concerning my departure, the Governor noted that:

> *The Employment Security Department under Gayton's leadership has been recognized nationally for innovative programs and achievements. Employment Security staff were always among the winners in the outstanding management and continuous improvement programs.*

> *Carver and his department overhauled services to bring new, more convenient options for customers. Because of Carver's efforts, never before have so many state agencies collaborated so closely. He gave private employers key roles in the Work-First program and championed strong partnerships to build the WorkSource employment and training, one-stop system.*

> *During his four years as Commissioner, Gayton embraced technology and contributed to Washington's three-time designation as the Digital State. Employment Security Internet websites are at the heart of customer services. The public can now file for unemployment insurance benefits, search through 17,000 available jobs in the state, and use their personal computers to access labor market information and additional job-finding assistance . . .*

On January 24, 2001, I sent an email to all employees of the Employment Security Department entitled "The Best Employment Security Department in America." The essence of my email expressed how proud I was of the entire ESD staff. When I came aboard as Commissioner in 1997 there were many who felt I was reaching too far by expecting ESD to become the best Employment Security Department in the nation by the end of my tenure. They said, "What is your plan B?" I replied that I had no plan B.

A major achievement of ESD employees was the launching of the historical WorkSource system. The structural changes by themselves were very significant, but these folks were also able to meet and *exceed* most of our ambitious customer goals during each of the past four years—and we received national recognition as a result. Benefits for low-income families increased. The agency was ranked number one in the nation for job placements. They also played a significant role in achieving a record low of welfare caseloads.

The restructuring had been quite a challenge for many of our ESD staff. Longstanding friendships got split up and people were faced with new colleagues. This took place during unbelievable stress on most employees. They persevered and maintained their commitment to the public to their great credit. Our teams became stronger than ever. I have never witnessed such dedication under such dire circumstances by employees in any other organization I worked for during my career. Yet they excelled.

In my good-bye message to everyone in ESD, I told them:

The most enjoyable times I have experienced over my four years as Commissioner were the fall tours and the brown bag lunches. It was on those occasions that I was able to talk directly to many of you about your concerns and observations. The open informal exchanges made a lasting impression on me. I was rejuvenated every time I participated in those meetings. I have always had a positive impression of public employees, but meeting with you face-to-face and hearing about how you responded to the gauntlet of issues strewn in your paths during my four years with you left me with a greater respect and admiration for you than I could ever have imagined in January of 1997.

The public owes you a debt of gratitude. You can rest assured that I will be on a personal mission the rest of my public life singing the praises of the wonderful team of ESD pioneers who changed workforce development forever during the years of 1997-2001.

As word spread throughout the agency about my departure, I was surprised by the many unsolicited remarks I received from employees such as the following example among many:

Good morning, Commissioner. Reading this morning's news, it was with deep emotion to learn that you will be leaving the ESD in February. I don't know if it is appropriate to share my feelings of admiration, but I will anyway. I just want you to know that I have the greatest respect for your passionate and outstanding leadership. I really like you as a person and highly respect you as the most effective and best leader I have benefitted from as a line staff. When I asked panelists what they found exciting about working there, two said "Carver Gayton." It is clear that your leadership is cherished! What a great legacy. One panelist said, "ESD is an honorable agency." Neat, huh?

What a great legacy indeed for the men and women working at ESD to be viewed as part of an "honorable agency." Public servants need to continually rcmind themselves that they can be productive and provide quality services to the people of the state and can do so honorably.

I am Inspired by the Remarks from Employees on My Departure

"Carver, I saw your announcement about moving from ESD. I wish you the best. I appreciated working with you very much. You definitely made my last years with ESD good ones. I also appreciated your calmness and persistent theme of making ESD the best in the nation. I also admired your solid professional reputation outside the agency with family, community, and spiritual leadership. Good going."

"Commissioner, I would like to thank you for the years you have given us. I have been in this agency for 14 years and have seen at least three commissioners come and go, but this is the first time I felt we will lose someone very valuable. . ."

"Commissioner Gayton: I have worked for this agency since last April and I wanted to thank you for fostering such a tremendous work environment. I have worked in many places over the years, and I am thoroughly thrilled at working here with such great people!"

"Commissioner Gayton: We have become the Employment Security Department of America because you had a vision. You shared that vision, we bought into the vision, and together with your outstanding leadership it was accomplished. In the twelve years I have been associated with this agency, I have seen commissioners come and go, but you were special. Thank you for the many opportunities you provided for us and your great leadership. We were blessed to have you come along and you will be missed. Best wishes in your future endeavors."

"Dear Carver, you are a wonderful leader and care about public service. It was a pleasure working with you. You inspired and motivated all who came in contact with you. Because of your leadership wonderful accomplishments were possible. I feel deeply honored to have had the opportunity to work with you. I admire your determination, courage, sensitivity, and commitment to customer service. Thank you, and I wish you luck as you continue your journey in public service. You are the BEST!!!"

"Dear Commissioner: Thank you for your charismatic leadership. Your commitment, dedication and energy will be a challenging role for others to follow. I have enjoyed the opportunity to work as a member of your ESD team. I have enjoyed the times we had to talk. . . and I always appreciated your multi-talents, and your great sense of humanity and humor. Thank you so much."

"Carver: What an honor it has been for me to serve with you at Employment Security. I have spent almost my entire career in the public sector, and you are the finest leader I have had the privilege of working with, and learning from, at any level of government.

"Carver: Thank you for being the most gracious, confident, ethical boss that you are! Your standards brought the best out of all of us. I hope ESD benefits from your leadership for several more years, but regardless of the number, you will have been the most positive influence ESD has ever had! Truly."

CHAPTER 29

Returning to
Seattle Public Schools

I HAD NO IMMEDIATE professional plans after I left ESD. I continued to be involved in volunteer activities with the University of Washington: I was a member of its College of Education Visiting (Ambassadors) Committee. I was also on the Visiting Committee of the Dan Evans School of Public Policy and Governance.

I didn't have anything else in mind for retirement other than reconnecting with my family and taking vacations in my favorite spots—the Caribbean and the Hawaiian Islands. That was my intention.

However, after working full time from ages 21 to 64, I found it difficult to manage all my free time. One morning I got into my car and started backing out of my garage. I realized I had a problem when heard a loud crunch—I forgot to open the garage door! Also, I had no idea where I was going. At that point, I knew I needed some meaningful activity(ies) to keep me busy and out of trouble!

Soon after that, I got a phone call from Joe Olchefske, the new Superintendent of the Seattle Public Schools. He'd read about my stepping down as ESD Commissioner, and he wanted to offer me a consulting opportunity. Our conversation was about a "small high school concept" that the Bill and Melinda Gates Foundation had been promoting. The theory was that teaching and learning would be more impactful and productive within small high schools, coupled with small classes of 15 or fewer students.

Joe knew of my background in education reform, especially in building education pathways between high schools and two-year colleges in the Two-Plus-Two concept that dovetails the last two years of high school with the first two years of community college. The upshot of the discussion was that he wanted me to work with his office and design an "academy of math, engineering, and science." The proposed high school would immerse students in a rigorous standards-based curriculum with the goal of providing a strong competency in academic and workplace skills.

I was excited about Joe's proposal. It seemed directly related to my work during my last few years with The Boeing Company.

My initial contact outside of Joe was Judy Peterson, principal of the Center School located within the Seattle Center. The Center School was a highly regarded small school model, but its curriculum didn't have a STEM-related focus. Another key contact was Tom Vander Ark, the Education Director for the Gates Foundation. Tom recommended that I visit five excellent small schools in California, Illinois, New York City, and Washington, DC. Most of the schools were part of their respective public-school systems. I considered them to be specialized magnet schools with a STEM focus. The intention of the visits was to get a sense of the possibilities of creating a similar school for under-represented students in the south end of Seattle. All of the schools were excellent, but my general impression was that most of the students were cherry picked for success.

I then I met with representatives of the Port of Seattle and The Boeing Company to get business perspectives on what I witnessed during my travels. I emphasized incorporating the Two-Plus-Two/Tech Prep I'd initiated at Boeing into a possible school. They were intrigued about what could happen in Seattle and wanted me to follow up with them. I made multiple in-depth visits with key folks at South Seattle Community College for the same reason.

A final draft of our plan was ready in June of 2002. The overview of the plan was as follows: "Through a collaborative arrangement between South Seattle Community College, and Seattle Public Schools, a new science, math, and engineering school has been proposed to open in September of 2003. This small school will provide a program of studies that will immerse students in the rigorous, standards-based learning environment, one designed to engage student interest in the fields of mathematics, science, and engineering."

Having worked for the Seattle Public Schools district before, I looked forward to making a presentation before the Seattle School Board in the fall of 2002 and gaining approval for the initiation of the project.

But alas—that was not to be!!

The Seattle Public Schools district announced that it had *overspent* its prior year budget by $23 million and was on track for a $12 million deficit by the end of the 2003 fiscal year!

Obviously, the financial situation made it impossible to initiate the "small school" project that I had worked on for more than six months and my role would change.[43]

The district took two actions to ensure that such a fiscal situation would not happen again. First, it engaged Moss Adams Advisory Services to conduct a performance audit. And second, the School Board appointed a Committee for Fiscal Integrity (CFI). The committee's charge was to evaluate the performance audit and then advise the district on implementing the audit's recommendations. The committee was co-chaired by me and retired King County Superior Court Judge Larry Jordan. The CFI included financial managers, other businesspeople, and a university business professor.

There were two principles that our committee decided upon before we began our deliberations: 1) We would not conduct independent fact finding (the auditor's role) and, 2) CFI members agreed they would focus on *preventing* future financial difficulties. In other words, no ad hominem attacks or inordinate dwelling on past non-essential problems.

———

The ultimate accolade for any organization is to have a positive case study written by the *Harvard School of Business*, right? In April of 2002, the *Harvard Business Review* provided a glowing perspective of the Seattle Public Schools district. The title of the study was "Transformation of the Seattle Public Schools from 1995-2002." At the start of the case study, Joseph Olchefske is quoted as saying, "I am an outsider to education and originally an investment banker. My predecessor and mentor was John Stanford, who was an Army general before he was a superintendent. Not surprisingly, the reforms that we pursued since 1995 reflect our exposure to well-run organizations outside of the educational establishment."

It is important to note that Mr. Olchefske had no prior experience in managing large organizations, though General Stanford had. The case study outlined the district's reform plan. The district's priority had been to decentralize its budgeting process and delegate that responsibility to individual school principals giving each school increased flexibility in managing resources, hiring staff, and designing education programs. Accordingly, the district's central office reduced its involvement in the school-based activities. This was obviously a reasonable business plan.

In 1998, John Stanford unexpectedly died of leukemia, and his protégé, Joe Olchefske, who was CFO, took over as superintendent. Again, it was observed that he had an outsider's view of education reform and an appetite for risk and change—a characteristic consistent of an investment banker who focused on raising capital from corporations, government, and other entities. He had the ultimate in academic credentials: a Bachelor of Arts degree from the University of Chicago and a Master of Arts degree in Urban Planning from Harvard University's Kennedy School of Government. He was also described by observers as quantitative, logical, and relentless, with a photographic memory.

A caveat in the *Harvard Business Review* case study pointed out that such case studies are not intended to serve as *endorsements* or illustrations of effective or ineffective management. However, the Seattle Public Schools case study concluded with these laudatory words: "To almost all observers, Olchefske had overseen the design and implementation of an ambitious and thoughtful reform plan, one that reflected leading thought from both the education and private sectors."

Similar positive indicators of the progress of the district were reflected by a speech given by a Seattle School board member to the Seattle Rotary in the spring of 2002, emphasizing the "great" accomplishments of the school district, with particular emphasis on its "business practices."

Ironically, just months before the district announced its financial crisis, UCLA business professor William Ouchi lauded the Seattle School Schools district in his newly published book *Making School Work: A Revolutionary Plan to Get Your Children the Education They Need*. Ouchi spotlighted three of the "best" school districts: Edmonton in Alberta, Canada; Houston in Texas; and Seattle. Ouchi believed that the success of these districts was demonstrated by their *entrepreneurial approach to management* rather than a bureaucratic one. This new approach allowed principals to control budgets and be accountable for their performance and budgets. This management approach also empowered the parent communities.

How could this financial mess happen to a school district that was regarded as one of the "best" managed districts in the nation?

In the spring of 2003, Moss Adams and our Committee for Financial Integrity revealed our devastating reports. Olchefske announced his plan to resign. The following fall, the wrath of the public was demonstrated by three school Board members being voted out of office and one deciding not to run again.

How could public confidence in the leadership of the Seattle Public Schools change so quickly and drastically?

Some of the broad observations of the audit conducted by Moss Adams helped answer that question. Significant mistakes were made in the district's budgeting processes. Moss Adams indicated that they had never seen such a poorly managed budget operation. Also, budgets were adjusted, or "plugged," to fix problems in hopes that future revenues would cover the short fall ($10 million picked out of the air). Added to such factors, *spending continued* even though funds were not available to back up expenditures.

The Moss Adams findings concluded that the primary problems that led to the crises were *people issues* and the organization's *cultural issues*. These permeated the budget processes. Other challenges, such as the economy, were out of the district's control (inferring also not computer problems or an individual person).

The Committee for Fiscal Integrity agreed with the 113 Moss Adams findings and recommendations. But our committee placed particular emphasis on the cultural/organizational problems. These had to do with how the top-down leadership style had inhibited two-way communication and caused dysfunction within the whole system. These were things the district could change.

The report indicated that certain cultural issues of the organization were big problems for the district. Central Office Departments operated in silos, resulting in a lack of communication within and between departments. I felt that the concept of "general systems theory" was ignored. In essence, the theory suggests the importance of working within a team environment. If one important element of an organization is dysfunctional—in this case the financial operation—the entire organization is at risk.

The philosophy of putting students first, and the mantra "Kids First," was pursued at the expense of good fiscal management. This cultural attitude permeated the entire school district and impeded the ability of running a tight fiscal operation. Though the focus on students is laudable, the two are not mutually exclusive. They are interconnected.

School Board leaders needed training in financial matters. They tended not to hold district staff accountable for implementing disciplined financial practices. Budget materials provided to the board were hard to understand but evidently *not challenged* by board members.

Moss Adams did an excellent job diagnosing the causes of budget problems. All 113 recommendations were accepted by CFI as well as by the board. The primary conclusions and the recommendation of the CFI were that improved business practices alone would not eliminate risks of financial crises. There must also be reform of the organizational culture. Reluctance to communicate bad news, managers consistently in a reactive mode and district and departments isolated from one another, all directly contributed to the budget crisis. It was also imperative that the culture must change to ensure sound financial management is an essential priority. Financial management does not supersede a focus on "Kids First"; it is necessary to complement it.

At the conclusion of CFI's work, I received a letter dated June 30, 2003, from Seattle School Board President, Nancy Waldman, which read in part:

Dear Mr. Gayton,

On behalf of the School Board, thank you for your valuable contribution to Seattle Public Schools as a member of the Committee for Fiscal Integrity. I know how hard this Committee worked over the past months, and we are truly grateful for your time and expertise as we worked together to address the fiscal crisis in which we found ourselves.

Carver Gayton and Larry Jacobs did an excellent job of presenting the Committee's final report and recommendations at the June 4th Board meeting. We found it to be thorough, thoughtful, and extremely helpful . . .

A June 12, 2003, editorial in the *Seattle Post-Intelligencer* pointed this out:

. . . it is imperative that the District institute business practices that create and sustain excellent school programs. "Co-Chairman Carver Gayton says that, over the long run, kids will be better served by recognizing financial realities.

There is hope for raising academic standards, eliminating achievement gaps, and improving all schools; first though, the District must invest in changing its disastrous finances."[44]

I would like to end the discussion of my role as co-chair of the Committee for Fiscal Integrity with an observation from the great scholar Peter Drucker. Concerning the desired skill set for a leader of a large organization, Drucker says it doesn't really matter whether the leader comes from the public or private sector. He observes that 90 percent of what executives do is generic, they all spend about the same amount of time on people problems. But the last 10 percent needed from a leader *must fit the organization's specific mission*, its history, and specific vocabulary.

In my opinion, much of General Stanford's success was related to the fact that he had been steeped in organizational management for many years. However, his successor, Joe Olchefske, had never been an executive within a large organization.

Raj Manhas succeeded Olchefske as Superintendent. Manhas came to the position with previous experience in executive management in the City of Seattle as well as Rainier Bank in Seattle. After following the recommendations of the Committee for Fiscal Integrity and the Moss Adams report, Manhas and his team was credited with closing the budget shortfall, balancing the annual budget, and returning the district to financial health with $20 million in reserves while focusing on what he called "child-centered education." He ended his term in June of 2007. In my estimation, the primary difference between the two superintendents was Manhas's extensive leadership and management experience in large organizations and bureaucracies.

I am very proud of the work of the Committee for Fiscal Integrity that I co-chaired. We had considerable independence from the school board. No micromanaging by the board was evident at all. We had the good fortune of having Moss Adams Advisory Services to conduct the performance audit. The relationship the CFI had with Moss Adams was exemplary. Periodic, public, open-meeting status reports also went extremely well. At the end of the process, I felt that we had contributed a great deal toward restoring public confidence in the Seattle Public Schools system. As of this writing there have been no similar fiscal problems within the district since the implementation of the recommendations of the Committee for Fiscal Integrity in 2003.

CHAPTER 30

Returning to the U of W

IN THE FALL OF 2001, I was asked by the new Dean of the University of Washington Evans School of Public Affairs (Now the Evans School of Public Policy & Governance) to be a lecturer on the school's academic staff. The evening course was entitled "Public Affairs 573: Strategic Leadership in Education and Workforce Development." The graduate course provided dual credits for Evans School students as well as graduate students in the Education Leadership Program within the College of Education.

I repeated teaching the class during the fall Quarter of 2003. The seminars were small, averaging 15 students per class. Most of the students worked during the day as professionals within governmental or educational sectors.

At the beginning of the course, I emphasized that business community leaders in the nation, like the Washington Roundtable, agreed that rapid changes in the global economy require new skills and knowledge profiles for our workforce of the future. As I also pointed out this situation has challenged the delivery systems of educational and governmental institutions. With that in mind, I said the course would examine education and strategic leadership initiatives being implemented between and within public and private sectors that are attempting to address this challenge.

An example of a major initiative discussed was the importance of expanding early learning programs, especially focused on poor children of color, such as the Head Start Program. Reliable research indicated that the social cost savings of effective programs to both the private and public sectors could be enormous.

Another innovative educational approach examined was the Two-Plus-Two/Tech Prep program, connecting high schools with community colleges. I initiated such programs while at The Boeing Company which gained international recognition. This also included work-based learning internships and apprenticeships, making schooling more relevant to real world industry needs.

The excellent career and technical academies I visited while a consultant for the Seattle School Schools was another example of considerable discussion in the class.

My lectures were interspersed with presentations from local, state, and national leaders from the private and public sectors who influenced the direction of the workforce of the future. Quite frankly, the students regarded the guest speakers as the highlight of the class. Looking back, I probably could have provided more insights on my personal view of the topics discussed, but my expectation was that the guest speakers and the assigned readings did indeed represent a great deal of my point of view.

I thoroughly enjoyed being back in the classroom, and the department wanted me to continue in that role.

———

In October 2003, a statue in the image of former U of W head football coach Jim Owens was placed on campus in front of Husky Stadium. The statue renewed a longstanding controversy surrounding Owens. Owens had coached the Huskies from 1957 to 1974 and had led three teams to the Rose Bowl. However, he was also at the center of racial turmoil and accusations of bigotry during that time. I was hired in 1968 as an assistant coach as a result of those racial tensions. I came to the position as a former player on Owens's victorious 1960 Rose Bowl team, as a Black U of W graduate, and as a graduate assistant on the victorious 1961 Rose Bowl team.

Owens suspended four Black athletes on October 30, 1969. Because of my background with the team and my new position as an assistant coach, I feel I was in an advantageous position to observe the events surrounding the suspensions. I resigned as assistant coach in protest of how Owens handled the episode.

The October 2003 installation of the statue kicked up a maelstrom. Before a decision was made regarding the statue, university administrators and supporters needed to have a better understanding of the lingering anger that existed in the African American community. A very positive reconciliation meeting between former players and Coach Owens took place two days before the October 25, 2003, USC game. I was very pleased to hear that during the meeting Owens expressed regret for any pain he may have caused in the lives of Black athletes in the past. However, it was unfortunate that the meeting, along with his expressions of regret, took place *only days* before the statue's unveiling. Such an approach could have lessened considerably the possibility of a public outcry if it had taken place months earlier.[45]

There are a few important reasons why so many people on both sides of the issue have been so reluctant to speak out over the years. First, the mistreatment revisits a very painful time in their lives, and they want to move forward. Second, there is fear among many prominent moderate Blacks that if they express what may be perceived by the White power structure as a negative view, they may be inviting retaliation against them and jeopardizing their careers. Third, Husky football players, both Black and White, do not want to damage the bonds they established as teammates.

The admonitions by some very well-meaning Blacks who stated that we as a people had bigger fish to fry rather than to protest the unveiling of a statue is a legitimate concern. There's no question that there are major problems in the African American community that must be addressed, especially those that impact our youth, i.e., drug use, lack of early childhood education, limited entry into institutions of higher education, etc. Having strategies that address these issues effectively is fundamental to the survival of our community. Working on these issues requires our long-term commitment.

However, those African Americans living in Seattle who regarded the statue issue as insignificant are either relatively young, new in town, or were incommunicado during those years of turmoil on the U of W campus. It is important for them to take note of the words of Santayana: "Those who do not learn from the past are bound to repeat the mistakes of the past."

The racial issues that emerged during the Owens years were not insignificant. Many individuals take for granted the large percentage of Black athletes currently on U of W teams, the wide variety of academic and support programs now available to students of color, and the increasing numbers of minority

Four Highly Successful Individuals

Regarding the four players—Gregg Alex, Ralph Bayard, Harvy Blanks, and Lamar Mills—suspended from the team in 1969), it is of value to note the following:

Gregg Alex is a well-known and highly respected minister and executive director of the Matt Talbot Center in downtown Seattle. He also was a spiritual advisor for the athletes within the University of Washington Athletic Department for many years. Gregg approached the Athletic Department with the idea of a reconciliation meeting with Coach Owens months before it actually took place.

Ralph Bayard currently serves as an executive with the Casey Family Foundation which serves foster care children nationwide, and previously served as senior associate athletic director in the U of W Athletic Department for a number of years under former Athletic Director Barbara Hedges. Ralph was also at that meeting.

Harvy Blanks was a successful actor, playwright, and director in New York City and Denver.

Lamar Mills is a prominent attorney in Seattle and serves as deputy director of the Northwest Defenders Association.

All have graduate degrees.

---

faculty and staff on campus. But all these outcomes were the indirect results of the confrontational events within the athletic department during Jim Owens's tenure more than three decades ago. The high visibility athletic programs and the issue of race led the university to examine other aspects of university life where inequities existed.

The current results are mixed—but certainly far and away *better* than they were in 1969. Regarding the athletic department's current programs, race is, for the most part, a non-issue, especially in terms of access, recruitment, and playing time of athletes. However, *all* of these were major concerns in 1969.

As to the viability of having additional reconciliation meetings over the statue matter, it is my view that the issue be put to rest and that we move forward. That does not mean that we forget what transpired 50 years ago. We all must be vigilant regarding such matters.

I do not profess to have known Jim Owens well, but within the context of what I have observed of his personality, I do know that it took a tremendous amount of courage for him to apologize to his former players at the Homecoming Game in October 2003. It was not part of his make-up to deliver what I am sure he considered as a very private statement, and in a public forum. It had to have been a gut-wrenching experience for him.

I am very pleased that Coach Owens expressed regret for what happened to Black athletes during his tenure. No one admired Coach Owens more than I. However, I could not stand by him after that hellish, cold, and rainy October evening in 1969 when he justified the suspension of four young African American athletes because they would not swear by an ill-conceived loyalty oath.

I had waited for years for a sign or gesture to allow myself to declare the wounds had finally been healed. Owens provided that gesture on October 25, 2003, with a heart-felt apology to his players for the pain he caused them. And he expressed this in front of 72,000 Husky fans, who responded with a resounding standing ovation. The irony of that day was that exactly 34 years earlier, a packed Husky Stadium gave Coach Owens a deafening ovation for *suspending* some of the same players he was apologizing to in 2003. Though I did not applaud Owens in 1969, I was compelled to do so in 2003. His gesture that day symbolized to me the end of an excruciating saga in the history of Husky sports.

It is crucial to point out that young men with less strength of character and determination would not have been able to survive and endure the "stigma" of being suspended from the University of Washington football team by a man who was at the time considered to be one of the most powerful and influential personalities in the state of Washington. Against the odds, each not only survived, but excelled—personally, professionally, and as citizens.

PART VIII

NORTHWEST AFRICAN AMERICAN MUSEUM

CHAPTER 31

Laying the Cornerstones

I WAS AWARE that a proposed African American Museum for Seattle had been deliberated by a variety of mayoral appointed boards beginning in the early 1980s. I followed newspaper accounts of the activities of those groups but had no direct connection with them. However, as 20 years passed by, I became concerned our Black community and city leaders could not come together and establish a Black Museum. I felt a museum was long overdue, one with an emphasis on our rich and unique culture, featuring our history, arts, customs, and achievements.

It appeared to me that the main issue the various groups *could* agree on was location. A museum committee comprised of activists and business and community leaders (these folks ultimately became board members of the African American Heritage Museum and Cultural Center—or the AAHMCC) agreed that the home of the museum should be the deserted Coleman Elementary School in

...it was especially important to have community involvement in developing our permanent exhibit. When people walked into the building, they needed to have a feeling of something *about themselves*.

---

the Central District. According to media accounts, that was basically the extent of their agreement. News of infighting, fist fights, and even death threats were prevalent. As a Black man whose family had lived in Seattle for more than five generations, I felt the Black community and Seattle deserved better.

By 2001, the project was dead in the water. Soon after, the Seattle Public Schools put the Coleman School up for sale.[46] It was at that point that the Urban League of Metropolitan Seattle (ULMS), then led by CEO James Kelly, contacted the school district and entered negotiations to purchase the property. With the Urban League officially attached to the project, financial support from individuals, private foundations, and community groups began to arrive, and in the spring of 2003 the sale was approved.[47]

The Urban League's concept was named the "Urban League Village." This called for the building to be repaired and divided into two sections. The top two floors would be transformed into apartments for low-income renters, and the bottom floor would house a museum and operate independently of the League. The proposed museum was named the Northwest African American Museum.

After the building's purchase, Kelly established an advisory committee of community leaders. This is when I became involved. This advisory committee included Dr. Constance Rice, Barbara Earl Thomas, and Mimi Gates among others, and eventually included museum professionals and an architect. Dr. Rice and I were named Honorary Co-Chairs of a broad-based fundraising effort for the entire project driven exclusively by the Urban League.

The project began with the selection of the architect, the construction contractor, and a professional fundraiser. Unfortunately, the fundraiser's initial efforts produced lackluster results. CEO Kelly felt that the time was right to search for a director for the project, someone with a strong background in fundraising. He initiated a national search yielding three finalists, all of whom were from large cities east of the Mississippi.

My fellow members of the museum advisory committee and I were asked to interview the candidates. After a morning of interviews, we gathered and reviewed our options. After much discussion, we did not come to a clear consensus on whom to select.

I was preparing to leave the meeting when Dr. Rice declared, "All of the candidates were good, but this position is so political, we really need someone who knows all the major players in the community." She went on to say, "I don't know why we are doing all of this, because the person we *really* need is Carver Gayton. Your family has been in Seattle a long time. And, since the focus of the museum is on the history of Black folks in the Northwest, you would be an excellent fit for the job."

I began to chuckle, not really taking her seriously. But I was certainly flattered by her comments. As I walked toward the door, I blurted out a very serious thought, "The only way I'd take on such a project would be if Barbara Thomas would agree to be my right hand as deputy director of the museum." I left the meeting, continuing to smile. I figured that any discussion of me taking on the job was over.[48]

In the early evening that same day, I received a phone call from James Kelly. He said, "Carver, after you left, the group decided that they would like you to take on the job as museum director. Barbara Thomas said she would seriously consider working with you if you accepted."

I was truly stunned! I replied, "James, out of respect for you and the group, I will consider your offer. But I first need to talk with my wife, Carmen, and think through the positives and negatives of taking on the task."

My first instinct was to turn down James's offer. Over the years I had read negative press about the serious divisions among the various boards and committees created by mayoral administrations from the early 1980s on. Those divisions precipitated actual *fist fights*! At the height of the conflicts, some committee members received death threats. Such threats led Kelly to be so concerned that he felt compelled to carry a handgun. He went to the extent of bringing the firearm into a community meeting at Rainier Beach High School. According to state law, bringing a firearm onto a school premises is a misdemeanor. Kelly said he purchased the gun after he had been threatened by Wyking Kwame Garrett, the son of activist Omari Garrett.

Outside of Kelly and the selection committee, no group or individual encouraged me to take the job. After several months of deliberation, as well as discussions with my wife and Barbara Thomas, I decided to take the job. Ultimately, the deciding factor was that I became peeved that a small group of individuals, the former occupiers of Colman School, felt entitled that the building was theirs, and that they were justified in making threats of violence to get their way, i.e., "the end justified the means."

Granted, their 8-year occupation was a sacrifice and commitment beyond measure. I can understand if they felt disappointed about not receiving more appreciation for their superlative efforts to secure a home for the museum. However, their continuous threats of violence and extortion against those who disagreed with their approach were—and continues to be—beyond the pale. Twenty-five years of that kind of behavior offered no rational reason to talk about reconciliation.

I concluded that the well-meaning but misguided group of ten men were, in effect, holding the entire African American community hostage. They were included in community-wide committees and boards to help establish an African American Museum, but they utilized force and intimidation in an attempt to get their way. I could not accept that approach. The community deserved better.[49]

The building of the museum had been in limbo too long. I was outright embarrassed by the in-fighting within my community for so many years. I felt I had to do my part to make sure the museum would become a reality. I quit teaching at the University of Washington and reconnected with Barbara. I asked her to team up with me to build the museum. She agreed to come onboard and concluded that the experience could be not only worthwhile but intriguing. Barbara had a strong background in the arts community as an accomplished artist, previous chair of the Seattle Arts Commission, and someone well connected with all major museums in the Northwest.

In November of 2004, Barbara and I met with Stuart Grover of the Collins Group who had been hired by the Urban League to develop a business plan for the proposed Northwest African American Museum. I fully agreed with Stuart's initial comments that a good museum tells a good story. We needed to gather the pieces and define the story we were going to tell. He said that the story should be active and engaging. The museum should have an ongoing education piece that's flexible, i.e., one that could change to accommodate the museum's rotating exhibits. But most importantly, the centerpiece needed to be historical. That history must be a living history: history as it happened and as it is happening now—and linked to the Northwest. One thing he did not emphasize, but I assumed was a given, was that we were focused on African American history.

Stuart talked about the importance of having a strategic plan, something Barbara and I had discussed before meeting with him. The essence of our discussion was to have a vision and broad concept of the museum. I'm a firm believer in continuing to improve on the goals and mission of an organization. I wanted to focus on having a "world class" museum within the framework of Northwest African American culture and history. The only slight disagreement Barbara and I may have had was when she cautioned that our eventual "Grand Opening" should not oversell our expectations to something that could never be topped. I understood her point, as long as our team had the commitment and desire to make the museum the best it could be, and we let folks know about it. That conceptual blip never hindered us from working hard throughout the three years we worked together. I feel our efforts resulted in a top-quality museum.

In 2004, Stuart's plan indicated that we should raise three to four million dollars by groundbreaking time in 2006 (Indeed, the groundbreaking took place June 1, 2006). That gave us a target of eighteen or nineteen months to accomplish that goal. We also agreed that we had to build excitement and commitment within the museum team, as well as the larger community. According to Stuart, previous efforts to create the museum had been missing that element.

We had additional discussions about the structure of our museum team and community groups, such as "community exhibit teams" focusing on past and contemporary history, the arts, and traditional African American roots. Within that context, Barbara and I agreed on the following:

- Establishing an independent advisory board and a steering committee focused on fundraising.
- Establishing a solid strategic plan with goals and timetables as well as a three-year business plan.
- Creating a board of directors with a 501© (3) nonprofit designation, independent and separate from the Urban League.
- Planning to have initial staff in place by December 15 and a strategic plan and steering committee in place by January 15, 2005.
- Having a development person in place as quickly as possible at Stuart's recommendation.

I, along with Barbara, committed to take on the jobs as executive director and curator respectively, by December 2004.

Follow-up discussions I had with ULMS executives, CEO James Kelly, and CFO John Chuta, led to some disturbing revelations. James said he wanted me to hold the title of Chief Operating Officer of the Urban League, with the added title of Manager of the Museum. I categorically refused; my title needed to be Executive Director of the museum. I felt that having the confusing dual title he suggested would have a negative impact on the museum's importance—and thus, it would hurt my ability to raise dollars.

I also explained that I'd immediately start the process of establishing an independent board for the museum and would create our own 501(c)(3) designation. Ultimately, we'd move as fast as possible to separate fiscally from the League. I advised that this was not meant to be disparaging to the League, but that the longtime community supporters of the museum expected a separate entity. James reluctantly agreed.

During the discussion, John Chuta said the museum's financial situation was such that it only had dollars for my salary for the next two months! And *nothing* for Barbara Thomas! He then asked, "What are you going to do?" By this point my blood was boiling. I asked, "What about the business plan of Stuart Grover which reflected dollars available for a curator and a development officer?"

He said, simply, that circumstances had changed. He asked me, "Is there any chance you could contact your former Boeing Company executive co-workers to see if they could bail *you* out?"

Fuming, I set up a meeting with one of my former colleagues at Boeing who was familiar with the ongoing difficulties with the museum. He was very supportive of the project and wanted it to succeed. As a result, a grant was provided that was helpful in sustaining the museum for several months. The grant was bolstered by my decision to forego 25 percent of my agreed-upon salary. That reduction remained in place during my entire tenure with the museum. Barbara also volunteered for a salary cut.

The lack of funds available from the League, as well as James expecting me to change my title, made me rethink my decision to take the job. But in view of the publicity surrounding my appointment—and especially the expectations of the African American community—I decided it was too late to change my mind. However, I justifiably became very cautious of my relationship with the League. They were embroiled in unpredictable circumstances with cash flow when we would soon face rapidly rising design and construction costs for the project.

The actions of James and his CFO became more understandable when they came to my office toward the end of December 2004. They brought the finance chair of the Urban League to discuss a proposal with me. The CFO began by saying there was a piece of empty property on the corner of 23rd and Union available at a cheap price which could provide a "wonderful" opportunity for the museum.

In essence, John said that the costs of remodeling Colman School, because of its *historical designation*, made the project prohibitive. He believed that if the League sold the Colman building and used the funds to build a new museum on Union Street and 23rd corner, it would end up costing much less than remodeling Colman School.

John and James wanted the approval of the finance chair and of me to sell the school building. In a June 11, 2007, article of *The Puget Sound Journal*, Kelly was quoted as saying that it would have been easier and less expensive to build a new structure rather than to restore the dilapidated school. James added jokingly, "After the Nisqually earthquake [Feb. 28, 2001], my prayer was 'Lord, let it fall down.' I went out there and it was still standing. Then I said, 'Lord, give me the strength of Samson to push it over,' but that didn't happen either."

I did not consider his statement a joke.[50]

I acknowledged that they were probably right concerning the reduced costs of their plan. But I said that the negative political consequences of their proposal would run all of us out of town. Thirty years of "blood sweat and tears" of the protesters as well as all the others within the community to have the museum at Colman would have been all for naught.

And then I could not believe my ears: the finance chair *agreed* with me! He added that the League Board would not approve their proposal. That ended the conversation.

There is no doubt in my mind that the League's CFO wanted his proposal to go into effect. Justifiably, he was concerned about the costs of the Colman project and did not have confidence that I would be able to raise the necessary dollars. It's important to note that I was hired to raise dollars for the *entire project*—not just the museum. The negative experience the league had had with their previous fundraiser for nonprofit endeavors did not give the CFO much hope that I, without any professional background in fundraising, would do any better. I believe he felt our team would fail, and he was doing his utmost to protect his boss from failure.

The CFO was attempting to discourage me from doing my job to justify implementing his 23rd and Union scheme. I could understand his position, but I could not support it.

My uneasiness with the fiscal relationship with ULMS made me realize the importance of having a separate NAAM 501©(3) tax exempt nonprofit organization. We needed to establish our own bank account as soon as possible. When I came aboard, all of NAAM's financial accounts, including fundraising, were under the control of the ULMS.

Another priority was to immediately hire additional staff members besides Barbara. At a minimum, I needed an administrative assistant as well as a development staff person to assist in our fundraising efforts. I had known Barbara Lavert and several of her relatives for many years and was aware of her office management skills. She also had outstanding academic credentials with a Baccalaureate Degree in Sociology and a master's degree in urban planning. She acquitted herself extremely well in her capacity during the entire time she was employed at NAAM.

Leila Miles read of my appointment as Executive Director through the media and contacted me about the possibility of being hired. I was impressed with her resume: she had graduated with honors from the prestigious Lakeside High School in Seattle, received her BA in business from Stanford University, and earned her master's in business from the University of Southern California. While I was interviewing her, she said her father was the world-renowned marine scientist, Edward Miles, from the University of Washington. I had known Ed through the Dan Evans School of Public Policy and Government where he had a dual appointment as a professor. I had lectured there and had served on the school's advisory committee. Leila's keen intellect and strong academic background in business made me feel she would be a perfect choice as the development manager of the office. The fact that she was the daughter of Professor Miles also made an impression on me. Leila's primary role was to assist me in fundraising planning as well as maintaining all our fundraising and financial records. She was also responsible for working closely with the ULMS Chief Financial Officer concerning those records.

When Leila came aboard, a Development Steering Committee was formed. It included leaders in the community, such as Ken Alhadeff, Pamela Eakes, Robert Flowers, Mimi Gates, Janie Hendrix, Leslie Jones, Ruby Love, Elizabeth Squires, Lenny Wilkens, and Starbucks executive Ken Lombard who chaired the committee. The role of the committee was to provide guidance concerning our fundraising activities. Hopefully, this group would morph into the museum's board of directors.

I was clear to me that our team needed to change the strategy of fundraising implemented earlier by the ULMS. I noticed that most of their efforts focused on raising small amounts of dollars from a large array of individuals—almost all of whom were from the African American community. This was a noble and well-meaning plan. However, with the rising construction costs of the project, I felt we needed to broaden our scope to include major individual donors, corporations, and family and community foundations. Also, more construction dollars were needed from local, state, and national government entities.

Criticism of our efforts came from some African American activists in the Seattle Community—in particular, followers of Omari Garrett and his son Wyking. They were angered because we were seeking dollars from "White" organizations and individuals. My response to such detractors was that we wanted to expose the *entire* Northwest population to the contributions of African Americans. We wanted to showcase our history, our culture, the visual and performing arts, and our role in the economic development of our nation. So, the African American community would drive the mission, vision, and objectives of the museum. And our team would make sure that we would not accept any donations that were outside of our community's desires, mission, vision, or objectives.

Barbara Thomas and I agreed that it was especially important to have community involvement in developing our permanent exhibit. When people walked into the building, they needed to have a feeling of something *about themselves*. Barbara organized NAAM volunteers who met with approximately 40 *community groups* in Washington, Oregon, Idaho, and British Columbia, asking them what they would like to see in the museum. They came up with wonderful suggestions!

Around the same time the community meetings were taking place, a young man named Brian Carter contacted Barbara. He had recently enrolled in the University of Washington Museology (study of museums) master's degree program within the College of Arts and Sciences. A professor had told him about NAAM, and he was keenly interested. Brian told Barbara he would be willing to do anything we needed.

She took him under her wing as an unpaid volunteer (which eventually became a paid position) with the title of Education Director, assisting Barbara with curatorial responsibilities. These included developing a categorizing system, acquiring collections, and researching other African American museums throughout the nation. Because of Brian, I was invited to speak to the museology graduate students at the U of W and provided an overview of the NAAM project. I had been unaware of the program before connecting with Brian. With Brian aboard, I felt we had the makings of a small but dynamite team of employees.

In January 2006, the NAAM Development Steering Committee chaired by Ken Lombard, held a meeting which also included me, CEO of ULMS James Kelly, CFO of ULMS John Chuta, and most of the members of the committee. The primary purpose was to discuss the establishment of NAAM's 501©(3) nonprofit status and the formation of a board of directors. It was my hope to have the committee morph into the new board.

To my surprise and dismay, several members of the committee began raising the question of possible NAAM *ownership* of the Colman building and/or the 20,000-square-foot museum space! None of the committee members had ever raised that topic with me before the meeting. James Kelly immediately and angrily declared that the entire building was owned by the Urban League, and his board intended to remain as the owner. He declared that NAAM ownership was not a negotiable issue.

Unfortunately, the discussion became a vitriolic exchange between James and Ken. James Kelly and John Chuta stormed out of the meeting in a huff. The meeting ended with no compromise between the two sides. Soon afterwards, Ken Lombard telephoned me and said he was resigning from the committee. I attempted to encourage him to stay, but he refused.

I was extremely discouraged. My first thought was that the entire project was collapsing. I was caught in the middle of two immoveable sides. No one from either the League or the Committee contacted me to provide consolation or advice. I had to get a grip on myself. I concluded that my commitment to the community was to complete the task of building the museum and have it open within the next two years.

Although the Development Committee had good intentions concerning ownership of the building or the proposed museum condominium, the fact remained that the League owned the building. And, as some lawyers say, "possession is nine-tenths of the law." I was not prepared to go into a long, protracted legal battle with either side. When it was clear that neither entity was willing to talk, I concluded that I would side with the League. The Development Committee was decimated and lost all but two members. Although I had in mind that the Development Committee would become the Board of Trustees of NAAM, it was clear that we had to start over from scratch.

On my own, I contacted an attorney who provided pro bono assistance to draw up by-laws of the Northwest African American Museum as a stand-alone nonprofit corporation separate from the ULMS. According to the Washington State Non-Profit Corporation Act, the board of directors had to consist of at least three members. I contacted two other members of the defunct Development Committee to be on the board. I included myself as Board Secretary. The first readily agreed to be a board member, but the other adamantly refused because of the ULMS position. I literally *begged* her to join, emphasizing our responsibility to the community to complete the project. I said the promise of a museum had gone on too long. It worked.

Finally, on June 19, 2006, NAAM received documentation from the Washington State Secretary of State that NAAM was now designated as a 501©(3) entity. The initial board members were Ruby Love and Jeff Coopersmith as co-chairs, me as secretary, and Janie Hendrix. NAAM was eventually designated a nonprofit by the IRS. NAAM could now raise funds that could be tax-exempt write-offs for donors.

The near-fatal chasm between the ULMS and our Development Committee did not become a reoccurring nightmare. I was pleased that the bitterness displayed, as well as the resolution of the problem, took place without an ill effect on the staff. Nor did any of the drama leak out into the community or the media. If it had, I feel that irreparable damage to the project would have taken place.

With our new by-laws, the success of our fundraising efforts, and the outstanding work of our small staff, we were now able to have several of the members of the former Development Steering Committee come back and become members of the board.[51]

CHAPTER 32

NAAM Becomes a Reality

IN EARLY 2006, after a national search, Barbara recommended that we hire an exhibit design company named Formations to create our permanent exhibit. Barbara insisted that we needed to have ULMS set aside $800,000 for the project. I agreed. With the "joined at the hip" philosophy of ULMS (i.e., mixing museum and ULMS funds), it was a difficult task. I stood firm regarding Barbara's recommendation, and the League gave in. This exhibit was to be the core, permanent exhibit of the museum and became known as the Journey Gallery.[52]

As donations began to flow into the coffers on a regular basis, there was no further talk from the League about selling the Colman school. Our team finalized our three-year strategic plan with our vision, mission, goals, and measurable benchmarks. We also assigned "process leaders" within our small operating team. To the dismay of our more creative members of the team—as opposed to the more bureaucratic folks like me—we held weekly staff meetings to determine progress being made on our targets and goals.

I also continuously emphasized that each team member, regardless of their primary role, had to see themselves essentially as *fundraisers*. All of us had some interface with members of the community, right? How they saw each of us would determine if they would support NAAM by their dollars or in other ways. To ensure success, we always needed to be customer oriented.

Carver Gayton, Barbara Thomas, and Brian Carter (left to right) stand in front of the hard-won site of the future museum during their push to fulfill the community's NAAM dream. (The Seattle Times, John Lok photographer)

As we became more focused, I felt it was important to build a more close-knit team. Having our offices spread out within the Urban League building worked against that goal. I contacted a good friend of mine, Jack Emick. He was the owner of EHS Design, a business office design corporation with contracts throughout the nation. I asked Jack if he knew of any office space in downtown Seattle that could accommodate our small team while construction and renovation were taking place in the Colman School. Discussions with Jack led to him providing pro bono office space at One Union Square—with only nominal charges for support needs! The move penciled out less cost than our rental charges at ULMS. Our phone and computer systems remained aligned with the ULMS.

The move allowed us to be closer to many of our business and nonprofit donors in downtown Seattle. As anticipated, it also created a closer, independent team. Jack was a great supporter of the museum and worked diligently to make our NAAM team feel welcome and comfortable in our new environment.

During the spring and summer of 2006, we made major strides in a variety of areas. Besides receiving our 501©(3) designation in June, NAAM had a groundbreaking ceremony on June 1. The crowd was overflowing, with many standing in the rain. ULMS Chairman of the Board Paul Childs was Master of

Ceremonies. Introductory speeches were by US Senators Murray and Cantwell. The media coverage was vast and very positive. Although Omari Garrett and a few other activists were across the street with placards denouncing the groundbreaking, there were no confrontations.

Soon after the event, Charlie James, another activist who occupied the building in the 1980s, telephoned me. I contacted him a few days earlier to see if he was interested in writing about his experiences during the occupation. I felt that having such an account was warranted and justified. Charlie, a highly regarded opinion writer for *The Seattle Times* and a variety of community publications, said he was open to discussing my offer. The only stipulation I had for the contract was that I did not want ad hominem attacks on any individuals.

Charlie's articles came out in the fall of 2006 and were very well done. I felt, at the time, that the animosity between his group and NAAM and the ULMS was beginning to die down.

During the late spring and early summer, the NAAM team worked under the guidance of Leila Miles, our development manager. Leila provided invaluable support for our fundraising efforts by assisting us in bringing in major grants in the $500,000 range! These came from organizations such as PAACAR, the Washington Housing Trust Fund, and the Washington State Heritage Capital Projects Fund. The new dollars also helped the staff and the NAAM Board move forward, and away from ownership battles.

We began to focus more directly on completing the construction of the building and preparing for the planned opening of the museum in early 2008.

Brian Carter, our part-time intern, finished his master's degree in Museology at the U of W in June of 2006. He would later be hired as our fulltime curator in January of 2007. His hiring, under Barbara's guidance, added considerable stability to the project.

Another step forward during the summer of 2006 was the work Barbara took on: overseeing the official startup of our community program with design consultant Formations Inc. Formation representatives conducted the Central District community meetings. They guided the meetings through discussions of all aspects of the museum programs, audiences, and exhibitions, etc. But their primary focus was on the planned permanent "Journey Gallery" Exhibit.

I also continuously emphasized that each team member, regardless of their primary role, had to see themselves essentially as *fundraisers*. All of us had some interface with members of the community, right?

Donald King, owner of DKA Architects, was the lead architect of the building. He also had a major role working with Barbara in facilitating the exciting community meetings.

As our fundraising continued to make progress, construction on the site started, and the Journey Gallery began to take shape. It became easier for us to recruit an array of outstanding board members from the business and not-for-profit communities. It was apparent by the fall of 2006 that the museum would become a reality no later than early 2008.

Grand Opening plans started in October of 2006. I began discussions with David Doxtater, CEO of The Workshop, whose company specializes in event planning. The target date for the festivities was the week of March 8, 2008.

David was highly regarded in his field, having created productions for many private and public organizations throughout the Northwest. He had submitted his draft proposal to me in November of 2006. I remember during one of our early conversations he asked me what I had in mind for the entertainment portion of the grand opening. I said I planned on having the renowned record producer and composer Quincy Jones recognized at the event with a Lifetime Achievement Award. I wanted to have at least three Grammy Award entertainers that Quincy had worked with to provide entertainment for the event!

I had known this former Seattleite for many years. Quincy, the iconic record producer, musician, and arranger, was also the winner of an unprecedented 27 Grammy Awards!

Barack Obama, who was running for President of the United States at the time, signed my copy of his book The Audacity of Hope while attending a NAAM event in 2006.

I participated as Seafair royalty in the 2006 Torchlight Parade as King Neptune with Karen Moyer was Queen Alcyone.

David looked at me in disbelief. He said "Carver, what is your plan B?"

I said, "I don't have a plan B."

He thought the mega star would be too hard to bring aboard. He replied, "Okay, let's see what we can do, but no promises."

Guidance for David included our Grand Opening Committee comprised of my wife, Carmen; Miki and Vicki Flowers; and Dana Looney, Quincy Jones's niece. We were on our way!

Toward the end of 2006, the NAAM Board of Directors began to take shape with Ruby Love and Jeff Coopersmith elected as Co-Chairpersons. I also recommended to the Board that my longtime friend, Fred Dean, CPA, should be elected to the board and chair the important Finance Committee. There were no dissenting opinions. Fred was General Manager of CFOsoft, LLC, an up-and-coming force within Seattle's financial community.

A formal vote was to take place in January of 2007. Tragically, Fred passed away a week before the Board meeting. Personally, I was devastated. I had known Fred since he was a young boy. We connected even more in that we both played varsity football for our beloved Huskies. It also was a significant loss to NAAM, the Urban League, and the community. At the time of his death, NAAM and the Urban League were on the verge of separating financially. We desperately needed his expertise. But sadly, that was not to be.

During the early months of 2007, Barbara Thomas was working diligently with NAAM's exhibit contractor. The plans for the Journey Gallery were nearing completion. Barbara was also providing plans for the first rotating exhibit which would feature the migration stories of the iconic painter Jacob Lawrence as well as the works of Seattle sculptor James Washington. Lawrence had been Barbara's mentor during his professorship at the University of Washington's School of Art.

The early months of 2007 were also devoted to fundraising and working on NAAM's lease agreement with the League. The agreement was signed by both parties on July 20, 2007. The NAAM team was led by NAAM Board Co-Chair Ruby Love and NAAM attorney Michel Stern. The NAAM team considered the finalized document as being fair. The lease was presented to the Board for approval and passed on August 14, 2007. The major elements were as follows:

Lease Term:

The term of the lease will expire forty-five (45) years after the commencement Date (commencement on or after March 1, 2008). NAAM will have the right to extend the term lease (3) periods of ten (10) years for each of its term extensions. It will have the option to purchase the premises. Price of the purchase, if exercised, will be by agreement or arbitration.

Rent:

The base rent shall equal one dollar ($1.00) per year.
Additional rent would include condominium charges and real estate taxes on the premises.

It was in the fall of 2007, as a very productive year for the museum began to wind down, that the strain on our staff began to show. We had been working hard to meet our ambitious goals. Our entire team was close knit and committed to doing our best to make sure that the community would be proud of our work. But our fast-paced and hard-driving culture had put considerable pressure on the entire staff.

It was within this pressurized office environment that Development Director Leila Miles left NAAM to pursue other opportunities in the late fall of 2007. Leila was the "process owner" of our fundraising efforts. She served as the administrative liaison to the board of directors with a primary responsibility of taking the minutes of our meetings. She prepared our budgets and was able to explain them in a clear and concise manner to the board, our clients, and the public. Her oral communication and technology skills were also exceptional. Her exit left a transfer of knowledge "vacuum" regarding our fundraising accounts and connections with ongoing and potential donors. This created a challenging learning curve for those who replaced her.

During this period, NAAM initiated a process of reconciling our fundraising account records with the ULMS records and the process revealed that thousands of dollars earmarked for the museum were inadvertently directed to the ULMS accounts. That led to the League setting up—within their overall account— separate identified accounts for *both* organizations. The agreed-upon intention was to go through another reconciliation exercise as soon as NAAM had a separate bank account established. In the rush to complete the construction of the NAAM-Urban League Village project and remain on target for the March 8, 2008, Grand Opening, the crucial reconciliation of those accounts did not take place during my tenure as executive director.

Since it was clear that we would indeed meet our March 8th Grand Opening deadline, most of my energy became focused on the details of the ceremony. Also at the top of my list was planning a musical celebration we called the Award Gala. It would be open to the public and give special recognition for Quincy Jones as the first recipient of the NAAM's Lifetime Achievement Award! I thought he would be the perfect person to be so recognized. The Award Gala would take place March 16th at Seattle's Paramount Theater, eight days after the museum's formal opening.

I initially called Quincy in October of 2006 and left a message with his administrative assistant saying that I would like to talk with him. He called me back on my office phone and my secretary answered. Quincy said, "This is Quincy Jones returning Carver's call."

She almost fainted! Then she screeched out, "Carver—Quincy Jones is on the phone, asking for *you*!"

I was surprised by his quick response. I told him how much I appreciated him getting back to me so soon. I gave my "elevator pitch" about the project and the fact that we planned on having a major entertainment gala as part of a week-long celebration of the opening. I capped off the conversation by saying that it was imperative for him to be a major part of the celebration and be recognized as the first recipient of the museum's Lifetime Achievement Award.

Quincy didn't hesitate for a second. He said, "Count me in, and let's continue the conversation. Let me know what you want me to do." That was it!

I followed up with a formal letter outlining what we discussed on the phone, and he responded with the following letter:

Dear Carver,

I truly look forward to attending the March 16, 2008, event in Seattle celebrating the Grand Opening of NWAAM.

I am especially pleased and honored the Board of Directors had selected me to be recognized during the event to receive their very first Lifetime Achievement Award.

Please keep me apprised of ongoing details surrounding the celebration that would assist in accommodating my visit.

Sincerely,

Quincy (signed)

Quincy and I had several phone conversations in the months leading up to the opening. I recall when I told him that I envisioned having top performing artists for our program, featuring him.

His response was "Who do you want?" and gave no parameters.

I replied, "Who do I want *in the world?*"

He said, "Sure!"

I said I'd get back with him. I looked back on the calls and can see our conversations usually took place in the late evenings on a Friday. He must have assumed that I had no social life by calling me at home then. He was right!

We usually talked for a few minutes about the subject at hand (i.e., the gala). But then for the next 30 to 40 minutes, he would regale me with wonderful stories! All about his glorious career and about growing up in Seattle. I cannot repeat many of his more colorful recollections. But he kept me in stiches!

There was a particular comment he made that really fascinated me. It related to what many considered his "business acumen." He said most admirers consider him an exceptional businessman. But, he said, "I'm fundamentally a musician.

And what I learned in that world I applied to business ventures, such as listening to my musicians and performers, respecting their talents, building upon their unique and positive characteristics—rather than having a cookie-cutter approach for all. Orchestration and arrangements translate into how best to utilize all the instruments and voices to become a beautiful and memorable whole."

I interpreted what he was saying by relating to the old adage that "the whole is greater than the sum of the parts."

The other element of his business and artistic sense was that he made people he worked with feel he truly cared about them, loved them.

In the fall of 2007, I sent Quincy Jones's administrative assistant a wish list of possible performers and celebrities for the gala. They included, among others, Carlos Santana, Patti Austin, James Ingram, Chaka Khan, Donna Summer, Yolanda Adams, Oprah Winfrey, Maya Angelou, Kenny G., Ernestine Anderson, Clarence Acox Jr., David Foster, Buddy Catlett, Diane Schuur, and Siedah Garrett.

I maintained contact with Quincy's administrative assistant, Debborah Foreman, consistently from late summer of 2007 through March of 2008, with primary focus on contacting the outstanding people listed above. Each of the letters I sent out had Quincy identified as having a copy. His name alone made my work an easy task. Of all those contacted, just *two* did not respond due to contractual commitments on the day of gala. I was overwhelmed by the responses. They were clear indicators of the respect and admiration all these performers had for Quincy Jones.

I worked closely with our Grand Opening Committee and our event consultant David Doxtater of The Workshop. Our plan was to hold three special events around the opening beginning with a Black-Tie Gala dinner at the museum for 250 major donors as well as representatives from the performing and visual arts communities on January 19, 2008. Guests had the opportunity to see NAAM before the general public and to enjoy an intimate evening, including a cocktail reception, dinner, and celebrity entertainment. Guests also received a tour of the museum by Barbara Thomas and other principals involved with the exhibits. Sponsors of the event had access to a very select group of leaders in the arts and cultural community.

The Gala's formal dinner was held in the museum's multi-purpose room then moved to the museum's largest room, the Legacy Gallery, which was

Carver Gayton (center) cutting the ribbon at the opening of NAAM, March 9, 2008, with city and state dignitaries at the time: (left to right) Seattle Mayor Greg Nickels, Governor Christine Gregoire, NAAM Board Co-Chair Ruby Love, US House Representative Jim McDermott, Carver Gayton, King County Councilmember Larry Gossett, and former mayor and civic leader Norman Rice.

transformed into an upscale jazz club by our consultants from the Workshop. The surprise for the guests was an evening-long performance by multi-Grammy Award winning singer Diane Schuur and her band. The former Seattleite was excited about coming to Seattle, not only on behalf of NAAM, but because Quincy Jones was to be recognized by the museum.

The performance by Ms. Schuur was truly memorable. The guests were thrilled and showed their appreciation by requests for multiple encores. The whole evening was an unabashed success!

The mention of Quincy Jones also significantly reduced the costs ordinarily charged by performers, for both the Diane Schuur event and the Quincy Jones celebration. All of the lead performers did the gig pro bono in honor of Quincy.

———

The official Ribbon Cutting and the Public Opening of the museum was held on March 8, 2008. A clarion call to the public about the opening museum was a stunning six-page insert published in *The Seattle Times* on March 1, 2008. The full-color story was entitled "Struggles and Triumphs: New Museum Presents a Compelling History of Black Experiences in the Pacific Northwest." The sponsor was the Seattle Art Museum. There is no question in my mind that the publication had an enormous impact on the community and contributed to the large turnout at the opening.

The day before the ribbon-cutting ceremony, I took the time to walk alone through the completed 20-thousand-square-foot museum and was simply amazed. Remembering the completely dilapidated structure in 2004, and now, four years later, seeing the new permanent Journey Gallery! It depicted two centuries of African American history in the Pacific Northwest. Chills of pride ran up my spine ran seeing the iconic paintings of Jacob Lawrence, having been shipped in from New York City, as well as the sculptures of Seattle's own James Washington in the rotating galleries.

The hard work of our team led by Barbara Thomas and Brian Carter came to fruition. It seemed like it was only a few months earlier that they were in the planning stages with the Formations exhibit company. Our new kitchen and café were bright and shiny, and the staff offices with new furniture donated by my longtime friend Martin Selig would make any other museum envious. The genealogy room, with equipment donated by the Church of Latter-Day Saints, was all wired up and ready to go. The gift shop was comparable to any other museums in the city. I was overcome with pride for our team, our donors, the African American community, and the community at-large.

Opening Day started with me taking invited dignitaries on a private tour of the museum at 10:00 a.m. At 11 a.m. As I approached the podium to begin the opening, I marveled at the crowd of thousands that showed up for the historic event. I gave a brief welcome, remarking that the "First leg of creating the museum had gone on for almost 30 years. We will not end our journey until we can ensure we have an African American museum at this site in perpetuity."

Reverend Dr. Samuel McKinney, pastor of the Mount Zion Baptist Church, gave the invocation. He appropriately referenced the museum's "difficult" birth by saying, "I want to thank all who labored and sacrificed to make this possible. . ." He also made mention of the activists who occupied the building for eight years.

I thanked Reverend McKinney and then introduced Anchor Joyce Taylor, of King TV, as the MC. I then sat down, and there was a slight lull with no one at the podium.

Suddenly a young Black man jumped up on the stage, took over the podium, and began talking. Knowing he was not part of the program, I casually walked up next to him while motioning to the police officers on the back of the stage to escort him out. The young man was Wyking Garrett, an opponent of the museum and the son of Omari Garrett, one of the activists who'd occupied the museum for eight years.

The festive atmosphere was broken as he began blasting the project yelling, "This is a disgrace. It is not what we sacrificed our lives for!" The crowd began booing. Wyking went on, saying "This is not what we asked for. We're gonna have a gang truce! We're gonna have a gang truce, and we're gonna fight for our community!"

At this point I was able to reach the microphone, still standing next to the young Garrett. I smiled at the crowd and said, "We are open to the opinion of others. They had a role in improving the visibility of the African American Museum. They were a part of that. But we are here to celebrate the opening of the Northwest African American Museum." The crowd gave a deafening cheer! The police on the podium then grabbed Wyking and took him away initially to the Seattle Police Department East Precinct, where he was booked on suspicion of criminal trespass and obstructing and then taken to the King County jail.[53]

Joyce Taylor came to the podium and spoke:

> This is indeed a historic moment for the City of Seattle. Many people were working toward the goal of having an African American museum at the Coleman School site for over a generation. However, it did not really gel until the Urban League of Metropolitan Seattle, under the leadership of Paul Chiles, Board Chair, and James Kelly CEO came up with the vision in 2001 of the Urban League Village, with the affordable housing on the top two floors of this building and the 20,000 square-foot ground floor being the Northwest African American Museum. The Museum did not become a reality until Carver Gayton took the helm as executive director and Barbara Earl Thomas joined him as curator. A mere three years from that time they came aboard until this month! You now see the wonderful results of their labors and that of their dedicated and talented team.

Joyce listed the dignitaries scheduled to speak: NAAM Board of Directors Co-Chair Ruby Love; SAFECO Foundation President Virginia Anderson; Mayor of Seattle Greg Nickels; King County Executive Ron Sims; US Senator Maria

Cantwell; and Governor Christine Gregoire. *The Seattle Times* described the celebration as a "Star Studded event."

After the formal ceremony, we opened the doors of the museum to the public. As I walked through the door, I looked to my left and saw Barbara lying on the floor of the museum's café. I was shocked! As I rushed over to her, she began moving and looked up at me. She said she was alright and not to worry. She got to her feet. I never found out what caused her to faint. With the thousands of people attending the opening, she probably was overwhelmed by the community response—along with being exhausted mentally and physically from the enormous pressure she endured over the previous three years! Barbara was relentless in her devotion to the project.

People were lined up from the large door of the museum, past the parking lot, on to all streets that converged with the museum! It remained that way for hours.

One of the highlights for me while watching the hundreds of visitors moving through the Journey Gallery exhibit was observing a group of young Black kids engrossed with the Tuskegee Airmen display. The display had the fight jacket, helmet, medals, and other paraphernalia of Colonel William Holloman, who flew a P51 fighter plane with the 99th Fighter Squadron in Italy during World War II. In 1944 and 1945, he protected American Bomber planes and strafed key enemy targets during his nineteen missions.

While observing these young boys, I mentioned to one of the museum volunteers, "It is really a shame that Colonel Holloman is not here to talk with the youngsters about his exploits and the story of the illustrious Tuskegee Airmen." Someone in the crowd said that they had seen Colonel Holloman standing way in the back of the line.

I immediately went outside and found him waiting patiently to enter the museum. I told him, "Colonel, you are the essence of the stories we tell about the accomplishments of our African American heroes! Come with me to the front of the line to your exhibit. There are some young folks who need to see you in the flesh and hear your story first-hand."

The kids were amazed, and Colonel Holman was excited about the opportunity to share what it was like as a Tuskegee Fighter pilot. I was so proud of him. I was also proud that the museum team was able to bring to life a very important phase of African American history. Colonel Holloman passed away two years later. To this day, his display continues to be a highlight for visitors at NAAM.

I was very pleased with all that transpired during that day of the opening, despite the attempt of Mr. Garrett to disrupt the festivities. I slept soundly that evening.

Reactions of some of the people within the community who toured the museum were as follows:

Upon seeing the artwork display of Jacob Lawrence and James Washington Jr., De Carla Estine Williams said, "It is breathtaking." She added, "We always had such hope [for the museum]. We as a community worked so hard to make it happen." Ms. Williams grew up in the Central Area neighborhood and attended Coleman School which houses the museum. She went on to say, "It's a very special place to me. So many times, I've driven past and wondered what would happen. To see it in a very powerful and special way gives me unspeakable joy."

—

"I'm really excited to finally come inside this building," said Rose, who grew up in the neighborhood. She said she had seen signs promoting the museum since 1995 and never thought it would happen. "I've been googling it for years."

—

Aimee Vaughn said, "I'm so excited. It's been a long time coming. Everybody is really ready for this. Carver took it on as a project and made it his."

———

The third event, the NAAM Lifetime Achievement Award Celebration for Quincy Jones, was held at the Paramount Theater on March 16, 2008.

Working with the various celebrities (and/or their managers) who were to perform at the Quincy Jones Gala was an especially fascinating aspect of my role as executive director of the museum. Everyone I had contacted was enthusiastic about participating in the concert and was elated Quincy wanted them involved. Only a few could not participate because of contractual commitments. Multi-Grammy awardees Kenny G and Yolanda Adams Two attempted to break their contracts in order to perform at the event. I had several conversations with their agents all the way up to a couple of weeks before, but the contracts were too restrictive.

None of the featured stars who agreed to perform were remunerated. They considered their performances *donations* to NAAM in honor of Quincy, which was an incredible gesture of the admiration they had for him. We would not have been able to have a production at nearly that scale without those commitments. The stars for the March 16th extravaganza featured Grammy award winners Carlos Santana, guitarist; James Ingram, singer; and singer-songwriter Siedah Garrett. Local performers included band leader Clarence Acox Jr. and the Seattle Repertory Jazz Orchestra, featuring jazz-great Buddy Catlett, as well as Ernestine Anderson, Steve Connell and Sekou, Laura "Piece" Kelly, Ruby Bishop, and Juan Huey Ray and Sound of the Northwest Choir.

The theme was to present an evening of history, music, and celebration weaving a musical story of the African American experience in the Northwest and beyond, with the incredible life of Quincy Jones. I came up with the concept and theme of the evening show and worked with the Doxtater team concerning the details. A program committee, chaired by myself and my wife Carmen, organized a variety of social events surrounding the Gala.

The narrator of the event was Vivian Phillips, well known within the performing arts communities throughout the Puget Sound area.

As the concert drew to a close, it was time to present Quincy with his recognition. Since Maya Angelo regrettably could not attend in person, she videotaped a beautiful tribute to Quincy and the museum. She expressed the importance of us all knowing about African American history and congratulated the community on the opening of the museum. She talked about Quincy, congratulating him on receiving NAAM's Lifetime Achievement Award. She expressed in heartfelt words what a loving person he is. She concluded by saying his music is a true treasure to our nation and the world.

At the end of the video, NAAM Board co-chairs Ruby Love and Jeff Coopersmith joined me at the microphone to present Quincy with NAAM's Board of Director's first annual Lifetime Achievement Award. He was asked to come on stage to receive it and make a few remarks.

Quincy, an engaging and humorous extemporaneous speaker, said receiving the museum's first annual Lifetime Achievement Award was a real honor, especially coming from his hometown. He said, "This is my city! This is my city! Seattle is my city! I've been crying all night anticipating this moment. I have so many great memories of my early days in Seattle—playing with outstanding musicians like Floyd Standifer, Buddy Cattlet, Billy Tolles, and Ray Charles. We started together!"

Quincy Jones was instrumental in the success of NAAM's opening events. He embraced the event, the city, and NAAM's dream of making the museum's opening truly special. He was recognized with NAAM's Lifetime Achievement Award at the Opening Gala.

He said he remembered being here at the Paramount Theater with his orchestra celebrating his own 50th birthday fundraiser for the Seattle Community Colleges—and he hoped to celebrate fifty more years.[54] "Being over the hill is not part of my thinking. No over the hill stuff. In fact, being over the hill is when you pick up speed." He remembered Frank Sinatra always saying, "Live every day like it's the last day of your life. One day you'll be right."

Quincy's final remarks were, "I love each and every one of you! I am so proud of NAAM and what you are doing for young people. I dreamt about this Carver! "Thankyou!"

The celebration ended with the entire group of entertainers coming together and singing Siedah Garrett's "Tomorrow (A Better You, Better Me)." And the entire audience joined in!

At the end, I came to the stage and thanked the performers, the entertainment committee chaired by my wife Carmen, our sponsors, Formations, our staff, NAAM Board of Directors, and special thanks and appreciation to our awardee and living legend Quincy Jones.

A follow-up reception for Quincy, the performers, and major donors took place at the Sorrento Hotel, owned by board member, Michael Malone. It was the icing on the cake for a glorious evening.

The next afternoon, I took Quincy and his family members on a private tour of the museum. All were elated.

I had made it clear when I first committed to being executive director that my major goal was to get the museum up and running. That goal had been met. At nearly 70 years of age, I wanted to move on to less intensive ventures during the winter of my years. On May 20, 2008, I sent the following email to the NAAM staff Board of Directors and community at-large:

Dear Friends,

After three wonderful and intense years as Executive Director of the Northwest African American Museum, I have decided to leave my position as of June 21, 2008. I will continue to assist NAAM in fundraising after I step down and will also begin serving on the museum's National Advisory Committee.

My job as Executive Director of this project has been more than three years of relentless pressure and emotional strain seven days a week. I can count the number of vacation days I've taken over those years on one hand. My passion for the museum kept me going, but I realize this kind of lifestyle cannot be sustained over time.

It is time for someone with a fresh perspective to help write the next chapter of the NAAM's remarkable story.

I am so grateful for what our team has achieved. Since 2005 the NAAM team has:

- *Led a capital campaign in raising over $15 million for the museum and another $10 million for the Urban League Village.*
- *Created both a NAAM Board of Directors and a National Advisory Committee.*
- *Achieved not-for-profit status for NAAM.*
- *Established a favorable long-term lease agreement (up to 75 years) with the Urban League, with sub-leases for a museum store and gift shop.*
- *Established an excellent and unique African American Museum with exceptional exhibits that already achieved national visibility.*
- *Held the Quincy Jones recognition gala and fundraiser on March 16, 2008, with attendees regarding it as one of the most memorable and uplifting concerts they have ever witnessed. Mr. Jones, also a member of NAAM's National Advisory Committee, indicated that he would like to have a significant role in the next gala.*

- *Hosted over 3,000 people who attended the ribbon-cutting for the opening of NAAM on March 8, 2008, and 2000 the following week.*

Finally, while the idea of having a museum at the Colman School had been in limbo for a generation, three years after our team arrived, and in partnership with the Urban League, the museum was built. And now our programs have been initiated.

A special note needs to be made of Barbara Earl Thomas, NAAM's Curator. Her excellent exhibits and programs are the heart and soul of the museum. The community is the true beneficiary of her talents. Barbara will serve as acting Director of NAAM after my departure.

Clearly, we all have much to be proud of. The creation of such a community gem is so much more than bricks and mortar. It reflects the relationships, partnerships, commitments, and sacrifices of scores of our friends, neighbors, and fellow dreamers.

I thank you for your support and encouragement during this remarkable and deeply fulfilling time of my life.

It's been a great ride!

Sincerely,

Carver Gayton

Once aware of my announcement, the University of Washington College of Arts and Sciences reported in their *Perspectives Newsletter:* "Some consider the mere existence of NAAM, after so many years of delay and disappointment, a little bit of magic. But it really boils down to finding the right people for the job." The article continued by quoting from NAAM's outstanding administrative assistant Barbara Lavert, "That we're actually here, and on time, is amazing," says Lavert. "I don't think anyone, but Carver and Barbara could have done this. Others have tried, but those two made it happen." I still choke up reading that statement. But Barbara Lavert needs to also realize we could not have made it without her.

That was followed up with a June 29, 2008, *Seattle Times* article: "Director Accomplished an 'Impossible' Task, Carver Gayton Retiring."

He Had Tough Job: taking African American Museum from Vision to Reality. Now that the seemingly impossible has been accomplished, perhaps mere mortals can take over.

Quincy Jones

QUINCY JONES WAS VERY MUCH involved in making the grand opening of NAAM a resounding success. All of the nationally recognized entertainers performed at his behest and free of charge. After the event, he sent me the song to congratulate me on the success of the opening as well as recognize the hard work I had put into the project. The sheet of music is titled "Carver Gayton," and the words and music were written by Quincy, Lionel Richie, and Rod Temperton. The tune was from the film Quincy produced, *The Color Purple.*

Quincy was probably the most famous person to graduate from Garfield High School in Seattle. With that in mind, I laughed heartily when I first read the final lyrics of the song: "Brother we sho' ain't got a whole lot of time, so shake your Gayton Carver, 'cus brother, Garfield is feelin' fine."

With slight exaggeration, that was the sentiment expressed Wednesday by some connected with the Northwest African American Museum when Carver Gayton announced that he would retire June 25, less than four months after the museum opening.

"If you're going to do the impossible, you need Carver Gayton," said Barbara Earl Thomas, the museum's curator, who will become acting director. "I couldn't have done anything so hard with anyone better."

Since he was persuaded to take the job in late 2004, Gayton, 69, helped turn the museum from a decades-long subject of discussion, proposals, and controversy into a $25 million reality.

"I just can't stay at the same pace that I've been going at for three years. I have to pull back," said Gayton, a former State Employment Security Commissioner, Boeing Executive, FBI Agent, and longtime educator.

Ruby Love, co-chair of the museum's board, said Gayton 'leaves a legacy of galvanizing the community' in support of the project.

"He's done remarkable work with remarkable collaborators and partners, and we want to celebrate an incredible museum he has taken to this point," Love said.

Quincy Jones presented me with a surprise gift in 2009.

The Northwest African American Museum has been in existence and thriving for 16 years. I am very pleased with its progress, despite the continuing disappointment of the same small group of community activists who attempted to take over the abandoned structure years ago. LaNesha Debardelaben, the immediate past CEO of NAAM, did an outstanding job of broadening community support for the museum during her tenure. She also made it clear to the activists that she and the NAAM team were and would be willing to work with them. A sign of the activists softening their position took place in May 2022 when a protest encampment they had in front of NAAM during the COVID-19 crisis was quietly taken down. NAAM closed during that time because of the coronavirus and had a grand reopening in the fall 2022. Debardelaben resigned in late 2023 to complete her work on her PhD at the University of Washington. Brandon Bird was named the new CEO in August of 2024.

During the lifetime of the museum, a wide variety of organizations, groups, and individuals have visited NAAM. They have represented various races, religious affiliations, and students from all grade levels. The museum's emphasis is on African American history, art, and culture, and the story of the museum itself is clearly of interest and value to the Northwest community and beyond.

Many of NAAM's exhibits and programs have received national and local recognition. One for which I have special interest is called the Dr. Carver Gayton Youth Curator Program. It is the brainchild of Barbara Thomas and Brian Carter, the museum's initial curatorial experts. It engages high school students in discovering the art and science of museum curation. The aim of the program is to bring a cohort of high school students together to produce museum-quality multimedia displays

Basketball great Bill Russell and journalist/ author Isabel Wilkerson tour exhibits with Carver Gayton.

that engage and educate the public on a theme. The theme is derived from the featured exhibit gallery. In 2019, NAAM was a finalist for the National Medal for Museum and Library Service Award. The Curator program was identified as a primary factor for that recognition.

The key reason for the success of NAAM I believe stems from the outstanding team we were able to bring together during the early years of the project. They were committed to the museum's vision and worked together as a tight-knit group during some very challenging times. Barbara Thomas, Brian Carter, and Barbara Lavert deserve special recognition. Many others on our operating team, on the board, and within the community at large and the business and non-profit communities, could also be named. However, the two Barbaras and Brian were with me daily through hell and high water for nearly four years. The community should be extremely grateful for their dedication. I certainly am.

Carver taking guests on a tour of the exhibitions. (Bill Kossen photographer)

Bill Gates Jr. and Mimi Gates attend a special NAAM event.

PART IX

ACROSS GENERATIONS

CHAPTER 33

Burdened, But Not Broken: A Family in Transition

MY MOTHER PASSED AWAY from Alzheimer's disease in 1993. She had been ill for years. During the illness her memory was poor, but she tended to be in a good mood most days. She could not remember the names of folks toward the end. However, one day I brought my two-year-old-son Chandler by her rest home. She smiled, blurted out his name, and reached out to give him a big kiss. It's amazing how the mind works in such circumstances. She did not remember who I was.

Mom connected well with all of my children, especially after the divorce. She was an important comforting influence for Cynthia, Clark, and Craig while I was away in Florida. I was looking through a large steamer trunk of hers after she passed away and discovered scores of letters and post cards that

Raising children is one of the most difficult responsibilities a person has.

they had sent her when they were away in college back East. I was amazed by the volume.

Cynthia sent the most communications. I was saddened by the tone of some of some of her letters, but glad that she had a sounding board like my mom. In a card dated May 1984, Cynthia had asked her grandmother, "Of the many things you have done in your life, what has made your life most enjoyable? Happiness seems to be something no one really has. There has to be something wrong when everyone is working so hard, and one is so alone."

Part of Cynthia's question was answered by the fact that in addition to raising a proud and accomplished family of eight children, her grandmother always found time to be involved in community activities, particularly those that enhanced the wellbeing of her children, grandchildren, and her race. Mom was recognized nationally in 1984 by the Schlesinger Library of Radcliff College as one of 72 "Black Women of Courage" for her outstanding professional and voluntary activities.

Cynthia apologized to my mom for writing such a "depressing letter." Cynthia said she was just looking for something to look forward to in life. She was asking her grandma a relevant question. Cynthia was 23 at the time and a semester away from graduating from college. Having trepidations about next

*Virginia Gayton connected with her grandson
Chandler and remembered his name even in her
later days of Alzheimer's disease.*

*My mother was recognized nationally by Radcliff
College and by the Schlesinger Library as one
of a group of Black women who significantly
impacted their communities.*

steps is understandable. Reading such letters makes me feel guilty and somewhat ashamed that Cynthia did not feel comfortable asking me that same question.

When she went away on scholarship to Howard University in Washington, DC, it was clear early on from letters she wrote that she was not enamored with the city. She had a difficult time with the general environment, and it didn't help that she was on a tight budget. After transferring to George Washington University and changing her major from Communications to International Relations, it was apparent to me from her letters that she was better adjusted academically and socially to her new city.

Cynthia is the true intellectual in the family. She always did well academically, from her years at Holy Names High School in Seattle through college and law school. After receiving her BA at George Washington University, Cynthia received her JD Degree in Intellectual Property at George Mason University School of Law. Then she became Attorney advisor in the Acquisitions and Intellectual Property Division of the US Department of the Interior, in Washington, DC. While there, she became Professorial Lecturer/Adjunct Professor of Engineering Law within the School of Engineering and Applied Sciences at George Washington

The family gathered when Virginia Gayton passed away in 1993.

University (a role she would fill for twenty years). She became Adjunct Professor in the University of Maryland School of Engineering, teaching Legal Aspects of Architectural and Engineering Practices in 2015.

Cynthia is currently the Solo Practitioner for her law firm, specializing in services to clients in information technology, engineering, entertainment, and the arts. She has written numerous articles in the field of intellectual property. Her primary publication is as editor of *Legal Aspects of Engineering*, now is in its tenth edition, an effort to raise engineering students' awareness of current problems and responsibilities that are faced during the course of a career. *Legal Aspects of Engineering* is a major textbook for Schools of Engineering across the nation.

As executive director of the Northwest African American Museum in Seattle, I learned of its reach when I hired a technician to adjust the museum's computer system. I noticed a copy of Cynthia's book next to his tool kit! I asked him why he had it and explained that my daughter was the editor of the book. He said he was a student in the College of Engineering at Seattle University, and that the book was a required text. That was the first time I truly realized the importance of Cynthia's work.

Cynthia visiting me on my birthday, October 18, 1982.

Cynthia married T. Jason Edwards in 2008 at Harper's Ferry. The historical surroundings added a special allure. It was a pleasant service attended by me, Carmen, her brother Craig, and their mother, Mona.

Jason graduated from the University of North Carolina School of the Arts in 2001 with a diploma in Scene Painting and Scenic Art. Since then, he has been a professional scenic, visual, and graphic artist. He also is the owner of Bot Studios, which provides regional video and video editing services throughout the Washington, DC, area. He is a wonderful match for Cynthia. He has a great wit, a sharp mind, and a laid-back personality. I agree with Jason when he says, "Cynthia is the most intellectually astute person I know." He knows how to stay in good stead with his father-in-law! I feel the same as Jason. My regret is that I didn't say that first to Cynthia. I am the luckiest man in the world having her as my daughter.

To get away from the hubbub of the DC metropolitan area, Cynthia and Jason spend the weekends at their home in Harper's Ferry, West Virginia. The arts and literary community there rejuvenates them. Since dividing her life between DC and Harper's Ferry, I've witnessed Cynthia being more relaxed, enjoying life, and having a greater appreciation of herself as a person and of all that she has accomplished.

Cynthia is imbued with high ethical standards. She also expects her friends and others she meets to have similar standards. To her credit, she has no problem respectfully pointing out to folks those occasions when they don't meet her standards.

She has helped me a great deal with my writings about her great-great-grandfather Clarke. She has a special interest in Great-Great-Grandpa's sister Delia Clarke and the terrible treatment she endured as a slave and has written several articles about her.

I truly relish talking with Cynthia over the phone. We stay on the phone for at least an hour each time. That does not happen for me when I talk with any other person. She is straightforward with me, especially in her adult years. Most of the conversations relate to the classes she is teaching or the books we are reading. We also discuss politics and history in general. She is a well-known expert in intellectual property law, but I don't have the competency to talk with her for long on that topic. I always look forward to talking with her.

———

Cynthia, Jason, and Clark recently completed a major project called *Hidden in Plain Sight*, revealing two concealed Harper Ferry Cemeteries. One cemetery, where Union soldiers were later buried, was set aside by the United States Armory at Harpers Ferry in the 1850s at the request of the citizenry. Another holds the remains of African American residents, including at least one African American Union soldier. Cynthia and Jason produced the documentary. Clark provided the background music. The 2021 production received a certificate for Exceptional Achievement from the Multi-Dimension Independent Film Festival.

———

Clark's lifelong devotion to music is summed up well in the New York publication *All About Jazz* in 2015:

> *You would be hard pressed to identify a musician as comfortable with classical music as he is with jazz, indie, folk and reggae. You would be equally hard pressed to identify a musician who can rock with Levon Helm (formerly of The Band) on weekends, fly to Istanbul for a command performance, pack the house weekly in New York at Nublu [night club], make recording sessions, wax eloquent about music history and the fundamentals of musicianship, tour with friends in support of their fledgling bands, and still find the wherewithal to record a big band piece from scratch in the remaining spare time . . . unless you happen to know Clark Gayton.*

The writer could have added that Clark has four Grammy awards for his recordings with Sting and Shaggy, Levon Helm, and Sturgill Simpson.

I have never met anyone more dedicated to his or her craft than Clark. He has been focused on music from the time he began to walk. That kind of dedication can be a two-edged sword. In 2017, Clark sent me a text with a picture of him in a hospital bed outside of Oslo, Norway. Tubes were attached all over his body. He was in Norway to perform at an international rock concert starting the next day. He had had a fainting spell resulting in a blood clot moving into his heart.

During my call to the hospital, he was very matter of fact about the situation and even joked about the tubing on his body. The doctors

My son Carver Clark Jr. was invited to perform as the featured performer at a Dollars for Scholars Foundation fundraiser event "For the Love of Jazz." Clark was backed up by the Johnny Lewis Quartet. The event was held at the Langston Hughes Arts Center in Seattle on March 28, 1999.

told him he had to stay in bed for the next ten days. Clark said he planned on performing at the concert.

I yelled at him, "Clark, are you crazy? You're going to kill yourself!"

His retort was, "I signed a contract. I have to play."

After the concert, Clark returned to the hospital for the remaining nine days. He said his treatment at the hospital was excellent and seemed much better by the time he flew home to New York. I believe he said that to console me. I was completely distraught!

When Clark got back home, he started a whole new regimen of changing his lifestyle around drinking, eating, and exercise. I felt he needed to do more than what he *told* me he was doing. Clark's regimen was working well, his health improving enough for him to accept a call to join Bruce Springsteen's band in January 2023 for a two-year world tour. Unfortunately, he suffered a stroke while rehearsing for the tour and is currently recovering in Brooklyn.

———

My son Craig graduated from Howard University School of Dentistry with the rank of Captain. He spent his first year in the military at Fort Benning, Georgia, for advanced training in general dentistry. He then volunteered for a role as assistant chief of Restorative Dentistry in South Korea. He later he returned to the Washington, DC, area as the assistant officer in charge at Fort Myer, Virginia. From there he volunteered for deployment to the NATO postwar humanitarian effort on Kosovo, serving as a brigade dental surgeon.

Craig and Fatisha marry in Atlanta, Georgia, with friends and family attending.

Craig's volunteer assignments in Korea and Kosovo were especially dangerous, i.e., serving at the 38th parallel border between North and South Korea, and in the battle area of Kosovo. Craig explained to me that such assignments allowed him a broad array of dental experiences that he would not have in private practice in the US. At home, most of the dental opportunities would be more specialized. He never mentioned any fear of the choices he made.

After five years as a general dentist, he was accepted to the Army's periodontal certificate program at Eisenhower Medical College Graduate Program in Augusta, Georgia. While there, Craig married Fatisha Tawana (Enahora) in Atlanta. Their wedding was attended by his mother Mona, me, Carmen, and several of his friends from Seattle. It was a wonderful affair.

Craig was assigned to Heidelberg Hospital in Germany soon after he completed his program. While in Heidelberg, Carmen, Chandler, and I visited Craig, Fatisha and their new baby Gabriela, my first grandchild. Gabi was a healthy, beautiful child. An added treat was visiting the sights in Germany and Paris, France. Being there with family made the vacation one of the most memorable of my life. Craig became a father, and I finally became a grandfather.

Craig resigned from the military with the rank of major after eleven years of honorable service. In 2016, Craig joined the US Navy Reserves as a lieutenant commander. That move, Craig explained, would be fun and interesting for his family because there would be ample opportunities to visit different parts of the world. The position also provided all of them additional health and retirement benefits.

Craig's retirement from military service led to the fulfilment of his dreams to treat patients in private practice. He became the owner of a very successful periodontal practice in Silver Springs, Maryland. He was very pleased with the idyllic situation in the DC area. Fatisha settled into her practice as an emergency room physician. Daughter Gabi acclimated to her new home, and her new baby brother, Bryce, kept the whole family energized. At the age of 51, Craig was exceptionally well established, personally and professionally.

Craig and his family visited Seattle in the early summer of 2017. One afternoon at our home as we were talking, he casually mentioned he had a slight pain on the right side of his lower back and asked if I had any idea what might be wrong. I didn't think the question was unusual. Craig often asked me such questions because I had had numerous college football injuries. I responded with a typical tough-jock assessment, "Craig, you should check with a physical therapist. Your pain seems like a muscle issue. A series of sessions with the therapist should take care of the pain."

Craig said, "Thanks Dad, I'll follow up with your suggestion."

I didn't hear back from him, and regrettably, I didn't give the matter another thought.

Fatisha insisted that he set up an appointment with a doctor when he returned to Washington, DC, because the pain was not going away. Craig delayed going. When he finally went, it was determined that he showed signs of a renal cancer issue, and the doctor recommended further tests. Sure enough, Craig had the beginning stages of renal cancer.

In the meantime, I was in ongoing conversation with Clark who was back in New York after his blood clot in Oslo, Norway. I advised him to call Dr. Sytman, a highly regarded cardiologist in Seattle and the resident physician who had *delivered Clark* in the University of Washington hospital emergency room fifty-three years earlier! Dr. Sytman and I had been on the same Garfield high school football team.

Dr. Sytman was very concerned that Clark may need surgery. The doctor suggested that Clark not travel anywhere and advised him to talk with a physician friend of his at the Columbia University Hospital to get further advice. In view of what Dr. Sytman said, I concluded that Clark's illness needed more immediate attention than Craig's, so I flew to New York to see Clark. Clark started a whole new regimen of lifestyle and medications that ultimately saved his life.

Craig's situation, to the surprise of his physicians, grew worse. Carmen, Chandler, and I flew to Washinton, DC, to see him during Christmas week, 2017. Cynthia and Clark also came. There was still the expectation that Craig would recover.

My son Craig Michael Gayton will always have a special place in my heart.

I was in an emotional daze with both my oldest sons being deathly ill at the same time. Carmen's understanding and courage kept me going. I'll always remember the slow, short walk Craig insisted we take with Gabi, Carmen, and Chandler around Craig's neighborhood. He attempted to laugh at my corny jokes, but it was clear that he was weak and in pain. But he never complained, and the walk was generally upbeat. I feel that by going on the walk with us, he was trying to say everything was going to be okay. We went home after Christmas with more than a glimmer of hope that Craig, with his well-known willpower, would overcome the disease.

That would not be. Fatisha informed us toward the end of January 2018 that Craig would pass away at any moment and encouraged us to return to the hospital in DC to say our goodbyes.

Craig was awake the day before he died and, as typical for Craig, was completing paperwork arrangements for his family. He assured me that his dental practice was in good hands and that I should not worry about the financial status of his family. He said it was sound.

I made a comment to him about not giving up and that he should stay strong. His last words to me were, "Aw, Dad, you've said that before." It was kind of a forlorn statement, like saying we both know that the end is near. I didn't want him to let go. He passed away February 14, 2018.

Cynthia was the primary organizer of Craig's beautiful "Service of Witness to the Resurrection" at Chevy Chase Presbyterian Church in DC. Craig's lifetime friends, Randy Wilkens and Doug Legters, gave deeply heartfelt remembrances of Craig. Clark played his trombone and provided a mournful New Orleans-style rendition of the spiritual "Swing low, Sweet Chariot" and closed with "Just a Closer Walk with Thee." There was not a dry eye in the sanctuary.

Craig was one of the finest individuals I have ever known. A fundamentally good person. Some may consider that a trite statement, but during these times we certainly need to be surrounded by more "good" people. Craig also worked harder than most, probably a result of his diagnosis of dyslexia at an early age. An aggressive listener, he certainly made me feel important by sincerely asking questions about relationships, management approaches to make his dental practice more effective, political issues, and so on. He made me feel like he truly wanted to know what I thought and felt, rather than just trying to make conversation. His attention created a bond that is beyond space and time.

Tearful moments of joy about Craig come out of nowhere when I see a beautiful sunset over the Olympic mountains, watch my grandkids playing, hear a moving melody, or run across a humorous Craig-like birthday card. Those moments also come when I'm kneeling in prayer for him each night. . . Those moments keep me upbeat. I am so blessed that Craig, my son, was in my life.

―――――

Carmen and I were also blessed to have a child added as a half-brother to the other three. Chandler was given more attention than the others since he was, in essence, an only child. Also, Chandler benefited from the fact that Carmen and I were better off financially than when Mona and I divorced. Nevertheless, I do not consider Chandler spoiled. In fact, he underplayed the benefits he had as an only child.

Chandler passed away on August 20, 2024, from injuries sustained while riding his motorcycle. His sudden death has caused incalculable grief to me and Carmen as well as hundreds of family members and friends.

Chandler was a very sensitive young man and had the innate ability to feel people out to determine whether he would like them or not. People gravitated to his winning personality. Like his mother, he had a wide variety of friends and remained close to the friends he went to preschool with. He was also very close to his mother's family in South Carolina and made a point to stay in touch with them. They doted on him down there and he loved it.

Chandler Gayton makes a spectacular catch for the Simon Fraser University football team.

Right: Carmen and I stand proudly with Chan as he graduates from Simon Fraser University in British Columba, Canada.

During high school, Chandler was a highly regarded football star at Seattle's O'Dea High School. He was a defensive back and a receiver and earned All-Metro League honors in his last two seasons. Several Northwest colleges were interested in him, including my alma mater, the University of Washington. However, the Huskies dragged their feet on offering him a full scholarship.

Coaches from Eastern Washington University were much more aggressive. Eastern had an excellent football program among the regional colleges in the Northwest and many of Chandler's friends had plans on attending. As a result, Chan accepted Eastern's scholarship offer. He redshirted (on reserve) his first two years, primarily due to shoulder injuries.

Though Chan was an honor student, he was not academically challenged at Eastern. After talking with Carmen and me, he decided to transfer to Simon Fraser University in Vancouver, British Columbia, where he was awarded a football scholarship. My mother's family had a long history in Canada before coming to Seattle so attending college in Canada was not far-fetched for Chandler.

His injuries limited him on the football field, but he enjoyed an outstanding academic experience at Simon Fraser. SFU was a godsend for him. He became an excellent and sensitive writer. He received his BA in Mass Communications/Media Studies in 2015. Then he continued graduate studies at the U of W's Evans

School of Public Policy and Governance. Chandler received his master's degree in public administration in the spring of 2022.

Chandler was extremely ambitious. He was a senior policy advisor for King County Council Member Girmay Zahily in Seattle. Chan focused on affordable housing and land use issues, making his mark by leading projects in low-income communities in South Seattle. He then took a position as strategic advisor for public safety for the Mayor's Office of Seattle.

Additionally, Chandler became a Certified Real Estate Broker with the Windemere Real Estate Company in 2015 under his mother's guidance. He also continued the Gayton Family tradition of community involvement as a volunteer on the Alumni Board of Trustees for O'Dea High School and serving on the Policy and Advisory Committee for Tree House, the state's leading nonprofit organization addressing education enrichment needs of youth in foster care.

Chan was an adventurer. He liked fast cars, snowboarding, and motorcycles. He loved traveling to different places in the world by himself. I wish I had had some of his mindset when I was in my youth. The closest I came to adventure was playing football and working in the FBI for a few years.

Raising children is one of the most difficult responsibilities a person has. A pet peeve of mine is when folks who haven't had children give advice about how to raise them. They need to have kids of their own, and then we can talk.

I really have no recollection of my mother or father lecturing me on how to act in public or at home. That is not to say I wasn't disciplined, but that I was guided primarily by their example. I loved and respected my parents.

When I married at the age of 21, I wanted to emulate my own father. I bought into my father's model of fatherhood and felt I was doing the right thing as a father. I saw my role very simply: fundamentally, I would be the bread winner, and my wife would raise the children. Like my father, I would attempt to be a good example by serving as a volunteer for worthy community services. I also tried to follow his example in such things as serving dinner every day at 6 p.m. with the expectation that every member of the family would be at the table unless excused in advance. (The two seasons I coached football were the exceptions.)

Societal and political upheavals during the 1960s and 1970s changed the role of the traditional family as I had experienced. In many respects, I failed as a father by not being involved in my children's lives as much as I should have been. As a father,

Carmen and Chandler made a great team as real estate brokers.

I spent more time with Chandler over the years than with my older children. Not spending more time with Cynthia, Clark, and Craig was a failing on my part. Despite my frailties as an absent father, by the grace of God, all of my children turned out to be good human beings with outstanding professional accomplishments.

Having two sons die within the past seven years has left me stunned. Nevertheless, I am committed to brace myself and celebrate, until the day I die, the memories of two of the most wonderful young men I have ever known.

———

Carmen, my beloved wife, adjusted very well to her home in Seattle. That did not mean she quit connecting with her friends and family in South Carolina or Georgia. She is on the phone every day with her mother and/or a friend in those areas of the country.

Carmen was initially employed for two years in Seattle as Human Rights Director for Coopers and Lybrand, a consulting group that provides marketing and operations strategies to organizations. She made very fast friends in this, and any, work environment as well as in the social and volunteer organizations with which she is associated.

While Carmen and I were looking for a new home, she became enamored with the real estate business. She joined Windemere Real Estate as a broker in 1995. When she decided on this career, her memorable words for me were: "I'll do this part time." I've had to make appointments to see her ever since! One thing I've learned about Carmen is that when she decides to get involved in a job or any of

The Gayton brothers gather for my birthday celebration in October 2005. It was the last time we were all together: (left to right) Gary, Leonard, me, John, and Phil.

her volunteer enterprises, she makes a 110% commitment! She revels in the fact that she is a "multi-tasker."

Carmen found her true niche in real estate. She loves her work, and her clients love her. She has created a very comfortable financial lifestyle for the family. She has done so well that she is now the owner of her own real estate LLC.

Many of Carmen's clients have in turn become close friends of ours. To a large degree, the business environment has morphed into a very interesting and fun social world. Much of that may just relate to Carmen's winning personality, because she also maintains close friends going back to the days when Chandler attended preschool, high school, and Simon Fraser University. In other words, she draws people to her, and the mutual admiration is not superficial.

I am still mesmerized by her beauty as well as her brains. From time to time, Carmen gets peeved with me for not getting more involved in helping her during tax time. Hey—Carmen was a math major in college, and I was a history major. Duh! Who should do the taxes? She would be spending so much more time teaching *me* what to do, we would miss the IRS deadline.

One thing I know for sure about Carmen: being with her is not boring. I would not want her to be any other way. She gives true meaning to my life.

To coin the phrase from the great composer and orchestra leader Duke Ellington: "CARMEN, MY DEAR, I LOVE YOU MADLY!!"

Carmen and I enjoy time with our grandchildren such as here with Gabi and Bryce, Craig's and Fatisha's children.

Family visiting Seattle in the summer of 2022: (back, left to right) me, Leonard, Gary, Fatisha, Gabi, Jason, (front, left to right) Bryce, and Cynthia.

CHAPTER 34

Honoring My Muse

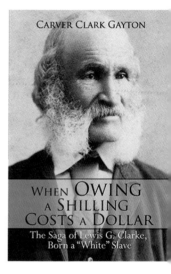

LEWIS G. CLARKE, MY GREAT GRANDFATHER, has in effect, been my muse for writing this autobiography. His spirit has unexpectedly come in and out of my entire life in ways that have encouraged me to remember his legacy. None of these serendipitous encounters were initiated by me.

Publishing the biography of Great-Grandfather Clarke, When Owing a Shilling Costs a Dollar: The Saga of Lewis G. Clarke, *fulfilled a dream of his, and mine.*

My first experience began around the age of four when my mother read excerpts from Harriet Beecher Stowe's book *The Key to Uncle Tom's Cabin* to my brothers and me. Mom always kept an 1853 original copy of *The Key* in a small cabinet in our living room. *The Key* was written to describe the real-life individuals on whom Stowe based her main characters in her famous classic, *Uncle Tom's Cabin*. Mom often read excerpts to us, particularly a section about George Harris, the quadroon, one-fourth slave, which stated that George was based upon the life of Lewis Clarke.

Stowe referred to Clarke's "Narrative" in the book and added that Clarke "... is an acquaintance of the writer." [Stowe] I did not realize that when Stowe mentioned "Narrative," she was referring to a published book. Nevertheless, even at the age of four, I was impressed that a member of our own family was once a famous man and that his name was in print. But throughout my entire childhood and through my early adult years, I considered the George Harris story as no more than interesting family lore. I also questioned that if Clarke was such a famous man, as my mother implied, why wasn't he brought up in my US History classes in high school? Or in college?

My view of Clarke changed considerably in 1972. A distant cousin of Mom's whom she had never met, Raymond Davis of Columbus, Ohio, contacted her by letter. He stated that he had located a book about Clarke. This cousin was the son of Mom's favorite Aunt Minnie (then deceased) who was also Great-Grandpa's eldest daughter.

Through Cousin Raymond, Mom found out that the "Narrative" Stowe had referred to in *The Key* was a copyrighted book titled *Narratives of the Sufferings of Lewis and Milton Clarke*. The Milton Clarke noted in the title was Lewis Clarke's younger brother. The book outlined the experiences the brothers had as slaves and their escape from slavery. The book ends with their arrival in Massachusetts in 1843.

The information Cousin Raymond related was news to Mom and to the entire Gayton clan in Seattle. Mom invited Raymond to Seattle in 1972 and he provided details of the book, which had been republished in 1969—more than likely through his own efforts. It was a wonderful reconnection of the Clarke and Gayton families.

The revelation of the book shed a whole new light on the Lewis Clarke story. First, I had not realized that Great-Grandpa had a brother named Milton and that they ultimately escaped from slavery together. The book covers Lewis's birth in 1815 in Kentucky through to the early 1840s, when he lived in Cambridge, Massachusetts. The *Narratives of the Suffering of Lewis and Milton Clarke* describes what Lewis endured as a child of a Scottish father and a quadroon mother who was a slave. They lived on a plantation in Madison County, Kentucky. Great-Grandpa tells of particularly horrendous experiences after having been sold to cruel plantation owners at an early age.

After having been sold a second time to a more compassionate owner, Lewis became fearful when a rumor indicated he was to be sold to a plantation in Louisiana. It was at this point that he decided to escape from bondage and seek refuge in Canada where he assumed his brother Milton had escaped to two months earlier.

Lewis made it to Canada only to determine that Milton had settled in Ohio. Lewis returned to the US, found Milton in Oberlin, Ohio, and settled there. Then Lewis decided to bring his youngest brother, Cyrus, out of slavery where he was held in Lexington, Kentucky. Lewis's *Narrative* also describes how he and his brother Milton were nearly captured by slave hunters in Oberlin.

The horrifying and heroic sojourn of Great-Grandpa attempting to seek out and free his brothers from slavery was discovered by abolitionists in the Oberlin area and passed on to the local newspapers. In turn, leaders of the American Anti-Slavery Society in New York and in Cambridge, Massachusetts, learned of Lewis's heroics. He and Milton were recruited by the Society to come to those cities and tell of their experiences to large audiences sympathetic to the abolitionist movement.

All this new information stoked in me a renewed interest in the life of Great-Grandfather Clarke. He was in fact an important person in American history, but his contributions were either forgotten or ignored. With this new impression of Clarke, I contacted a highly regarded US History professor whom I admired at the University of Washington. I told him the story of Clarke and gave him the *Narratives* publication. I was very excited about the family's discovery, and I expected him to feel the same.

However, he said that the narrative had been *dictated* by Lewis Clarke to an active member of the American Anti-Slavery Society. As such, the account was not truly legitimate in his mind. He said that such White abolitionists tended to exaggerate the treatment of slaves like my great-grandfather to embellish their cause. Clarke did not know how to read and write when he dictated his story. The professor considered the stories like those of freed slave Frederick Douglass more legitimate because Douglass knew how to read and write.

Overall, it was a depressing conversation. My excitement about Great-Grandpa waned considerably.

In 1977, I was hired as assistant professor at Florida State University in Tallahassee, Florida. While there I would jog periodically with a newfound friend, Peter Ripley. Peter was a history professor at the university and had a wealth of information about Great-Grandfather Clarke that my mother had never related to me. After discovering the connection, Peter provided me with a treasure trove of articles and papers about Great-Grandpa. Think of it! Here I was—3,000 miles away from Seattle—finding out about the significance of this ancestor by happenstance! Peter was one of only a handful of people in the nation who knew about the significance of Clarke's life.

My interest and appreciation of Clarke multiplied, especially after Peter gave me the box-load of papers on Clarke. Regrettably, I did not delve into the material then, because soon afterwards I was hired by The Boeing Company as Corporate Director of Education Relations and Training and returned to Seattle. I wholeheartedly took on the exciting, time-consuming role for almost twenty years! Meanwhile, the box of the Clarke material was stashed away in a closet at home.

After retiring from Boeing, I took on two consecutive full-time jobs: one as Washington State Commissioner of Employment Security, and the other as Executive Director for the Northwest African American Museum (NAAM) in Seattle. I finally began evolving into a retirement lifestyle after leaving NAAM. The box continued to sit.

On June 23, 2009, I received an email from Gregory Wilson, director of the Sugar Grove Historical Commission in Sugar Grove, Pennsylvania. He said, "I had the good fortune of reading a 2005 article in *The Seattle Times* in which you mention that Lewis Clarke is a maternal great-grandfather. I want to tell you that your great-grandfather once lived in Busti, Chautauqua County, New York— which is directly across the border from Sugar Grove. Clarke was considered a hero in these parts, while he was a conductor of an Underground Railroad for escaped slaves during the 1850s!" Mr. Wilson was interested in learning more about the Clarke family. I followed up with him and would continue corresponding with him for several years.

I had no immediate knowledge of Great-Grandpa living in Busti, nor the fact that he conducted an underground railroad. I immediately went to the closet for the box from Peter Ripley. Peter's information not only verified all that Mr. Wilson said but brought much more information to light that none of us in Seattle had known before. For example, Mom's cousin Raymond Davis had told us about the *Narratives of the Sufferings of Lewis and Milton Clarke,* published in 1846, and dictated by both Lewis and his brother Milton. This led us to believe that *Narratives* was the only book Lewis had published. But Peter's material revealed that Clarke's first book, dictated by himself and published in 1845, was exclusively about him. It was titled *Narrative of the Sufferings of Lewis Clarke During Captivity of More than Twenty-Five Years Among the Algerines of Kentucky, one of the so-called Christian States of North America, Dictated by Himself.* That book was the first work authored by a slave to be acquired by the Library of Congress and placed under copyright! It was also published *before* the iconic Frederick Douglass had his first narrative published!

At the time I received Mr. Wilson's email, I was beginning to write my autobiography, with an emphasis on the Gayton family side. But these revelations about my great-grandfather made me change course. The Clarke story had national, historical implications. I *had* to focus on Clarke.

Another factor that made me zero in on Great-Grandpa was reading an 1890 *Boston Globe* interview with him, written by a young Black reporter. In the article, Clarke said he had a manuscript about his entire life and was hoping to have it published. I have made considerable effort to follow up statements Great-Grandpa made in newspaper interviews he gave in other cities mostly related to speaking engagements he was invited to make in those cities in the late 1800s— such as Lexington, Kentucky; New York, New York; Detroit, Michigan, and others. But my searches through the hundreds of articles and papers provided to me by Peter and Gregory Wilson—as well as many hours on the internet—have *not* been successful in finding the manuscript. I've been searching since 2010.

I wanted to fulfill my great-grandfather's dream. I had discussions about this with my daughter Cynthia and decided to revitalize Clarke's story by writing an introduction to Clarke's historic *Narrative of the Sufferings of Lewis Clarke During Captivity of More than Twenty-Five Years*. I published a facsimile edition in 2012 with the University of Washington Press. I followed that in 2014 with my full biography of Clarke entitled *When Owing a Shilling Costs a Dollar: The Saga of Lewis G. Clarke*.

In *When Owing a Shilling Costs a Dollar*, I describe the lifetime contributions of Great-Grandpa and his role in American history throughout the anti-slavery and human-rights movements of the last half of the 19th century. Great-Grandpa's story provides insights into why the remnants of slavery and color lines remain with us today. Nevertheless, his perseverance against slavery and racism provides hope and inspiration to all who believe in the ideals of America.

Throughout Great-Grandpa's life, he pointed out that the physical sufferings of the slaves were not nearly as bad as the moral and intellectual degradation they had to endure. The wounds from whippings and floggings would heal. But the psychological scars were passed on to future generations.

Great-Grandpa said that the worst kind of torture he witnessed in Kentucky was seeing a slave woman stripped naked, hung up by her hands, and whipped till blood ran down her back. The act was even more degrading when carried out by a young master or mistress (*White children*) against an aged mother or even a grandmother.

One can imagine the feelings of degradation, not only by the woman being beaten, but by the grieving children and grandchildren who witnessed such atrocities. The scene speaks volumes of the power implication embedded in the minds of the slave and slave master. The slave master designed the whippings to crush the spirit and will of the woman as well as the slaves observing. Keep in mind that such atrocities went on for nearly 300 years, longer than we have been an independent nation.

Recognizing that these practices went on for generations, it defies reason to assume that all the vestiges of the culture of slavery have been eliminated from how Blacks and Whites see each other today! Great-Grandpa's story underscores William Faulkner's observation: "The past is never dead. It isn't even past."

Great-Grandpa's most impactful speech was delivered to a large gathering in 1842, where he spoke for three days. Lydia Maria Child, editor of *The National Anti-Slavery Standard,* captured his speech in an article titled, "Leaves from a Slave's Journal of Life." While addressing the crowd, Great-Grandpa made this profound query: "My grandmother was her master's daughter, and my mother was her master's daughter, and I was my master's son, so you see I haven't got but *one-eighth* of the [Black] blood. Now admitting it is right to make a slave a full Black nigger, I want to ask gentlemen acquainted with the business whether, because I owe a shilling [approximately 25 cents], I ought to be made to pay a dollar?"

Great-Grandpa was never ashamed of his Black blood. Nevertheless, his riveting question made abundantly clear the irrational, greedy, and racist basis of the "one-drop rule," which meant that anyone with a known Black ancestor was considered Black, thereby increasing the number of slaves and bolstering the burgeoning cotton economy to the benefit of slave owners.

Great-Grandpa's 1842 query continues to be an issue of discussion in modern-day America. I continue to support his opinion on the one-drop rule. Though it was fashioned out of ignorance and greed with the intent to further subjugate Blacks, in some respects the one-drop rule backfired on the slaveholders. It helped unite an oppressed people, a people who could be proud of their customs and heritage as well as could fight against racial injustice.

Toward the end of his life, Great-Grandpa gave one of his most revealing interviews to a young Black reporter for the *Boston Globe* in the spring of 1891. It provided insights into his legacy and the hopes and dreams for his race. Despite all the pain and suffering he endured, he remained positive about the future of his people. Great-Grandpa told the reporter, "I want my work to be a history of the times that have passed. You and your generation and those who are coming after you can never know or feel what we who have been slaves endured. You are surrounded by golden opportunities such as I never dreamed would come."

Great-Grandpa also expressed the importance of *perseverance* in challenging continuing injustices: "I have great faith in the rising generations of my race. Let us not be judged by a quarter of a century; give us 50 years, and then we will show what we are going to be."

A constant character trait of Clarke's was to be proactive rather than reactive to the social, political, and economic challenges that faced African Americans. He was a victim of the institution of slavery, which was entrenched in America longer than we've been a nation. Nevertheless, he envisioned slavery's ultimate demise.

Great-Grandpa's vision takes us to the cusp of the civil-rights movement, including the GI Bill of Rights of 1944 and 1952, the Brown v. Board of Education US Supreme Court decision of 1954, the Montgomery Bus Boycott of 1955, the emergence of the Reverend Martin Luther King Jr., the Civil Rights Act of 1964, and the Voting Rights Act of 1965.

The struggle continues. I am sure that if Great-Grandpa were alive today, he would agree with the words of Langston Hughes: "America never was America to me—And yet I swear this oath—America will be!!" I can hear Great-Grandpa saying loud and clear, "AMEN!"

———

In June of 2014, I was close to finishing the biography of my great-grandfather. I was invited to Transylvania University in Lexington, Kentucky, to talk with students about the work I was doing. I asked my daughter Cynthia to meet me in Lexington—not only to go with me to talk with the students, but to visit the areas around Lexington where Great-Grandpa was born and raised. We would explore Garrard County (named after the former governor of Kentucky) and the towns of Lancaster, Paint Lick, and Berea. The intention was also to take photos to incorporate into the book.

Think of the uninitiated, serendipitous people and events in my life that stretched over almost 40 year! That, capped by the out-of-body episode on the Garrard County courthouse steps, finally convinced me that I was destined to publish Great-Grandpa's biography.

One spot I had special interest in was the Garrard County Courthouse in Lancaster. This was just a few miles from Paint Lick, where Great-Grandpa was a slave. Paint Lick was also a site depicted in Stowe's *Uncle Tom's Cabin.*

The Garrard County Courthouse was the place where Clarke was put up for sale in 1841. The sale fell through, partly because Clarke was considered too uppity and as having too many privileges—in other words, according to Clarke, a "spoilt nigger." The other reason was that there were *three mortgages* on him that had not been settled. Soon after the failed sale, Great-Grandpa learned that he was to be sold to a plantation in Louisiana. He was determined at that point to escape, and to seek out and free his brothers Milton and Cyrus. His mind was made up. He decided he would not lend credence to the institution of slavery because no man had the right to own another human being. He would not allow himself to be sold again. Great-Grandpa began his journey North in July 1841.

I vividly remember the day that Cynthia and I visited the Garrard County Courthouse. I had an eerie feeling knowing that in that same spot over the years, hundreds—if not *thousands*—of human beings were bartered off like cattle to the highest bidders. While Cynthia and I were walking up the front steps, something happened in the exact spot where Great-Grandpa was put up for sale. I didn't know if was in my imagination or not, but I could feel him. I had an out-of-body episode that I had not experienced before, nor have since. I felt my left leg separate from my body, as if it had suddenly disappeared, and I immediately fell flat on the stairs! Cynthia, who was by my side, cried out, "What's wrong, Dad?"

I said, "I don't know. It feels like my leg is gone . . ." I waited for a few minutes. Then I got up and began walking again, with no after-effects.

I considered this episode a message from Great-Grandpa. Not a message to be fearful, but an assurance. It was as if he were saying, "I'm watching over you, son. I am elated that you are publishing my biography. Exactly what I intended to do before I passed away."

Think of the uninitiated, serendipitous people and events in my life that stretched over almost 40 years! My interactions with Cousin Raymond, Dr. Peter Ripley, and Gregory Wilson, capped by the out-of-body episode on the Garrard County courthouse steps, finally convinced me that I was destined to publish Great-Grandpa's biography. Taken as a whole, those same experiences inspired me to write and publish my *own* story. Thus, *this* book.

CHAPTER 35

Influence and Perseverance

LOOKING BACK ON MY LIFE I can identify a wide array of influences that have guided me and I'm thankful for them. My family, friends, and mentors form the cornerstones of who I am. They helped shape my sense of self and self-respect, my passions and drive.

As a young boy, I was aware that my paternal grandfather, John Thomas Gayton, aka J. T., was a true pioneer. He'd arrived in Seattle at the age of 23 from Yazoo County, Mississippi, in 1889, just months before Washington Territory became a state.

After settling in Seattle, he did many things, including working at the Rainier Club and catering. He completed his education at Seattle's Wilson Business College. He remained at the Rainier Club for fourteen years and became the Club's head steward. He then was hired as a Federal District Court of Appeals bailiff and subsequently its librarian. He was a leader and founder of a variety of Black community organizations, such as the First African Methodist Episcopal Church, the East Madison Young Men's Christian Association (YMCA), and the Black King County Republican Club. He became a pillar of the city, especially within the Black community.

My father, John Jacob Gayton, and his siblings, and their children followed suit when it came to community involvement. I did not wear this pride on my sleeve. Growing up, I was very proud of my family and their accomplishments. I wanted to emulate them, but I did not feel pressure to do so.

I am grateful for my family experiences during my formative years. I cannot recall my parents or siblings telling me how to act outside our home or in school. I learned from their example. Generally, a raised eyebrow or side glance gave me the correct message if I was out of line. I must say, however, that as the sixth child among eight siblings, I learned a great deal about how to comport myself from the discipline the older brothers and sisters received. Frankly, my mom and Dad were probably a bit worn out by the time I came along. Folks we knew in both the Black and White communities respected us, and we were taught to show respect in return. My early family experience certainly gave me confidence, but hopefully not arrogance.

––––––––

I feel that many teachers do not realize how important they are in the lives of students, especially in the early learning years. When I was a five-year-old first grader and the only Black child in the class, my teacher told me, "I just don't trust you." She truly frightened me because I had no idea what she was talking about. But I knew it was something bad. When I got home, I asked my mother what "trust" meant, and she told me. I didn't say anything more to my mother about what happened. Out of fear, I could not function in that class the rest of the semester.

Alternatively, a different school incident indirectly related to race had the opposite effect on me. In 1951, when I got into a terrifying fight in the in the boy's restroom with a White boy at Meany Junior High, I thought I could talk the bully out of fighting. But he surprised me and broke my two front teeth with a blow with his fist and brass knuckles he'd made in our metal shop class. I arranged for a continuation of the fight for the next day and came armed with brass rings I'd borrowed from a friend. I initiated the fight and would not let him quit. After ten or fifteen minutes, Miss Peterson, the vice principal, came and commanded us to stop. That was it. The crowd dispersed. The next day my opponent came to school with his arm in a cast and sneered at me. That was the first and last fist fight I ever had. I frightened myself with my own fearlessness!

I still don't know if Miss Peterson talked with my mother after the fight, but Miss Peterson rescued me. Under similar circumstances nowadays, I would

I began thinking about the possibility of becoming a teacher and realized the important positive impact teachers can have on the lives of young people. To this day I consider myself a teacher and educator, regardless of the roles I've had over the years...

have been expelled from school for what I did. Miss Peterson evidently saw me as a boy worth saving. She saw positive characteristics in me that many other educators would not have recognized—or if they had, would have done nothing to help me. She took me aside and gave me some responsibilities. She put me on a positive track. Before that point, I truly hated middle school. But she saved me from possibly being labeled as a problem student for the remainder of my school years. I cannot thank Ms. Peterson enough for what she did for me.

My junior year Language Arts teacher at Garfield High School, Mrs. Miriam Eskenazi, rescued me in a different way. She got into my face one day and admonished me for not working harder on my studies. She sternly said, "I'm going to make sure you work up to your potential!" She was the first academic teacher who really gave me tough love and convinced me that I could be a top-level student. After her admonitions, I earned nothing but "As" and "Bs" in my remaining classes at Garfield. From that point forward, I began thinking about the possibility of becoming a teacher and realized the important positive impact teachers can have on the lives of young people. To this day I consider myself a teacher and educator, regardless of the roles I've had over the years, most of which lay outside of traditional educational institutions.

My involvement in sports at high school and university levels taught me a lot about leadership and made me a strong advocate of the concept of "teams" throughout my professional career. I've been fortunate to be both a player and a coach for outstanding football teams at Garfield High School and the University of Washington.

At Garfield, I was a 145-pound fullback for two back-to-back city championship teams. I was captain, All-City and All-State, on our 1956 team. That team had a record of seven wins and zero losses. We accumulated a total of 132 winning points to our opponents' combined total of 37 points! As mythical state champions, that team is arguably the best team in Garfield High's 100-year history.

I had to literally beg Head Coach Darrell Royal at the University of Washington to recruit me for his team. He initially said that 170 pounds was too small to play for him. But with the help of my Garfield Coach, "Swede" Lindquist, Royal finally broke down and said he would give me a full-ride scholarship for the first year. And if I displayed the kind of determination, dedication, and perseverance I had at Garfield, I'd have a full scholarship for the remaining years on the team.

I played well enough to be the starter at halfback in the first game of the season against the University of Colorado in 1959. The team ultimately went on to win the 1960 Rose Bowl. This was the Husky's first Rose Bowl win in the University's history and the first Husky Football team, of which I was a member, to be inducted into the Husky Hall of Fame. The *1960 Rose Bowl Program* pointed out:

> *Carver Gayton, the fleetest Husky, scampered at will in Washington's opening victory against Colorado, 21-12, then was injured. . . Carver Gayton, 160-pound [actually 155 pounds] halfback lettered as a sophomore and junior year and was headed for a great season this year until injured in a game against Idaho. . . He was considered out for the season, but through sheer determination kept working out and finally rejoined the squad for the Cal game. Small and elusive, he has fine speed and breakaway ability, and is hard to bring down.*

During the 1960 season, after receiving my BA in History, I became a graduate assistant coach while taking classes toward receiving my teaching credentials at the U of W. That team went on to be selected as a co-national champion, the first Husky Football team to be so honored.

The common elements of those high school and college teams included the importance of working together for the common good, respecting the abilities of each team member, believing that the whole is greater than the sum of its parts, and having the insatiable desire to win. Much of what were considered "our winning ways" were essential intangibles: things that cannot be measured. Like our respect for our teammates, the desire to win—and our conviction that when a team drives to the twenty-yard line, getting a touchdown is a given. It's a *mindset*.

Steadfast belief in these essential intangibles helped us continue to win. We often played against teams with better individual athletes. They may have been bigger, stronger, and more athletic than we were, yet we could beat them because of our commitment to teamwork and our focus on winning. We never went into any game thinking we might lose. If we did lose, we considered it an anomaly.

These essential intangibles related directly to the successful experiences I later had with The Boeing Company, the Washington State Employment Security Department, and the Northwest African American Museum—a project had been in limbo for nearly 30 years. All the winning teams I've been associated with on the playing field, or in business, government, or the nonprofit world, have shared many characteristics, such as the standard we highlighted at Boeing that new hires would have a *fundamental understanding and commitment to teamwork*, as well as being good communicators, being flexible and adaptable, and having the desire to continuously learn.

———

Throughout my adult life I had to deal with issues of race and equity. However, during most of my professional career, my job descriptions did not emphasize those specific matters. Being Black in America made me aware of such issues as the norm. I had to learn when to address such things head on and when to let them pass. All along I had to make sure that whatever I did, my self-worth and integrity remained intact.

In 1969, I got embroiled in the race controversy of four Black players being dismissed from the University of Washington football team—because, according to the coach, they would not swear by a loyalty oath to him and the team. Many on the team were concerned about the poor treatment of the Black players. I was the university's first fulltime Black coach. I felt that football Head Coach Jim Owens was forcing me to side either with him or with the four players whom I highly respected. I considered the dismissals to be racially motivated and I sided with the players by resigning my position in protest.

At that time, I remember talking with the nationally recognized and respected Tacoma lawyer and civil rights leader, Jack Tanner. He told me, "Carver, I certainly respect the stand you took against Coach Owens. However, you are a young man, and you must decide, in terms of your career, whether you want to be a civil rights leader or an outstanding coach. You can't be both."

Jack's viewpoint really put me in a quandary for a few days. There was no one I respected more than Jack Tanner. But I was also aware of a statement made by the iconic Mississippi voting rights leader, Fannie Lou Hammer. To Blacks who were hesitant about getting involved in civil rights matters, she said: "When you say, 'I'm not going to get in the mess,' honey, if you were born in America with a Black face, you were *born* in the mess!"

I agreed with Fannie Lou Hammer. As a Black and often confronted with race matters, I have to make decisions on what to do. It is part of my life in America. I felt that I had to take a stand on this issue as a human being. My integrity was at stake, and in the case of those young men, their lives and careers were at also stake.

Surprisingly, in early 2021, I was contacted by Jennifer Cohen, director of athletics at the University of Washington. She had been reading a 2004 article I had written for Historylink.org about the dismissal of the four Black football players from the team in 1969 and my subsequent resignation. She had been unaware of the incident and wanted to know more about it. Jennifer asked if I had any problem with her talking with any of the four ball players. I said no and encouraged her to do so. Later she contacted me again, saying in effect that she was disturbed by this incident and wanted the university to make amends for what had happened. She added that she wanted to have me and the four ball players interviewed to get a more in-depth account of what had happened.

A while after the interviews, the five of us were informed by Director Cohen that we were selected by the prestigious University of Washington Tyee Club to be inducted into Husky Hall of Fame. The Tyee Club supports the Athletic Department through their financial gifts. Seven other individual outstanding

The football team members suspended in the fall of 1969 were honored and inducted into the U of W Hall of Fame in October 2021. The "Five Who Dared" were (top left to right) Gregg Alex, Ralph Bayard, and Harvy Blanks, (bottom left to right) Carver Gayton, and Lamar Mills.

athletes from a variety of sports were also selected to be inducted into the Hall during a planned ceremony on October 17, 2021.

After our story was presented to the large audience at U of W's Hec Edmundson Pavilion, "The Five Who Dared" received a standing ovation. We were the only inductees to be so recognized that evening.

My prayers are with Harvy Blanks who passed away three months after the induction ceremony. I found out after he passed that he had been diagnosed as terminally ill before the induction. Even though he must have been in pain, he was smiling and in good spirits throughout the evening. He even gestured toward me so I could hear him during the dinner, saying to his wife, La La, "Look at Coach, isn't it great seeing how happy he is." Rest in Peace, Harvy, knowing that our names have been carved into the Husky Hall of Fame *forever*.

Husky Hall of Fame Program Notes

1969—The Five Who Dared: Gregg Alex, Ralph Bayard, Harvy Blanks, Lamar Mills And Carver Gayton (Football)

During the 1969 football season four Black members of the Washington football team—Gregg Alex, Ralph Bayard, Harvy Blanks, and Lamar Mills—were suspended from the team after refusing to pledge personal loyalty to head football coach Jim Owens. In the face of racial tension and adversity the young men stood by their actions, believed in themselves, and stayed committed to an intense personal sacrifice for the greater good.

Later that week before departing for a road game at UCLA, remaining Black members of the team travel party got off the buses carrying the team to the airport as a show of solidarity. Assistant coach Carver Gayton, a former U of W letterman and first full time Black coach in Athletic Department history, resigned to show solidarity with the players.

Under pressure from the public and campus groups, three of the four players were reinstated to the team just before the final game of the season, the Apple Cup vs Washington State. In that game, Bayard caught two touchdown passes to lead the Huskies to their only victory in a 1-9 season.

Despite all the adversity that they faced, all five of these men went on to distinguished careers outside of football. Bayard, who earned a PhD from the U of W, eventually returned as an assistant athletic director in the 1990s. He has spent much of his time since then working in the child welfare field. Alex, who has run an addiction treatment facility, served 13 years as a team chaplain for the Husky team and was key in supporting U of W players. Mills became an attorney in Seattle, focusing on public defender work, while Blanks [since deceased] who had been injured at the time of his suspension and who was never reinstated, earned a master's degree from Cornell and became an actor, director, and playwright. Gayton earned his bachelor's, master's, and PhD from the U of W. He's worked as an FBI Agent and had a long career as an executive at The Boeing Company, among many other pursuits. Gayton has been an advocate for education reform and served as a keynote speaker on the subject all over the world.

Martin Luther King would often say that "The arch of the moral universe is long but bends toward justice." That is certainly the case regarding the "Five Who Dared" story. It took the moral courage of Athletic Director Jenn Cohen, together with University President Ana Mari Cauce, to correct the wrong that those young men had to live with and have nightmares about for most of their lives. It took 52 years for true justice, especially for Gregg, Ralph, Lamar, and Harvy, to be recognized and honored for the pain they suffered from the unjust actions they endured.

———————

As I've grown older, people have approached me asking what has made me go in so many directions personally, professionally, and in community endeavors over the years? I began to ask myself the same question while writing this book. I've concluded that, without realizing it, the Zen proverb "Expect nothing, appreciate everything." has been a guiding light. The concept helps me focus on the positive aspects of my life and builds relationships with others. I don't regard it necessarily as a moral concept. I consider it a survival concept. So many things that I've learned to appreciate have changed my direction in life. Things that I learned from a broad range of people and circumstances. Some of the issues are small, others are large. All are appreciated.

EPILOGUE

Blessings From My Odyssey

1997 – Husky Football Legend Award

I retired from The Boeing Company in early 1997 and was then appointed by Governor Gary Locke as Commissioner of the Washington State Employment Security Department.

On November 8, 1997, I was individually honored as a "Husky Football Legend" at halftime ceremonies during a game against The University of Oregon. I was totally surprised when first notified by Athletic Director Barbara Hedges. It made me think of all the great football players who were so recognized in the past that I had followed as a child!

Having the announcer present my name and background, followed by the loud roar of 70 thousand fans was a moment I will savor forever! During

I was honored as a "Husky Football Legend" in November of 1997 at a U of W football game half-time ceremony.

the announcement, I had a flashback to my teenage years dreaming of possibly playing football at the University of Washington, but thinking it was a far-fetched notion. But here I was at Husky Stadium, standing on the shoulders of great football players I had idolized in the past. The moment also reminded me of how a fellow Husky teammate admonished me during practice my sophomore year. "Gayton, don't work so hard. You'll get your varsity letter." I didn't take his advice. I continued to work hard and was guided by my inner self.

And here I was, before an overflow crowd, having received three varsity letters, a member of the Husky Rose Bowl Hall of Fame team, and hired as the first person of color to be a full-time coach in any sport at the University of Washington. And being named as a Husky Football Legend. That moment on that November day in 1997 brought tears of joy and pride to my eyes. What an honor!

2005 – Honoring Homer Harris at Garfield's "First Annual Legends Dinner"

In 2005, I was working as the executive director of the Northwest African American Museum in Seattle and received a call from Dorothy Harris, the wife of Dr. Homer Harris, MD. She wanted me to speak on Homer's behalf because he was being inducted into Seattle's Garfield High School Foundation's First Annual Legends Dinner. I immediately agreed.

I had known of Homer Harris from my childhood days because Homer's family and the Gayton family had been close for many years. My parents would talk about his achievements as a scholar and a star football, track, and baseball player while at Garfield, as well as the University of Iowa. Homer could not play football at the University of Washington where he wanted to attend because of his race. Homer told me that the head coach at the U of W said Homer could only sit on the bench if he came but could have all the ice cream cones he desired. Homer decided to attend and play football at the University of Iowa. In 1937, he became the first African American to captain a Big Ten Conference team and was named the team's Most Valuable Player.

After graduation from the U of Iowa, Homer entered the Historically Black University, Meharry Medical College in Nashville, Tennessee, where he graduated with his medical degree.

I had learned about many of Homer's accomplishments from my parents and by viewing his awards in the trophy cases in the halls at Garfield. I did not meet Homer until 1955 when he came back to Seattle to set up his dermatology practice.

After he arrived, our two families got together for me to meet his stepdaughter who was my age. During the summer of 1955 we would meet, play tennis periodically, and go on picnics with Homer's family. Homer and I connected well because of our athletics background as well as our connection with Garfield. From time to time, he would say that he envied me because I played in the Rose Bowl in 1960. He was attempting to flatter me because I considered his athletic accomplishments as second to none. I regard him as one of the most outstanding scholar athletes to ever attend a State of Washington high school.

My connection with Homer lasted many years. I would look for excuses to have appointments in his dermatology office just to talk. He followed my football and professional careers over the years and related how proud he was of me for what I achieved.

In 2005, three years before his death, I was honored to be asked by his wife Dorothy to introduce Homer at Garfield High School Legends event recognizing his many achievements. She knew how much I admired Homer. Imagine, fifty years had passed since I was first introduced to Homer! What a privilege it was to be regarded as one of his friends. I considered him a father figure.

Homer died not quite three years after the Legends event.

2008 – Museums Without Walls

Toward the end of 2008, I was contacted by a teacher who was heading a project called Museum Without Walls. This was a joint project comprised primarily of White students from suburban Mercer Island High School outside of Seattle and students from Seattle's Franklin High School where the enrollment was predominately Black. The point of the project was to bring these young people from diverse socio-economic backgrounds together and to interview individuals in the metropolitan Seattle area who were leaders in the civil rights movement during the 1950s through the early 1970s.

I was one of the dozens of individuals the students interviewed. They had read about my contributions to the movement in the 1960s and 1970s while I was an administrator and coach at the University of Washington, as well as my role as a member of the Seattle School Board.

I was very flattered to find out that of all the people interviewed, I was selected as one of three whom the students wanted to honor. Another was Larry Gossett, a former Black Panther, president of the Black Student Union at the University of Washington during the late 1960s, a founder of the university's Minority Affairs Department, and president of Martin Luther King County Council at the time. The third person selected was a woman named Rita Schwerner, an attorney.

I had known Larry for many years and admired his commitment and dedication to the civil rights cause. The name Rita Schwerner made me pause, and I asked the teacher on the phone "Could you tell me about Ms. Schwerner? Because the only Schwerner I can recall is Michael Schwerner—the voting rights worker from New York City, who was murdered in Philadelphia, Mississippi, in 1964." The teacher responded, "Mrs. Schwerner is the *widow* of Michael, who had gone with him to Mississippi to help Blacks register to vote." I was speechless! Rita and Michael Schwerner had put their lives on the line daily in Mississippi to help ensure that Blacks had the right to vote. Michael paid with his life. Rita has lived on to tell of their heroism and commitment to human rights. She had been living in Seattle and working in the area as a lawyer.

When I accepted the award at the Mercer Island Jewish Community Center on Mercer Island, I mentioned my indirect connection with the Philadelphia, Mississippi, story. I found myself choking up realizing that the students were placing me in the same company as Rita Schwerner and her heroic acts on behalf of African Americans. I knew all the details she and her patriotic colleagues endured. I was truly humbled knowing that the students admired me similarly. I have received many recognitions over my lifetime, but the Museum without Walls honor, in light of its context, will always remain as one of the most significant.

2008 - Centennial Celebration of the FBI

After my years as an FBI agent, I continued to have periodic contact through the retired agents associations in various parts of the country. I've been invited to public relations gatherings of community leaders sponsored by the Seattle Field Office. I was especially pleased to be invited by the Seattle Field Office in July 2008 as their keynote speaker celebrating the centennial anniversary of the Bureau. William Mueller was the director of the FBI in 2008.

There were approximately 100 special agents and staff at the gathering. I related my experiences as an agent with emphasis on being the only Black agent serving in the Kansas City and Philadelphia Field Offices during my tenure. All in all, I was respected while in the Bureau and I in turn respected the Bureau. I considered it the best federal investigative/law enforcement agency in the nation. I have not changed that perspective. There were race-related incidences that I did not approve of, but that is par for the course for most public and private institutions in America. As a Black American I've had to determine when and how to pick my battles to maintain my integrity and self-worth. I did so while I was a special agent of the FBI.

2018 – Reminiscing with Reverend Samuel McKinney

Revered Samuel McKinney, pastor of the Mount Zion Baptist Church in Seattle and civil rights leader, was terminally ill and residing at an assisted living residence in April of 2018. Reverend McKinney had been a good friend of Reverend Martin Luther King. A *Seattle Times* reporter, recalling King's visit to Garfield High in 1961, wanted Reverend McKinney and I to reminisce together about that historic day nearly 57 years earlier. I was asked to join the meeting because Reverend McKinney had introduced me to Dr. King on that day at Garfield. During our April conversation, I emphasized that Dr. King's visit emboldened me to include in the US History and Contemporary Problems classes I was teaching the contributions, roles, and achievements of African Americans relevant to all aspect's American history, culture and science.

As we talked, I forgot about the reporter taking notes. Reverend McKinney's quick wit and turn of phrase gave no sign that he would be joining Dr. King in a matter of days later. I was joyously uplifted by that meeting with the pastor.

2021 – Celebrating the 60th Anniversary of Dr. King's Visit

LaNesha DeBardelaben, recent past CEO of the Northwest African American Museum, wanted to create an event celebrating the 60th anniversary of Dr. King's 1961 speech in Seattle. LaNesha asked me to be on the steering committee to help plan the event because I was one of the few people living in Seattle who had met Martin Luther King during that November 1961 visit. I was flattered by being asked and readily accepted.

I was also honored to be named to the first Martin Luther King Elders Circle for Exceptional Black Leaders over the age of 75 who have "led and won victories in the struggle of civil rights, social equity, and opportunity in Seattle's Central District and greater Pacific Northwest."

The large turnout for the various events that weekend to celebrate Dr. King's 1961 visit demonstrated to me that his message concerning civil rights, social equity, and opportunity are as relevant today as they were 60 years ago.

2022 – Garfield High School's Centennial

Seattle's Garfield High School had its Centennial celebration on September 27, 2022. As a member of Garfield's Hall of Fame, I was asked to be a keynote speaker at the event. Other keynote speakers included Steering Committee Chair Lynn Jaffey, Mayor Bruce Harrell, Seattle Schools Superintendent Brent Jones, PhD, and Garfield Principal Tarance Hart, PhD.

I was proud to serve in that role considering all of the exceptional alumni of the school, including such luminaries as Quincy Jones, Jimi Hendrix, and Homer Harris among others.

As I looked out on the crowd of thousands of alumni and community members, I was reminded of the time I served on the Seattle School board in 1974. The Washington State Superintendent of Public instruction office was considering closing Garfield because it was a "segregated school" with 90 percent Black enrollment. I couldn't believe my ears. During a board meeting I blurted out "Not on my watch. What about Roosevelt High School with 90 percent White students?" Led by me and School Board President Phil Swain, the entire board and key staff sought an alternative. We came up with the current model of Garfield, approved by the entire board on June 12, 1974, as an "exemplary" magnet school with an emphasis on science and math, and open to students throughout the district. Today, Garfield is ranked as the number one high school in the district, knowing that they will always work on continuing to improve.

I'm in my 86th year on this plane, I could not have been prouder to have the opportunity to praise this elite educational gem!

Acknowledgments

I AM FORTUNATE to be married to a woman who is the whole package of being bright, compassionate, beautiful, and strong willed.

Carmen Walker and I met one day over thirty years ago in Houston, Texas, and married six months later. Life has been exciting ever since. Our years together have not been perfect, but they are as close to perfection as I've had with any person during my lifetime. I would not have been able to write this book without her love, support, and encouragement.

I also thank my developmental editor, Jenn Hager, for all the guidance and assistance she has provided in writing this book. Her interpersonal skills are way beyond what I expected when I asked her to be my editor. She drew out of me important aspects of my life that I had buried in my mind, both positive and negative, that I feel have truly enriched my story. Her approach also provided a better picture of how I see myself. Thank you so much, Jenn.

I'd like to acknowledge and thank the publishing team at Documentary Media, Petyr Beck and Tori Smith especially, for their outstanding work organizing and clarifying the final manuscript.

As I have reflected in the body of my book, members of my family have made a profound and positive impact on my life, particularly my mother and father. I am forever grateful to them.

As indicated in the book there are many former teammates, friends, mentors, and professional colleagues who have influenced me in very beneficial ways. Attempting to mention all of you would necessitate an endless number of volumes of work, but you know who you are, and I thank you from the bottom of my heart.

Finally, I am so grateful for my role, from the time I was a child, in my loved ones' lives. I have loved and have been thoroughly loved in return. That is the essence of a blessed life.

Carver

Honors

Member of University of Washington Championship Rose Bowl Team, 1960.

University of Washington Oval Club, upperclassmen scholastic and activities honor society, 1960.

University of Washington, Husky Legend, 1987.

Frederick Douglass Distinguished Scholars Honor Society, National Council for Black Studies, Pacific Northwest Region, 1988.

Blacks In Government, Region 10 Outstanding Citizen Award, 1989.

National Association of Partnerships in Education, Mckee Award, the organization's highest recognition, honoring the "school to career" program created at The Boeing Company under the leadership of Dr. Gayton, 1993.

University of Washington Athletic Department, Husky Hall of Fame, 1994.

Employment Management Association, Pericles Service Award, 1995, honoring the "school-to-career" program, presented each year to the most innovative and effective human resource program in the nation.

The National Alliance of Business (NAB) recognized The Boeing Company as having the best school-to-work program in the nation in 1997 because of the leadership of Dr. Gayton.

University of Washington Alumni Association, Distinguished Service Award, 1997.

University of Washington Football Legend, 1997.

National Network Consortium, Augustus F. Hawkins Meritorious Service Award, recognizing distinguished leadership and contributions in the field of workforce development, 2001.

Named by *Seattle Magazine* as "one of the twenty-six most influential people [in Seattle] of 2006," November 2006.

Cornish College of the Arts, Honorary Degree of Doctor of Fine Arts, 2007.

Loren Miller Bar Association, Community Service Award, "To honor your exceptional contributions to Seattle's African American Community," 2008.

University of Washington, selected as one of the "Wondrous One Hundred Living Legends," recognizing one hundred ". . . living alumni who have made or are making their mark outside the University bounds." 2008.

Garfield High School, Hall of Fame "Golden Graduate," 2011.

Pacific Northwest Football Hall of Fame, 2012.

University of Washington College of Arts and Sciences, Timeless Award, honoring 150 Distinguished Alumni For their Timeless Achievement, 2011.

Central Area Chamber of Commerce, Phenomenal People Award, recognizing ". . . outstanding work in helping others to rise to their full potential." 2016.

University of Washington Department of Political Science, Distinguished Alumnus Award, 2016.

Professional and Community Involvement

Commissioner, Washington State Youth Commission, 1969–1970.

Board of Trustees, Opportunities Industrialization Center, Seattle, 1970–1973.

Commissioner, City of Seattle Women's Commission, 1971–1972.

Vice President, National Affirmative Action Officers' Association, 1971–1977.

Director, Seattle School Board, 1973–1975.

Board of Trustees, Pacific Science Center Foundation, 1975–1977.

Chairman, Seattle Chamber of Commerce Higher Education Committee, 1981–1982.

Washington State Governor's Temporary Committee on Education, Policy, Structure and Management, 1982–1986.

Vice President, Board of Directors, Leadership Tomorrow, Chamber of Commerce, Seattle, 1982–1987.

Commissioner, Northwest Association of Schools and Colleges, 1984–1990.

University of Washington Executive MBA Program Advisory Committee, 1984–1992.

Washington Roundtable Working Committee on Education, representing Boeing,1984–1991.

President, University of Washington Alumni Association Board of Trustees, first minority, 1985–1986.

University of Washington College of Education Visiting Committee Ambassadors, 1985–1996 and 2001–present.

National Advisory Panel/National Center for Post-Secondary Governance and Finance, Washington, DC, 1986–1990.

Board of Trustees, Seattle Community Colleges, 1989–1999, Chair 1994 and 1997.

Director, Virginia Mason Hospital Board of Directors, 1991–1994.

Board of Trustees, National Center for Occupational Research and Development, 1992–1998, Chair 1997.

Chairman, University of Washington President's Club, 1993–1994.

Trustee, KCTS, Channel 9 Association Board, 1993–1999.

President, Independent Colleges of Washington Board of Trustees, 1994–1997.

Trustee, Association of Governing Boards of Universities and Colleges, 1997–2001.

Co-Chair, Seattle Public Schools Committee for Fiscal Integrity, 2003.

Chairman of the Board, BlackPast.org, 2011–2013.

Emeritus Director, University of Washington Foundation Board, 2012-present, Recognition Committee for selecting the Bill and Melinda Gates Volunteer Service Award 2012-2015, Co-chair 2015.

University of Washington Foundation Executive Committee, 2013–2015.

Evans School of Public Policy and Governance Visiting Committee, 2013–Present.

Keynote speaker at international, national, state, regional, and local conferences regarding educational reform and global education issues over the years, including representing The Boeing Company as a featured speaker in Noordwijk, The Netherlands, as guest of the US Department of Education and the European Community, speaking on the subject *Schools and Industry: Partners for Quality Education.*

Notes

1 My mother was a founding member of the Seattle chapters of the Delta Sigma Theta Sorority in 1932, as well as the Links Inc., in 1955. In 1984, she was nationally recognized by the Schlesinger Library of Radcliff College as one of 72 "Black Women of Courage for their Outstanding Professional and Voluntary Activities."

2 Neal, Steve, and I have continued to be friends through high school and beyond, although I have not seen Steve for many years. Neal and I see each other regularly and currently serve together on a committee for Garfield High School's centennial anniversary, our alma mater. Steve is a retired University of Oregon professor and Neal is a retired attorney and public sector executive.

3 Songs played included those by Big Mama Thornton (Hound Dog); Jimmy Forrest (Night Train); The Clovers (One Mint Julep); Big Joe Turner (Shake, Rattle and Roll); Faye Adams (Shake a Hand); Ruth Brown (Mama, He Treats Your Daughter Mean), and The Spaniels (Goodnite, Sweetheart, Goodnite).

4 Of my three older brothers, John, Gary and Phil, only Phil made the cut to play freshman ball, but he did not play beyond that year. However, all were excellent trackmen, with Gary and Phil becoming exceptional. Gary won the All-City mile event and was captain of the team, and Phil became the second-best pole vaulter in the state his senior year. Gary went on to excel at the University of Washington as an 880-yard runner in track and the first African American team captain of any varsity sports team at the U of W.

5 I worked the night swing shift at The Boeing Company as a "maintenance electrician" attempting to make ends meet to support my wife and new baby girl.

6 In the spring of 1965, I was selected to attend a special class of agents who had shown skills in developing informants. The class took place at the FBI's academy in Quantico, Virginia. Felt was one of the primary presenters. By that time, he had been promoted to Chief of the Inspection Division of the Bureau. The classroom environment, with questions being allowed from the agents, gave me a more in-depth assessment of Felt. He came across as a very devoted "company man" and not the kind of personality who would become a whistle blower. That was precisely the reason why he was so effective as "Deep Throat," even though there were a few within President Nixon's inner circle who had their suspicions about him.

7 Years later, in 1985, I was invited to a barbeque sponsored by the Seattle FBI field office at the firing range in Everett, Washington. Invitees were local business leaders such as Bill Boeing Jr., son of the corporation's founder; and Eddie Carlson, founder, CEO and Chairman of United Airlines as well as Western Hotels Inc. [Westin] among other business notables. I had the opportunity to test my skills with a .38-caliber Smith & Wesson, the same model I carried with me every day for nearly four years when I was in the Bureau. I had not fired a gun for over seventeen years, but the superb training I had years earlier had remained with me, and I hit six rounds of bullseyes!

8 John Dean, "The Enemies List Revisited," *Boston College Magazine*, Winter 2005.

9 Arthur M. Schlesinger, Jr., *Robert Kennedy and His Times*, (Boston: Houghton Mifflin, 1978), 640.

10 Ibid., 641.

[11] Ibid., 273.

[12] Tim Weiner, *Enemies: A History of the FBI*, (New York, Random House, 2012), 292.

[13] Ibid., 293.

[14] Ibid., 293-294.

[15] Ibid., 294.

[16] Ibid., 296.

[17] Ibid., 299.

[18] Ibid., 300.

[19] Schlesinger, 642.

[20] Ibid., 642.

[21] Ibid., 641-644.

[22] Ibid., 641-644.

[23] It was my understanding that Mr. Hoover did not want the Bureau to have any responsibility for drug crimes because too much money was involved. He felt human nature was such that his G-men could be too easily enticed to be on the take. The "straight arrow" image of special agents could more easily be tainted by being involved in drug investigations. Whether such FBI lore is true or not, it is interesting to note that the Agency did not investigate drug crimes until Hoover was no longer at the helm of the Bureau.

[24] Before I left KCMO, I introduced my informant Charlotte to my friend and fellow agent Tom Trettis. She agreed to work with him and her file was passed on to Tom. A few months later after I was assigned to the Philadelphia field office, Trettis telephoned me and laughingly told me he had to close her file because "She was a psychopath." Admittedly, she could be scary but would tend to go into such fits when she didn't feel comfortable with a person. I empathized with Trettis that she was like a lit stick of dynamite. Luckily, she did not blow up when she worked for me. She represented the challenge of working for many criminal informants because their moral perspectives, lifestyles, and worlds in general are the direct opposite of what most agents experience. Those juxtapositions, in my mind, were fundamental parts of the excitement and fascination of working with them.

[25] Craps is a dice game in which the players make wagers on the outcome of the roll or a series of rolls. The "floating" aspect is that the games would move from location to location to avoid detection from authorities.

[26] Reverend Sullivan was nationally recognized as the founder of Opportunities Industrialization Centers (OIC), a very successful jobs program which focused on urban Blacks. OIC became a national network of centers throughout the United States. Sullivan was also the author of the "Sullivan Principles" which encouraged corporations not to do business with apartheid South Africa.

[27] Carr subsequently worked for TRW as Director of Security and gained notoriety, unfortunately, as the supervisor of Christopher John Boyce who was convicted in 1977 of spying for the Soviet Union while at TRW. See *The Falcon and the Snowman* by Robert Lindsey.

[28] Jim Dent, *The Junction Boys*, (Thomas Dunne Books, 2000).

[29] "Carver Gayton Named Full-Time Husky Aide," *Seattle Times*, July 3, 1968.

30 Dave Dupree, "Blanks: Complex Kid from the Strip," *Seattle Post-Intelligencer,* November 12, 1968.

31 Georg N. Meyers, "The Sporting Thing: Husky Gridiron Crop, the Letter's Message," *Seattle Times,* April 3, 1969.

32 John Underwood, "The Desperate Coach: 'Shave off That Thing,'" *Sports Illustrated,* September 1, 1969.

33 Bob Schwarzmann, "Gayton Leaving is Regretted," *Seattle Times,* November 11, 1969.

34 Georg N. Meyers, "The Sporting Thing: The Husky Question, What Happens Next," *Seattle Times,* November 2, 1969.

35 Don Hannula, "The Longest Saturday: The 1969 Football Season is Over, but for Jim Owens the Agony Lingers," *Seattle Times,* December 14, 1969.

36 Stephen Dunphy, "Black Boycott of U of W Sports Unfolds," *Seattle Times,* January 2, 1971.

37 Georg N. Meyers, "The Sporting Thing: What's Going to Happen to Jim and Joe?" *Seattle Times* January 17, 1971.

38 "Dismiss Owens," *University of Washington Daily,* January 19, 1971.

39 John de Yonge, "Fire Owens, Kearney, Urges Rights Panel," *Seattle Post-Intelligencer,* January 1971.

40 A hiring goal could be set, for example, on the percentage of Blacks who live within the metropolitan area of a university. Not meeting the goal would not lead to a penalty by the government if the university could document "good faith efforts."

41 The Arab League was established in 1945 to strengthen ties among its 22 member states to coordinate their policies and promote common interests.

42 Lyle's agency had 20,000 employees and a budget of $14 billion. ESD had 2,500 employees, a budget of $500 million, and an unemployment insurance trust fund of $1.6 billion.

43 *Report of the Committee for Fiscal Integrity,* Seattle School District, June 4, 2003.

44 *Seattle Post-Intelligencer* editorial, June 12, 2003.

45 John Iwasaki, "A Controversial Statue Creates Dissent, Healing: Jim Owens, Former UW Football Coach Apologizes for his Actions in '60s," *Seattle Post-Intelligencer,* October 24, 2003.

46 Just weeks before the Grand Opening of NAAM in March of 2008, I had a conversation with Bob Watt, former deputy mayor under Mayor Norm Rice during Rice's two terms. Watt congratulated me on the imminent opening of the museum. He also pointed out the that he considered the inability of the Rice team to make the museum a reality as its biggest disappointment.

47 Florangela Davila, "Contributions Pouring in for Black Museum." *Seattle Times,* September 26, 2002.

48 I had been an admirer of Barbara Thomas for many years, beginning in 1969 when she worked for me as an instructor and team leader for a summer Youth Program at the University of Washington. I followed her career as a nationally recognized artist, protégé of the legendary painter Jacob Lawrence, and her role on the City of Seattle's Arts Commission.

49 It is important to note that I had known both Omari Garrett and Charlie James for many years and had respect for them. I knew Omari from the days when I was a city park instructor during the summers in the early 1960's at Washington Park in the University of Washington Arboretum. In those days, Omari was called Cordell. Additionally, I was his teacher and coach

at Garfield High School. I remember him as an exceptionally bright and gifted student in my United States history class. He was also an exceptionally gifted football player. I could have utilized him in several different positions, however, I had him play as the starting quarterback, a position usually for brightest football player on the team and the best leader, in addition to being a good passer. I thought to myself that this young man has great potential and will make significant contributions within the community in years to come. When we talked then, he really brightened up my day.

Charlie James and I connected when I was working at the University of Washington. I admired his writing in community newspapers as well as his blogs over the years we worked together on issues of common interests concerning the African American community while I was commissioner of the Washington State Department of Employment Security Department, and also during the few years I was the executive director of NAAM. I suspect that Charlie has ongoing concerns regarding the direction of the museum, but I feel we could have come together on some matters of mutual interest if I had remained longer at NAAM.

50 Linda Thomas, "Builders Tear Into Colman School's Challenges," *Puget Sound Business Journal*, June 11, 2007.

51 NAAM Activity Highlights, May-July 2006.

52 Formations had also designed main exhibits for the Muhammad Ali Museum Center in Louisville, Kentucky, among others.

53 Susan Gilmore, "A New Look at the Past: Northwest African American Museum," *Seattle Times*, March 9, 2008.

54 I co-chaired the event, along with Morrie Alhadeff, in March 1983.

Bibliography

Abram, Eva, and Minnie Collins. Community Conversation, Mt. Zion Baptist Church, August 27, 2006.

African American Heritage Museum and Cultural Center. African American Museum Project Records, Record Series 5751-05, Boxes 1, 2, and 3. Seattle Municipal Archives.

Allison, James. "The Historical Background of Harriet Beecher Stowe's Uncle Tom's Cabin." *Evansville (IN) Journal*, April 15, 1881.

Barker, Joseph. *The Lives of Lewis, Milton and Cyrus Clarke: Three Celebrated Fugitive Slaves.* London: Wortley, 1846.

Beason, Tyrone. "We Have a Unique Story to Tell," *Seattle Times*, January 16, 2005.

Bigglestone, William. *They Stopped in Oberlin: Black Residents and Visitors of the Nineteenth Century*, Scottsdale, AZ: 1981. Revised edition, paperback. Oberlin, Ohio: Oberlin College, 2002.

Cruse, Harold. *The Crisis of the Negro Intellectual.* New York: William Morrow, 1997.

Clarke, Lewis Garrard. *Narrative of the Sufferings of Lewis Clarke: During Captivity of More Than Twenty-Five Years among the Algerines of Kentucky, One of the So-Called Christian States of North America.* Boston: David H. Ela, 1845.

Clarke, Lewis, and Milton Clarke. *Sons of a Soldier of the Revolution During Captivity of More Than Twenty-Five Years Among the Slaveholders of Kentucky, One of the So-Called Christian States of North America.* Boston: Bela Marsh, 1846.

Davila, Florangela. "Contributions Pouring in for Black Museum." *Seattle Times*, September 26, 2002.

Davis, Charles T., and Henry Louis Gates, Jr., eds. *The Slave's Narrative.* Oxford: Oxford University Press, 1985.

Debow, Samuel P., and Edward A. Pitter, eds and comps. *Who's Who? [African Americans] In Religious, Fraternal, Social, Civic and Commercial Life on the Pacific Coast—State of Washington.* Seattle: Searchlight Publishing, 1926–1927.

Drucker, Peter F. *Post-Capitalist Society.* New York: Harper Collins Books, 1993.

Erickson, Olivia Littles. "Co-Constructing Racial Identities at Seattle's Northwest African American Museum." PhD diss., University of Washington, 2015.

Eurich, Nell P. *The Learning Industry.* Princeton, New Jersey: Princeton University Press, 1990.

European Communities Commission/United States conference proceedings. "Schools and Industry: Partners for a Quality Education." Noordwijk, the Netherlands, June 25-26, 1992.

Fryer, Alex. "African American Museum Up Against Oct. 31 Deadline." *Seattle Times*, September 12, 1999.

Gayton, Carver Clark. "Employer Needs of the Future." Unpublished convocation speech presented at Saint Martin's University, Lacey, WA, May 10, 1997.

——. "Federal Funding and its Impact on the University." PhD diss., University of Washington, Seattle, August 20, 1976.

—— "Martin & Malcom and the Legacy of African American Leadership in the United States." Unpublished paper for a Martin Luther King Day speech, Mt. Zion Baptist Church, Seattle, WA, January 15, 1993.

——. *Narrative of the Sufferings of Lewis Clarke*, A Facsimile Edition, Introduction by Carver Clark Gayton. Seattle and London: University of Washington Press, 2012.

——. *When Owing a Shilling Costs a Dollar: The Saga of Lewis G. Clarke, Born a "White Slave."* Ann Arbor, MI: Edwards Brothers Malloy. 2015.

Hess, Frederick M. *Urban School Reform*. Cambridge, Mass.: Harvard Education Press, 2005.

Kaplan, Morton A. *System and Process in International Politics*. New York: John Wiley & Sons. 1997.

Kerber, August, and Barbara Bommarito, eds. *The Schools and the Urban Crisis*. New York: Holt, Rinehart and Winston, 1965.

Levine, Marsha, and Roberta Trachtman, eds. *American Business and the Public School*. New York and London: Teacher's College Press, 1988.

Marsh, David D., Judy B. Codding, and Associates. *The New American High School*. Thousand Oaks, CA: Corwin Press, 1999.

Mills, Kimberly, "Whose Dream is it—Overcoming Infighting is Key to African-American Museum's Success." *Seattle Post-Intelligencer*. August 18, 1996.

Morison, Samuel Eliot, and Henry Steele Commager. *Growth of the American Republic*. New York: Oxford University Press, 1980.

Mumford, Esther Hall. *Seattle's Black Victorians, 1852–1901*. Seattle: Ananse Press, 1980.

National Advisory Commission on Civil Disorders. Report. Washington, DC: The Government Printing Office, 1968.

National Center on Education and the Economy. "America's Choice: High Skills or Low Wages." Rochester, NY, 1990.

National Commission on Excellence in Education. "A Nation at Risk: The Imperative for Educational Reform." Washington, DC., April 1983.

Northwest African American Museum. "Mission and Vision." n.d., Northwest African American Museum. http://www.naamnw.org/mission-vision/.

Packer, Arnold H., and Marion W. Pines. *School to Work*. Princeton, NJ: Eye on Education, 1996.

Porter, W. Thomas. *A Football Band of Brothers: Forging the University of Washington's First National Championship*. Victoria, BC: Trafford Publishing, 2007.

Porter, Tom, Carver Gayton, Trish Bostrom, and Richard Redman. "From the Playing Field to Organizational Leadership." CD recording from panel discussion, Michael Foster School of Business, University of Washington, October 4, 2007.

Potter, Edward E., and Judith A. Youngman. *Keeping America Competitive*. Lakewood, CO: Glenbridge Publishing, 1995.

Schlesinger, Arthur M. Jr. *Robert Kennedy and His Times*. Boston: Houghton Mifflin, 1978.

Shenon, Philip. *A Cruel and Shocking Act: The Secret History of the Kennedy Assassination*. New York: Henry Holt, 2013.

Stowe, Harriet Beecher. *The Key to Uncle Tom's Cabin; Presenting the Original Facts and Documents Upon Which the Story is Founded.* London: Clarke, Beeton, and Co., and Thomas Bosworth, 1853.

———. *Uncle Tom's Cabin: or Life Among the Lowly.* John P. Jewett, 1852.

Tahir, Kwame, Merciful Allah, and the Youth Action Committee, 1997 Memorandum to the AAHMCC Board, August 27, 1997. http://www.aahmcc.org (accessed on October 6, 2007).

Taylor, Yuval, ed. *I was Born a Slave: An Anthology of Classic Slave Narratives.* Vol.1: 1772–1849. Chicago: Lawrence Hill Books, 1999.

Taylor, Quintard. *The Forging of a Black Community: Seattle's Central District from 1870 through the Civil Rights Era.* Seattle and London: University of Washington Press, 1994.

Thurow, Lester. *Head to Head: The Coming Economic Battle Among Japan, Europe, and America.* New York: William Morrow and Company, Inc., 1992.

Tully, Andrew. *The FBI's Most Famous Cases.* New York: William Morrow, 1965.

Van Horn, Carl E. *No One Left Behind: The Report of the Twentieth Century Fund Task Force on Retraining America's Workforce.* New York: The Twentieth Century Fund Press,1996.

Whitehead, Alfred North. *The Aims of Education.* New York: Collier Macmillan, 1957.

Suggested Reading

Ambrose, Stephen E. *Undaunted Courage*. New York: Simon & Schuster, 1996.

Baldwin, James. *Baldwin: Collected Essays*. New York: The Library of America, 1998.

Conrad, Joseph. *Lord Jim*. New York: The Modern Library, 1931.

Coates, Ta-Nehisi. *Between the World and Me*. Boston: Spiegel & Grau, 2015.

Cone, James H. *Martin & Malcom & America: A Dream or a Nightmare*. Maryknoll, NY: Orbis Books, 1991.

Cruse, Harold. *The Crisis of the Negro Intellectual, from Its Origins to the Present*. New York: William Morrow, 1967.

Douglass, Frederick. *Narrative of the Life of Frederick Douglass: American Slave*. Edited by John Blassingame, John R. McKivign, and Peter P. Hinks. New Haven, CT: Yale University Press, 2001.

Du Bois, W.E.B. *The Souls of Black Folk*. Introduction by John Edgar Wideman. New York: Vantage Books, 1990.

Dunbar, Paul Laurence. *The Complete Poems of Paul Laurence Dunbar*. New York: Dodd, Mead, 1944.

Franklin, John Hope. *From Slavery to Freedom: A History of Negro Americans,* 3rd ed. New York: Alfred A. Knopf, 1969.

Freire, Paulo. *Pedagogy of the Oppressed*. New York: The Seabury Press, 1973.

Grier, William H. and Price Cobbs. *Black Rage*. New York: Basic Books, 1968.

Hacker, Andrew. *Two Nations: Black and White, Separate, Hostile, Unequal*. New York: Macmillan Publishing,1992.

Haley, Alex. *The Autobiography of Malcom X*. New York: Penguin Books, October 29, 1965.

Hemingway, Ernest. *For Whom the Bell Tolls*. New York: Scribner's, October 21, 1940.

Hughes, Langston. *The Panther and the Lash: Poems of Our Times*. New York: Alfred Knopf, 1969.

Lewis, David Levering. *W. E. B. Du Bois: Biography of a Race*. New York: Henry Holt, 1993.

Morris, Milton. *The Politics of Black America*. New York: Harper & Row,1975.

Ripley, C. Peter, et al. *The Black Abolitionist Papers*. Chapel Hill, NC: University of North Carolina Press, 1985.

Shirer, William L. *The Rise and Fall of the Third Reich*. New York: Simon & Schuster, 1960.

Wilkerson, Isabel. *The Warmth of Other Suns: The Epic Story of America's Great Migration*. New York: Random House, 2010.

Wyatt-Brown, Bertram. *Lewis Tappan and the Evangelical War Against Slavery*. Baton Rouge, LA: Louisiana State University Press, 1969.

Index